A Gazetteer
of Prehistoric Standing Stones
in Great Britain

Olaf Swarbrick

BAR British Series 558
2012

Published in 2016 by
BAR Publishing, Oxford

BAR British Series 558

A Gazetteer of Prehistoric Standing Stones in Great Britain

ISBN 978 1 4073 0960 6

BAR Publishing is the trading name of British Archaeological Reports (Oxford) Ltd.
British Archaeological Reports was first incorporated in 1974 to publish the BAR
Series, International and British. In 1992 Hadrian Books Ltd became part of the BAR
group. This volume was originally published by Archaeopress in conjunction with
British Archaeological Reports (Oxford) Ltd / Hadrian Books Ltd, the Series principal
publisher, in 2012. This present volume is published by BAR Publishing, 2016.

Printed in England

BAR
PUBLISHING

BAR titles are available from:

BAR Publishing
122 Banbury Rd, Oxford, OX2 7BP, UK
EMAIL   info@barpublishing.com
PHONE   +44 (0)1865 310431
FAX   +44 (0)1865 316916
www.barpublishing.com

Contents

ACKNOWLEDGEMENTS

I am very grateful to many helpful people throughout Great Britain who cheerfully undertook considerable work and effort on my behalf to provide help, information and references on various aspects of the Standing Stones and associated monuments in Great Britain. They are far too numerous to mention individually and I did not know who many of them were. Without their help much of this work would not have been possible. They include private individuals, the librarians, public servants and employees of numerous public, private and academic institutions and companies, professional and amateur archaeologists, authors and writers, the boatmen who ferried me around the islands and the many individual landowners, farmers and householders who gave me access to their Standing Stones and showed me where they were, often in their gardens and beside their houses, and everyone else who provided help and information. I have received invaluable help from Philip Kuhn to organise the typescript, Dr. Rob Ixer FRS for vital advice on geology and the development of the grooves and rock drills, Dr. Mike Pitts for much background information and Dr David Davison for assistance to arrange the text. I wish to acknowledge the great value of the Ordnance Survey Landranger maps (scale 1 : 50 000) without which many of the Standing Stones could not have been found and the project accomplished.

INTRODUCTION

This gazetteer is not the work of an archaeologist and nor is it an academic report. These are practical field observations, which can be made by anyone, of most of the prehistoric Standing Stones in Great Britain (GB) and some 'Other Stones' which post-date AD 1. The gazetteer is not comprehensive. It includes a list of 34 prehistoric Standing Stones known to be extant but which I have not been able to visit, a list of Standing Stones of unknown provenance and of interesting 'Other Stones'. The motivation for this work was the Wimblestone *(24, Somerset, ST434585, photo. 1)* which is an extant prehistoric Standing Stone hard by my childhood home and which started my interest in these monuments. In September 1996 I set out to find, visit and sketch the prehistoric Standing Stones in Great Britain and soon discovered that there was no readily available and comprehensive list or lists of Standing Stones and their exact locations, so that there were numerous Standing Stones unknown to me and others which were very difficult to find. I decided to attempt to produce a readily usable gazetteer of all the prehistoric Standing Stones in GB with the National Grid reference number for each to enable easy location in the field together with colour sketches, photographs, field records and relevant information gathered from various sources, but excluding stone circles, long stone rows, burial chambers and dolmens. Some Standing Stones were not visited because they were inaccessible for various reasons and these are separately listed . These and the other Standing Stones and some other stone monuments which post date AD 1 are recorded in the gazetteers but are excluded from the analysis. Apparently unrecorded Standing Stones continue to be found. The national grid references are essential for accurately establishing and finding the locations of Standing Stones. It is probably not possible to produce a totally comprehensive gazetteer of all the prehistoric Standing Stones in Great Britain.

PREFACE

Standing Stones are the simplest and most numerous of prehistoric monuments. There is no real information about the prehistoric Standing Stones of Great Britain because they were set up before literacy and records and thus the date of origin and the methods of transport and erection and the use of these enigmatic and often magnificent monuments are totally unknown. As a group the Standing Stones are highly pleomorphic and very varied. Some are dominating features within their landscape, whereas others are insignificant and uninteresting. It has been suggested some may be phallic symbols. Many Standing Stones are visually arresting and appear today as significant works of art in their own right but so far no attention has been given to the aesthetic aspects of Standing Stones.

This gazetteer sets out to list the prehistoric sites with Standing Stones in Great Britain between the Scilly Isles and Shetland Isles. The prehistoric Standing Stones are thought to date from between c. 5000 BC to c. 1750 BC (Service and Bradbury 1993a). Single or paired Standing Stones from the second or third millennium BC (Williams 1988a) are common and widely distributed (Cope 2004) in western and northern areas of Great Britain (GB), but accurate dating is not possible. This gazetteer has no Standing Stones attributed to the period from 1500 BC to AD 1. Although most Standing Stones occur as a single Stone on 708 sites there are also 188 sites with two or more Standing Stones (Table 1), leaving aside the many Stone Rows containing larger numbers of stones which are not included in this work. The intention was to visit, measure and list all the prehistoric sites in Great Britain which contain one or more prehistoric Standing Stones. This proved to be impractical and not all the extant Standing Stones were visited or are listed and this gazetteer is thus not comprehensive. It was not intended to include stone circles, longer stone rows, burial chambers, barrows and dolmens, but some of these became included because of the intrinsic interest of associated Standing Stones and difficulties and ambiguities of assessment.

Numerous Standing Stones of post AD 1 origin and Stones of unknown provenance were included to complete the record. This gazetteer records visits to a total of 1068 sites with 1502 Standing Stones of both prehistoric and post AD 1 origin (Appendices 1, 2 and 3). 896 of these sites are presumed to be prehistoric with 1228 prehistoric Standing Stones which are summarised, with the heights of the Stones in metres, in Table 1. Appendix 4 includes 35 prehistoric sites with 36 other prehistoric Standing Stones which were not visited but are known to be extant, so the total number of prehistoric sites here recorded in GB in 2010 is 941 with 1264 prehistoric Standing stones. Appendix 5 records 128 other sites with Standing Stones which were Not Found or are now Lost or Destroyed. It is probable that there are other unrecorded prehistoric Standing Stones which will continue to be found, such as that about which I was recently told and then visited *(1183 Exmoor SS465443 Photo 2)* and which is not marked on the OS map nor recorded by the County Archaeologist; one wonders how such an obvious large Standing Stone has not been mapped, recorded or listed.

753 *(85.9%)* of all the prehistoric Standing Stones visited in this work lie within the littoral counties on the west coast of GB from Cornwall to the Western Isles where they are especially found on the peninsulae and islands, and along the east coast from Flambourgh Head to Duncansby Head and on the Orkney and Shetland Islands (Figures 1, 2 and 3). The average height for all the prehistoric Standing Stones (as measured by me) is 2.0 metres with an overall range from 0.3 metres to 8.2 metres (Table 1). 708 of the prehistoric sites *(79% of all prehistoric sites)* have one Standing Stone, 188 prehistoric sites *(21%)* have two or more Standing Stones and some of the multiple sites are complex and difficult to characterise. Standing Stones may have many different shapes (Table 5), and some Stones are aesthetically pleasing. 264 of the prehistoric Standing Stones *(21%)* are leaning (Tables 1 and 8), one at 50° from the vertical, and many have shallow sockets (Table 9). Thom and Thom (1990a) have suggested that many sites and Stones are associated with various astronomical observations but this has been criticised by Heggie (1981). The rock for most Standing Stones is of local origin, but some appear to have been transported for up to 15 to 20 kilometers and it is not possible to determine whether this movement was by human or geological and glacial, activity. There are 28 Stones with well marked 'grooves' due to weathering which have now become a distinctive and obvious feature of these Stones (Table 15). There are ten Stones with holes which perforate the thickness of the Stone., six of which are in granite (Table 16). There are 'cup marked' Stones in Scotland and Northumberland, but they are infrequent elsewhere. There are

no apparent or obvious differences between the overall dimensions, shapes and other features of the prehistoric Standing Stones in England, Scotland and Wales and they are all considered together, although they are not a homogeneous group.

Although many sites and Standing Stones are leaning, have fallen over or been destroyed it is suprising that so many have survived down the millennia and are still vertical. The prehistoric Standing Stones are under researched and need further assessment and conservation.

INTRODUCTION TO THE GAZETTEER

The Literature on Standing Stones

Relatively little has been specifically written about Standing Stones. Service and Bradbury (1993) and Jean-Pierre Mohen (1989) discuss and describe Standing Stones on a world-wide basis with good maps of the distribution in Europe, North Africa, and southern Asia, which indicates there are none in Australia or the Americas except in Columbia. The Inuit Peoples in northern Canada build interesting multi-stone stone 'inuksuit' in many different forms (Hallendy 2000), which are different from Standing Stones and with which they should not be compared. Some iuksuit have been erected within living memory and there are in these areas also some single stones which appear like the GB Standing Stones (pages 33, 34, 71, 72 and 89).

The Standing Stones of GB are under-researched (Field D., English Heritage, personal communication 2007) and relatively little has been specifically written about them. There is a good 'Note on Dating' by Service and Bradbury (1993a). It may be that some Standing Stones are assessed as being prehistoric without any real evidence. 'The Ancient Stones of Wales' have been listed and described by Barber and Williams (1989) who effectively provide a gazetteer for Wales (but I was unable to find some of them). Thom and Thom, with notes by Burl, (1990 parts I and11) describe numerous sites, Standing Stones and Stone Rows in GB with site plans and astronomical observations (which were Alexander Thom's real interest) and Williams (1988) in 'The Standing Stones of Wales and South-West England' describes many features of the Standing Stones in that area and provides an extensive bibliography and distribution map. Burl (1988) describes the Bronze Age 'Four Poster' circles of Western Europe. Some individual Standing Stones are mentioned and described in various publications such as 'Kilmartin' (RCAHMS 1999), 'The Standing Stones of Europe' (Service and Bradbury 1993), 'Shell Guide to British Archaeology' (Hawkes 1986) and 'Circles and Standing Stones (Hadingham 1975). The books 'Magic Stones' by Jan Pohribny (2007), 'Megaliths' by Corio and Corio (2003) and 'The Megalithic European' by Julian Cope (2004) contain many excellent photographs of Standing Stones and other stone momuments in Europe and elsewhere and a useful bibliography, but they offer very little real information.

TABLE 1 SITES WITH STANDING STONES IN GREAT BRITAIN
(WITH THE AVERAGE HEIGHTS OF PREHISTORIC STONES IN METRES)

	number of sites	number of Stones	prehistoric sites	prehistoric stones (% of Stones)	leaning stones (% of Stones)	average height (% of Stones)	range of height	prehistoric sites with 1 Stone	(% prehistoric sites) with >1 stone
England	229	382	160 (83%)	238 (62.3%)	53 (23%)	2.0	0.4 – 8.2	128 (80%)	32 (20%)
Scotland	547	745	484 (88%)	668 (90%)	150 (22%)	2.0	0.3 – 5.7	364 (75%)	120 (25%)
Wales	292	375	252 (86%)	322 (86%)	61 (19%)	1.9	0.4 – 4.5	216 (85%)	36 (15%)
Great Britain	1068	1502	896 (84%)	1228 (82%)	264 (21%)	2.0	0.3 – 8.2	708 (79%)	118 (21%)
Add other extant prehistoric sites & standing stones not visited			37	39	I have little or no specific information about these individual Stones				
Total number of prehistoric sites & Standing Stones recorded in this work			933	1257	it is probable that more Standing Stones will be found				

The Definition of 'Standing Sones'

Standing Stones have been defined (Monuments Protection Programme 1990, cited by Jason Dodds, West Yorkshire Archaeology Service, personal communication 2004) as "a ritual or ceremonial monument of prehistoric date which comprises a single or occasionally a pair of upright orthostatic slabs, sometimes worked to shape, which may be surrounded by other smaller, stone settings, pit burials and timber structures. The main upright stones vary in size from less than 1.0 metre to 6.0 metre high". This definition specifies a prehistoric origin, but overlooks the Standing Stones which are over 6.0 metres high (*48 and 49, Yorkshire, SE389663, and 50, Yorkshire, TA098677*) and that there are numerous groups of Standing Stones (other than Stone Rows) which comprise three or more Standing Stones *(710 Lewis, Western Isles NB164343)* and the numerous rectangular settings known as 'four posters' (Burl 1971) *(204, Angus, NO196515, photo 3)* and does not define 'orthostatic slabs'.

Jean-Pierre Mohen (1999 a) defines a "Standing, or raised, Stone as any stone used by human beings to mark a place, a recollection, an homage or a veneration and also referred to as a menhir or peulvan". He writes that "peulvan" is the Ancient Breton name for a Standing Stone in the area around Audierne. For menhirs he states "the term became common among devotees of Celtic practices at the end of the 18th. century" which should now be discarded, and describes megaliths as 'a block of stone of large dimension installed and incorporated into an architecture called megalithic' and an orthostat as a 'standing stone slab that forms the wall of a megalithic tomb or an element of such a wall". This definition by Mohen does not imply any particular age, group or the actual numbers of Stones at the site nor the dimensions and arrangements of the Standing Stones, other than the subjective 'large dimension' for megaliths. These definitions thus appear to include circles, dolmens, stone rows and the other megalithic monuments of whatever age and conformation, and to confine orthostats to the walls of tombs and burial chambers thus excluding the term from the free-standing Standing Stones. Daniels (1958) describes three types of prehistoric megalithic monument in Western Europe, indicating that these are not hard and fast categories, namely:

1. the chamber tomb,
2. the single standing stone,
3. the grouped standing stones.

There are numerous synonyms for Standing Stones which are shown in Table 2.

A Standing Stone is defined in this work as a Stone raised by human agency for some specific purpose which may be single and isolated or in groups, rows or complex configurations. This definition, as with Mohen (1999 a), says nothing about the age, size and shape, the numbers of Stones on a site, and the orientation and site arrangements. 'Standing Stone' is a simple and accurate description providing an obvious definition of these highly pleomorphic Stones and groups thereof so that the inclusion or exclusion of some Standing Stones within this gazetteer and some of the Stones included as "Other Stones" may be subjective, ambiguous and anomalous. In this text Standing Stone is usually abbreviated to 'Stone', which unless used otherwise indicates a prehistoric Standing Stone.

Materials and Method

The sites and Stones referred to in this gazetteer, in the field records and in the text are identified first by the dated 'drawing number' in my sketch books, and then by the county in which the site and Stone is located, followed by the Ordnance Survey national grid reference number with three digits each for easting and northing. The national grid reference is the definitive identification for the location of each site. It can be difficult, and often impossible, to find Stones in the field without a grid reference. The 'drawing number' together with the County provide for easy reference within the Appendices 1, 2 and 3 which form the gazetteer lists. The 'drawing numbers' are the chronological order in which the sites were visited, some more than once. Sites and Stones can be found within the Appendices by the 'drawing number' followed by the County and then the national grid reference, all of which is given in the text in parenthesis and italics, thus *(216, Angus, NO280507)*. For easy reference the gazetteer lists of Stones are grouped under England (Appendix 1), Scotland (Appendix 2) and Wales (Appendix 3) and the Stones are listed under each County. Exmoor includes sites in both Devon and Somerset and is shown anomalously as a separate 'county'. Anglesey, the Isle of Man, Orkney, Shetland and the Western Isles of Scotland (ie. the Outer Hebrides) are each shown as separate counties. The smaller islands around the coast of GB are listed under the county within which the island is included, but are shown separately from the rest of that county. Some sites, such as the Shap Alignment comprising twelve Stones *(170 to 176a, Cumbria NY558152)* and The Six Stones on Dunruchan Hill *(736 to 741, Perth from NN792178)* and the Stones on the Lleyn peninsula are shown separately within the county lists. Many examples of the particular features of sites and Stones are provided to illustrate the text but do not include all the sites and Stones which display these features. The Stones of the Channel Islands and Ireland are not included in this work.

It was intended to exclude the dolmens, quoits, burial chambers, circles and the longer stone rows of over six Stones, but some of these interesting Sites and Stones were perforce included; as Daniels (1958) pointed out there can be no hard and fast categories. Stones included are the outliers and centre Stones of stone circles *(132, Cumbria, NY570372, photo. 4 and 1173, Cornwall, SW412273, photo 5)*, henge Stones *(131*

Cumbria NV5344296), Stones associated with small and large ring cairns *(364, Argyll, NM 90290 photo 6 and 927 Highland NH679359)* and the portal Stones of some long barrows (*756 Oxford, SU281851*) and burial chambers *(966, Galloway, NX517538, photo. 7)*. The inclusion of some of these Stones is ambiguous because for some Stones it became an arbitrary choice rather than an objective decision. Numerous Stones of post AD 1 origin are included in Appendices 1, 2 and 3 such as Stones of Roman origin *(158, Dorset, SY708913)*, Pictish 'symbol' Stones *(1013 Aberdeen NJ610303, photo 53)*, an 8th. century Stone with both Pictish symbols and a Christian Cross *(1036, Aberdeen, NJ703248, photo 8)*, Ogham Stones *(209, Isle of Gigha, Argyll, NR642482)*, mediaeval *(503, Cornwall, SX112252, photo 9)* and later Stones *(602, Lleyn peninsula, Gwynedd, SH526397, dated 1712, photo 10)*, together with modern Stones *(601, Gwynedd, SH553422, photo 11, ploughed up by the farmer and erected as a 'joke' in a prominent position)* which are included because they are clearly Stones which are significant, interesting or obvious and must be included within a gazetteer of Standing Stones. The provenance of some of these Stones of post AD 1 origin is not clear *(30 and 42 Somerset ST773509)* and all the Stones post AD 1 are excluded from the analysis and discussion, because they form a separate group.

The synonyms for Standing Stones are shown in Table 2. English Heritage (1990) has a classification of Standing Stones and associated monuments with much extra information. In this work I exclusively use Standing Stone, which is usually abbreviated in the text to 'Stone'.

The arbitrary age criteria for the Stones used in this gazetteer is shown in Table 3. Prior to AD 1 the ages of the Stones are uncertain and inadequate (Ritchie 1997) and the inclusion of some Stones within the prehistoric

TABLE 2 SYNONYMS FOR STANDING STONES

OTHER NAMES	NOTATIONS USED ON ORDNANCE SURVEY MAPS
MONOLITH	STANDING STONE
ORTHOLITH	STONE
ORTHOSTAT – in tombs & burial chambers	LONG STONE
HIR (prefix or suffix in Wales)	BROADSTONE
MEGALITH – may indicate part of a complex structure or site rather than single stone	MENHIR (also used in France) obsolete & should not be used
	MEAN (Wales
STELE – monolith of modest size (<0.75 metres) with one face decorated in low relief	HIRION
	CLACH (Scotland)
PEULVAN (ancient Breton name around Audierne)	LECH
	CARREG (Wales)

era may be open to speculation. From AD 1 onwards sites and Stones are usually reliably dated. There are many post AD 1 Stones which fall within the definition of Standing Stone as defined for this work and these are included in the gazetteer because they are obviously Standing Stones. Some are listed as 'Other Stones' in Appendix 6. These include various memorial Stones *(Other Stones 93, SU282868)*, Christian crosses *(Other Stones 95, NZ207225)* and 'refuge stones *(Other Stones 88NT991728)*, Pictish stones *(Other Stones 98, NJ876154)*, boundary markers which are especially numerous on Dartmoor and the North Yorkshire Moors *(Other Stones 86)* but the list is not comprehensive. In AD 2000 numerous unrecorded 'millenium stones' were erected throughout GB.

The Sources of Information

The Ordnance Survey 1:50 000 scale 'Landranger' series of maps was the major source of information for this work. Most Stones were found because they are marked on these maps. The Landranger maps do not mark all the Stones, and some marked 'Standing Stone' are no longer extant as shown in Appendix 4 under 'Stones Lost or Destroyed'. The national grid reference number and altitude for every site was obtained from these maps. The 1:25 000 'Pathfinder' series often mark Stones not shown on the 1:50 000 scale, but it was impractical to purchase the necessary large number of Pathfinder maps. It can be difficult or impossible to locate Stones without the grid reference. Lists of Stones and information were also obtained from County Archaeologists, local Antiquity Societies, English and Scottish Heritage, RCAHM in England and Scotland, CADW in Wales, the National Trust, publications in various journals, archaeology and guide books and some individuals. An interesting feature of these lists is that almost every list included Stones not shown on other lists and excluded Stones recorded elsewhere. These lists, like the OS maps, may include sites where the Stone is no longer extant having, presumably, been lost or destroyed , but again the lists are different. Most, if not all, of the 'official' lists are thus incomplete and inaccurate.

TABLE 3   THE HISTORIC ERAS OF STANDING STONES,
AS USED IN THIS WORK

	abbreviation in appendices	
prehistoric	*before AD 1*	PH
medieval	*from AD 1 until AD 1500*	M
later	*from AD 1500 until AD 1850*	LL
modern	*post- AD 1850*	Md

Appendix 4 lists the 'Stones not Visited, Not Found or Lost' which are subdivided between

36 'STONES STILL EXTANT but NOT VISITED' often because of inaccessibility, some of which have been seen from a distance, or are otherwise known to be extant from reliable information,

54 'STONES NOT FOUND or LOST which appear to be no longer extant on the site,

74 'STONES of STATUS NOT KNOWN' , which although marked on the OS map or otherwise recorded have not been visited or could not be found or otherwise verified as extant, often because they were inaccessible.

Some Stones have been recently destroyed *(Stones Lost 50, SO084598)*. Many Stones listed by the County Archaeologists and others could not be found *(Northumberland NU062002)* and are presumed to be lost. It can be impossible to find Stones within forestry and undergrowth *(Northumberland, NZ067771 was searched for four times and not found, and 114 Perthshire NN700061 – two searches, stated to be extant by farm manager)*. There are numerous Stones which were not visited because access is difficult *(126, two Stones on Switha Island, Orkney HY365909 and HY362606)* or too dangerous *(Other Stones 149, Islay NR224605)* visible across 1 km. of abandoned waterlogged peat cuttings or on distant hill tops *(App. 4 Stones Extant 191 Dyfedd SN734447)* visible from 2.5 KM distance, or just impossible *(Stones still Extant 11, Argyll NR703124)* visible across 500 metres of impenetrable gorse). All these are listed as 'Not Visited' in Appendix 4.

Appendix 5 lists 'Other Stones' on 144 sites. These Other Stones and some of the sites are significant Stone monuments which fall outside the definition of Standing Stones and include prehistoric and later monuments such as stone circles, dolmens, burial chambers, memorial and millennium Stones, Christian Crosses, stepping stones, constructed stone columns and other stone monuments and some natural features such as glacial erratics which are obvious stone features of the local environment. It is not a comprehensive list of all these 'Other Stones' and they are not further considered.. The 'Stones Not Found. Lost or Destroyed' and 'Other Stones' are briefly discussed later. All these Stones are excluded from the analysis of the prehistoric sites and Standing Stones.

The field work was carried out between 1996 and 2009. Site visits were made to Stones between the Scilly Isles and Lizard Peninsula in Cornwall and Unst, the northern-most island of the Shetland Islands, including the intervening archipelagos and islands. At each site a colour or pencil sketch of the Stone(s) was made, photographs obtained and an A5 size field record (Table 4) was completed.

These records were completed on the site (some are consequently untidy, especially when made in rain) and observations relevant to that site and the associated surroundings were noted. Two basic photographs were obtained for each Stone, one from the South and one from the East or West, depending upon the bearing of the sun. A 1 metre measuring stick is included in the photographs. Measurements are in metres to the nearest 0.1 metre, but ground measurements of the size of sites and other distances are estimates. Other relevant photographs showing features particular to that Stone or group, the site and its surroundings were also obtained, so that for some sites there are several photographs (some of which may be on two films). The Stones were measured for height, width and thickness, the angle of lean if present and the compass orientation of 'slabs' observed to the nearest 5°, the shape was assessed (Table 5), the geology of the Stone (where known – my knowledge of geology is limited), the extent of any lichen cover (on the later visited Stones), carvings or markings and grooves, fissures and cracks or other features were recorded and photographed as appropriate. Any calculated numbers are rounded to the nearest digit. Sketch maps of sites are not to scale.

The field record sheet (Table 4) proved over-optimistic and it was not possible to obtain all the indicated data. In addition published and other information from numerous sources about many of the Stones is included with the field record for that Stone. Some Stones are Scheduled Ancient Monuments which is noted on the Record sheet where this information was known.

TABLE 4 FIELD RECORD FORM

Olaf Swarbrick FRCVS Date   200   in spreadsheet   photo   negatives   **DRAWING No.**
STANDING STONES   **SITE**
STONE ROW   **COUNTY**
COMPLEX SITE   **LOCATION**

NUMBER of STONES

OS map 1:50 000 SHEET no.   not marked - GRID REF   altitude*

COMPASS ALINGMENT of Stone   °   alingment BETWEEN STONES   °   SAM**
                                            DISTANCE between STONES*

VERTICAL FALLEN LEANING   ° to   "NATURAL" STONE   DRESSED

HEIGHT*   overall WIDTH/DIAMETER   MAXIMUM THICKNESS   HISTORIC PERIOD

MORPHOLOGY   **LICHEN**   %   approx. section at base   north ↑
                                            COVER

GEOLOGY

ASSOCIATED FEATURES

CARVINGS & MARKS
* measurements in metres ** Scheduled Ancient Monument *** Sites & MONUMENTS no.

The shape and geology of the Stones is arbitrarily described as shown in Table 5, and recorded in the gazetteer lists by the numerical code also shown in Table 5. Pillars are tall and thin *(photos 14 and 16)* whereas columns are thicker and shorter *(photo 6)*, the differentiation being somewhat subjective. 'Stumps' with the width more than 50% of the height *(photos 2, 18 and 37)* are somewhat different from amorphous lumps and cuboidal Stones *(1094 Lothians NT149744, photo 25)*. Some Stones are distinctly triangular *(photo 1 and 52)*. For 'slabs' the width of the Stone is more than 2.5 times the thickness *(photos 26 a and b and 32 a and b)*.

TABLE 5 NUMERICAL NOTATION FOR THE SHAPE AND GEOLOGY OF STANDING STONES AS USED IN THE APPENDICES

	SHAPE		GEOLOGY
1	tall slim pillar	1	sandstone
2	thick column	2	granite
3	stump – width >50% height	3	slate
4	slab – width <25% thickness	4	quartz
5	conical or triangular	5	puddingstone
6	amorphous lump	6	conglomerate
7	lies flat (total length measured)	7	gritstone
8	slab with man-made hole(s)	8	metamorphic / igneous
9	dumbell shape	9	limestone
10	rounded glacial boulder	10	sarsen
11	Christian Cross	11	dolerite – Prescelli bluestone
		12	gneiss

The sketch books are numbered from 1 to 47, each containing 21 to 24 sketches. All the negative photographic films are stored in numbered envelopes or containers providing for easy recovery. The films are numbered consecutively in the order in which they were exposed from 1 to 208. The number of the film containing the negative of each individual photograph is noted on the reverse of the photograph and on the field report form; some films contain negatives of other unconnected items. The field records and photographs together with references and photo-copies of information relating to that Stone which form the definitive records for this gazetteer are contained in 25 A5 size loose leaf files, each of which contains the records of the Stones from two sketch books. All these books and files are numbered accordingly to show the numbers of the Stones therein. The field record sheet (Table 4) proved over-optimistic and it was not possible to obtain all the indicated data. In addition published and other information from numerous sources about many of the Stones is included with the field record for that Stone.

Various other sites and Stones which post-date the prehistoric era are shown separately in Appendix 5.

Observations on the Stones

There are no records and only sparse information relating to the sites with prehistoric Stones in GB and relatively little has been written about them. The only real information that is usually available for prehistoric sites and Stones are the geographical location of the site, the number of Stones and their physical dimensions, characteristics and geology together with any associated features and archaeological findings . There is no known way of determining when the Stones were put into their present positions (Service and Bradbury 1993). These prehistoric Stones were erected during a period of more than four millennia (between c. 5000 BC and c.

1500 BC) and modern ethnic, national and county boundaries within Great Britain have no relevance. There must have been many different ethnic peoples and factors involved and all are unknown. Given that these Stones were erected over several millennia between Cornwall and Shetland they are clearly not a homogenous group and there is a total lack of data with which to make sensible groupings or assessments,. Arranging them under the counties in England, Scotland and Wales is merely a modern convenience. In this work the Stones are considered together. It is important to keep these factors in mind and not to speculate. Given the substantial and sustained manual efforts required to transport and erect these Stones it is clear that they were very important to our prehistoric forebears.

The gazetteer lists are the important part of this work, and are intended to be a practical list of the location all the sites in GB which have prehistoric Standing Stones for the use in the field. It does not deal with archaeological interpretations. Many sites have multiple numbers of Stones in complex configurations (179 Kilmartin, Argyll NR834964, photo.12 and 710 Lewis Western Isles NB162343) and it is obviously important to consider both the site as a whole and the individual Stones together with any other associated features, but this has not been attempted in this discussion. Occasional Stones, not recorded on the Ordnance Survey maps or on any list or elsewhere, continue to be found. One may be told about these by the farmers on whose land they stand (1152 Cardigan, SN345476) or they are just observed in the landscape (110, Lancashire, SD633667) and the quartz Stone 2.0 metres high at (1183 Devon, SS465443, photo 2) is too large to be overlooked but has not been mapped or recorded. 39 Stones on 37 sites known to be extant were not visited (see Appendix 4). It is unlikely that an accurate and comprehensive gazetteer of all the prehistoric sites containing Standing Stones in Great Britain can be compiled.

This work records a total of 1068 sites with 1512 Stones in GB from the combined prehistoric and post AD 1 eras.

The analysis is confined to the 896 prehistoric sites *(84% of all sites)* with 1228 prehistoric Standing Stones *(81% of all Stones)*. All the fallen Stones and Stones of post AD 1 origin are excluded from the analysis. For easy reference in the appendices the sites and Stones are grouped first under England, Scotland or Wales (see the lists of sites in Appendices 1, 2 and 3) and then within the current administrative counties. The detail in Table 6 shows that there are 708 prehistoric sites with one Stone *(79% of all prehistoric sites)*, 117 sites with two Standing Stones *(13.% of all prehistoric sites)*, 46 sites with sites with 3 Standing stones *(5% of all prehistoric sites)*, 14 sites with 4 Standing Stones *(1.5% of all prehistoric sites)* and 11 sites with more than four Standing Stones *(1.5% of all prehistoric sites)*. For some sites with complex features or which have two or more Stones a brief sketch plan, without a scale, was drawn on the reverse of the record form.

TABLE 6 THE DISTRIBUTION OF PREHISTORIC SINGLE AND MULTIPLE STONE SITES

	Number of prehistoric sites	Number of prehistoric standing stones	Number of prehistoric sites with 1 or more Standing Stones				
			1 Stone	2 Stones	3 Stones	4 Stones	>4 Stones
ENGLAND	160 *100%*	238	128 *80%*	18 *11.5%*	5 *3%*	4 *2.5%*	5 *3%*
SCOTLAND	484 *100%*	668	364 *75%*	77 *16%*	31 *6.5%*	6 *15%*	4 *1%*
WALES	252 *100%*	322	214 *85%*	22 *8%*	10 *4%*	4 *2%*	2 *1%*
total for GREAT BRITAIN	896 *100%*	1206	708 *79%*	117 *13%*	46 *5%*	14 *1.5%*	11 *1.5%*

Many sites, including some with only one Standing Stone, are complex *(179 Kilmaartin Argyll NR 834962, photo 12, and NM908290, photo 6)* and it is difficult to categorise some of the sites together with their Standing and fallen Stones and other associated features which requires archaeological assessement and expertise. Some sites and Stones dominate their surroundings *(185 Argyll NR720864, Sketch 3, 208 Argyll mainland NR728861, 417 Shetland HU490429 , 498 Powys SN92419, 669 South Uist, Western Isles NF770320, photo 13, and 1155 Pembroke SN100370)* whereas other Stones are insignificant *(702 Lewis, Western Isles NB507638, 0.4 metre high, photo 15)*. Some Stones may be almost lost within their surroundings *(33 Dorset SY922805)* or in broken ground *(359 Argyll mainland NM840040)*. Some dolmens, stone circles , burial chambers, henges and barrows (many of them ruined), and Stone Rows longer than five Stones have obvious and interesting associated Standing Stones. These sites include outliers of stone circles *(536 Mull, Argyll NM618251, photo 16, 3.0 metres high)* and centre Stones within stone circles *(1173 Cornwall SW412273, photo. 5)*, Stones with attached curb cairns *(364 Argyll NM908290, photo 6)*, probable unfinished stone circles which now appear as Standing Stones *(10 and 11, Islay, Argyll, NR187560)*, cove stones *(19, Avon, ST601631, photo. 17)*, burial chambers *(151, Oxford, SP378238 and 924, Sutherland, NC629092)*, henge Stones *(980, Fife, NO286303)*, the portal Stones of barrows *(756, Oxford, SU281851)* and the blocking Stones of some stone rows *(654 Dartmoor Devon SX556748 and 655 Dartmoor Devon SX690798)*. Some Stones are at considerable altitudes *(520 Powys SN755473)* at 390 metres and *(898 Powys SN943699, , photo 14)* at 460 metres. There is often no clear criteria upon which some of these should have been included or excluded as Standing Stones

Some of the prehistoric Stones are magnificent and beautiful and these aesthetic attributes have, so far, been overlooked and have received no comment but are an important feature of some Stones. Some of our prehistoric forebears produced what are now well known works of art such as the many cave paintings that are well appreciated today although it is not known if they were produced for recreation, beauty or practical purposes. It seems most unlikely that Standing Stones, involving as they did enormous labour, would have been erected for their intrinsic beauty. Some Stones can, nevertheless, today be appreciated today in this light. They can dominate their surroundings with visual impact attracting interest, thought and curiosity. Fifteen of these sites and Stones, some of which may be easily visited, are listed below and illustrated in the sketches and photos with this text, but there are others.

Long Meg,	3.4 metres,	*(132 Cumbria NY507372, photo 4)*
Upper Fernoch	2.4 metres	*(185 Argyll NR720864, sketch 3)*
Strontoiler,	3.75 metres,	*(364 Argyll NM908290, photo 6)*
Maiden Stone,	3.1 metres with 8th. or 9th. century carvings	*(1036 Aberdeen NJ703248, photo 8)*
Garth Farm,	2.6 metres, modern Stone erected 1999	*(601 Gwynedd SH553422, photo 11)*,
An Cara,	4.75 metres,	*(669 South Uist Western Isles NF770320, photo 13)*
Stones of Stenness,	4.7, 5.0 and 5.5 metres	*(942 Orkney HY308126, photo 19)*
Lundin Links	5.5, 5.2 and 4.2 metres	*(66 Fife NO405026, frontispiece and photo 23)*
Mains of Gask,	3.1 metres, tall thin slab	*(927 Highland NH67935, photo 26)*
Pipers west Stone,	4.0 metres with substantial splits	*(319 Cornwall SW435247, photo 30)*
Balinaby Stone,	4.9 metres, tall thin slab	*(13 Islay NR220672, photo 32)*
Queen's Stone,	1.7 metres, with 13 deep narrow grooves	*(415 Hereford NZ561181, photo 34)*
Auchencorth Farm,	1.8 metres,	*(868 Lothians NT204567, photo 44)*
Tolvan Stone,	1.6 metres with hole 0.25 metre diameter	*(501 Cornwall SW706277, photo 52)*
Barnhouse	3.5 metres, only 0.3 metre thick	*(937 Orkney HY312122, photo 27)*

The geology of the Stones was incompletely recorded because my knowledge of geology is inadequate; this is an unfortunate omission. Where the geology is recorded sandstone is the most frequent, occurring as it does in many areas of GB, and being particularly prominent in north-east Scotland and Orkney. Here most of the Stones are 'slabs' of varying height up to 5.5 metres *(942 Orkney HY306128, photo 19)* and some slabs are only 0.15 metre thick because the sandstone rock in these areas has very thin but well marked bedding planes. There are a pair of slabs of metamorphic rock *(260 Maeni Hirion Penhros Feilw Anglsey SH228819, photo 20)* which are 2.85 metres high but only 0.35 and 0.2 metre thick. It is difficult to comprehend how they were produced. Many Stones in Cornwall, Dartmoor, much of Wales and Scotland are granite. Stones formed from the other rocks which occur in GB are at a much lower incidence. Almost all the Stones in Pembroke are of the local dolerite, better known as Prescelli 'bluestone'. All the 14 Stones and the 'polishing stone' in Wiltshire are sarsens and all Stones in the Cotswold area are much weathered oolitic limestone. This distribution emphasises the use of the local rocks for the Standing Stones.

28 quartz Stones *(2.2% of all prehistoric Stones)* form a particular but small group within the GB Stones. They can be an arresting sight glistening in the sun. They are clearly a feature where they occur as follows -

England	6	*(2.7 % of English stones)*
Scotland	2	*(0..3% of Scottish Stones)*
Wales	18	*(3.2% of Welsh stones)*
Total for GB	26	quartz Stones

The physical features of the quartz Stones, such as the size and shape, are generally similar those of all the other Stones -

pillars or columns	8
stumps	8
slabs	5
amporphous lumps	2
lying flat	4

The heights of the quartz Stones are shown in fig 7, the average height being 1.8 metres with a range from 0.8 metres to 3.3 metres. Seven are 2.0 metres high or more. The large white Stone at *(1112 Aberdeen NJ735241)* is 3.3 metres high and is a magnificent sight in the sun. It is an outlier to a recumbent stone circle. The physical features of the quartz stones, such as size and shape, are similar to those of all the other Stones. Five of these quartz Stones in England are on Exmoor, one of which *(190 Exmoor SS601439)* was broken by lightning in 1996 (personal information from the farmer 1998) but the stump is still 2.5 metres high; it was originally much higher. The Boscowen Un circle *(1173 Cornwall SW412273, photo 5)* has a leaning central pillar of quartz which is 2.7 metres high. Wales has a much larger number of quartz Stones for which there is no obvious explanation. In Wales two of these Stones are at altitudes of 480 metres *(897 Powys SN925925)* and 545 metres *(899 Powys SN863620, photo 18)*. Assuming that quartz boulders are not found at these altitudes it would have been a big sustained effort to get them up to these heights. Stones of other rock also occur at similar high altitudes in Central Wales. There is a row of seven Stones *(882 Powys SN835145)* of which six are quartz and one of sandstone. One large quartz Stone was moved for use as a war memorial and now stands at *(1101 Gwynedd SN661856)*. Individual quartz boulders may occasionally be seen in Welsh fields *(Other Stones Wales 135 SN467505)* but this had been removed by 2010. They are often used for embellishments along driveways and in gateways in west Wales but not in England or Scotland.

41 other Stones *(3.2% of all Stones)* have well defined crystalline inclusions of quartz -

8 in England	*(3.5% of English Stones)*
23 in Scotland	*(3.5% of Scottish Stones)*
11 in Wales	*(3.1% of Welsh Stones)*.

These vary from well defined quartz veins to individual crystals or pebbles. The equivocal sarsen at *(414 Sussex TQ288060)* is the only sarsen with quartz inclusions. There are no Stones with quartz inclusions in the sandstone areas of north-east Scotland, Orkney or in Shetland, although there are three Stones with quartz inclusions in the Western Isles. There is little mention of quartz Stones in the literature. In Ireland Burl (1993 c) records 'huge' quartz portal stones at the Slaney circle and also at Athgreaning and there are quartz pebbles within the circle at Reanascreena (Burl 1993 d), but nothing like this is recorded in GB.. Were quartz Stones, or those with well marked quartz inclusions considered to be valuable and especially selected for these features or were they just the most readily available local stones? The stone row at *(897 Powys SN925925)*, the quartz Stones on hilltops in Wales, and the quartz centre Stone within the Boscowen Un stone circle *(1137 Cornwall SW412273, photo 5)* and the use of quartz recorded in Ireland by Burl (1993 d) might suggest that quartz did have a special significance for some of our Forebears.

The Distribution of Standing Stone Sites

Sites with prehistoric Stones are present in most areas of Great Britain, except in the South East, the Pennines, Snowdonia and the Scottish Highlands in all types of landscape, terrain and most geological formations except rugged mountain areas, from the sea shore *(667 South Uist Western Isles NF745145)* to the top of high hills *(898 Powys SN943699 at 460 metres photo 14, and 899 Powys SN863620, photo 18,* amongst sand dunes *(310 Argyll NR657245)* and in river gorges *(71 Powys SO183198)*. In this gazetteer there are only two sites south and east of the line from Hull to Southampton, well shown in *(fig.1)*. There is little suitable stone in this area of England, although Lincolnshire has a ridge of excellent building stone but does not have prehistoric Standing Stones (J. S. Catney Lincolnshire Archaeological Officer 1997, personal communication). Sarsen stones were present on the South and North Downs, and it is speculated that there may have been numerous sarsen monuments in these areas which have been lost over the centuries. These chalk Downs still have three sites with sarsen Stones including the equivocal Gold Stone *(414, East Sussex, TQ288607, which has been moved and has a dubious provenance)*, the impressive Coldrum Burial Chamber *(732, Kent, TQ288060)* and Kit's Coty House chambered tomb *(Kent, TQ745608, which is not featured in this work)*. It has been suggested that in the south-eastern areas where wood was plentiful there were wooden prehistoric monuments, analogous to Standing Stones, which have been lost as is suggested in some areas of Cornwall (Barnatt 1982a). The recent finding of 'Sea Henge' at Hunstanton in Norfolk (Brennand 2004) may support this opinion. Much of these areas were probably densely wooded lowland which were avoided by the limited population (Hawkes 1986a). Norfolk has glacial erratic boulders which can be seen on village greens, three of which may have been set up as Standing Stones in prehistoric times (E. J. Rose, Norfolk Landscape Archaeology, personal communication 1997). The Downland areas of South-Eastern England have been farmed for many centuries so that prehistoric sites and any Stones are more likely to have been lost or cleared and wooden monuments will have disintegrated.

Sites are predominately situated along the western and the north-eastern seaboards of Great Britain and on the western and northern archipelagoes (figs. 1 England, 2 Scotland, and 3 Wales) where there are 698 prehistoric sites with 915 prehistoric Stones *(76.8% of all the prehistoric sites and 75.8% of the all the prehistoric Stones)*. Some are almost on the foreshore *(675 Isle of Harris Western Isles NG020939)* and others overlook substantial lengths of coast from cliff edge sites *(106 Pembroke SM862148)*. Along the West coast of Great Britain from the Scilly Isles and the Lizard Peninsula to Little Loch Broom and including the inshore Argyll archipelagos and the Western Isles there are 414 prehistoric sites with 529 Standing Stones *(46% of all prehistoric sites and 43.7% of all prehistoric Standing stones)*. On the North-East Coast of GB, from Flamborough Head northwards to Duncansby Head and including the Orkney and Shetland Islands there are 218 prehistoric sites with 386 prehistoric Stones *(23.9% of all prehistoric sites and 32% of the prehistoric Stones)*. All this is clearly shown in Table 6 and figs. 1, 2 and 3, illustrating that the prehistoric sites and Stones are concentrated within the peninsular and island areas of West Cornwall, Pembrokeshire, the Lleyn Peninsula, Anglsey, Galloway, the Kintyre peninsula, and the archipelagoes of the Firth of Clyde, the Inner Hebrides, Western Isles, Orkney and Shetland. This clearly indicates that many of the early peoples dwelt in coastal areas and presumably they were effective seafarers. The Minch is a difficult sea passage and there are over 60 miles of open ocean between Orkney and Shetland. On the Scottish West Coast north from Loch Sunnart there are only three recorded prehistoric Standing Stones *(555 Argyll, NM527625, 765 Highland NM659493 and 1125 and Ross and Cromarty NH080916)*. Along the east coast north from Flamburgh Head there are sites somewhat inland on the North Yorkshire Moors, in Northumberland and many sites amongst the inland areas in Fife, Angus, Perthshire and Aberdeenshire. Other sites are situated along the coast to Inverness and thence northwards to the Pentland Firth. The two large counties of Perth and Aberdeen have many inland sites, some deep within the glens (fig. 2). The Scottish brochs (Childe V. G. 1940), dating from almost two millennia after the Standing Stones, are also essentially distributed along the coasts and islands of western and northern Scotland and Shetland (Graham and Anna Ritchie 1991).

The inland areas have much lower concentrations of Stones except, as noted above, for the hinterland of Aberdeen and Perth. There are numerous sites on the hill areas of Dartmoor (17 sites) and Exmoor (10 sites), the more southerly of the Cambrian Mountains (58 sites many at around 500 metres altitude) and on the hills of the Scottish Borders (8 sites). Along the Cotswold Hills there are 15 sites to the south-west of Oxford but

Fig. 1 Distribution of Standing Stones in England

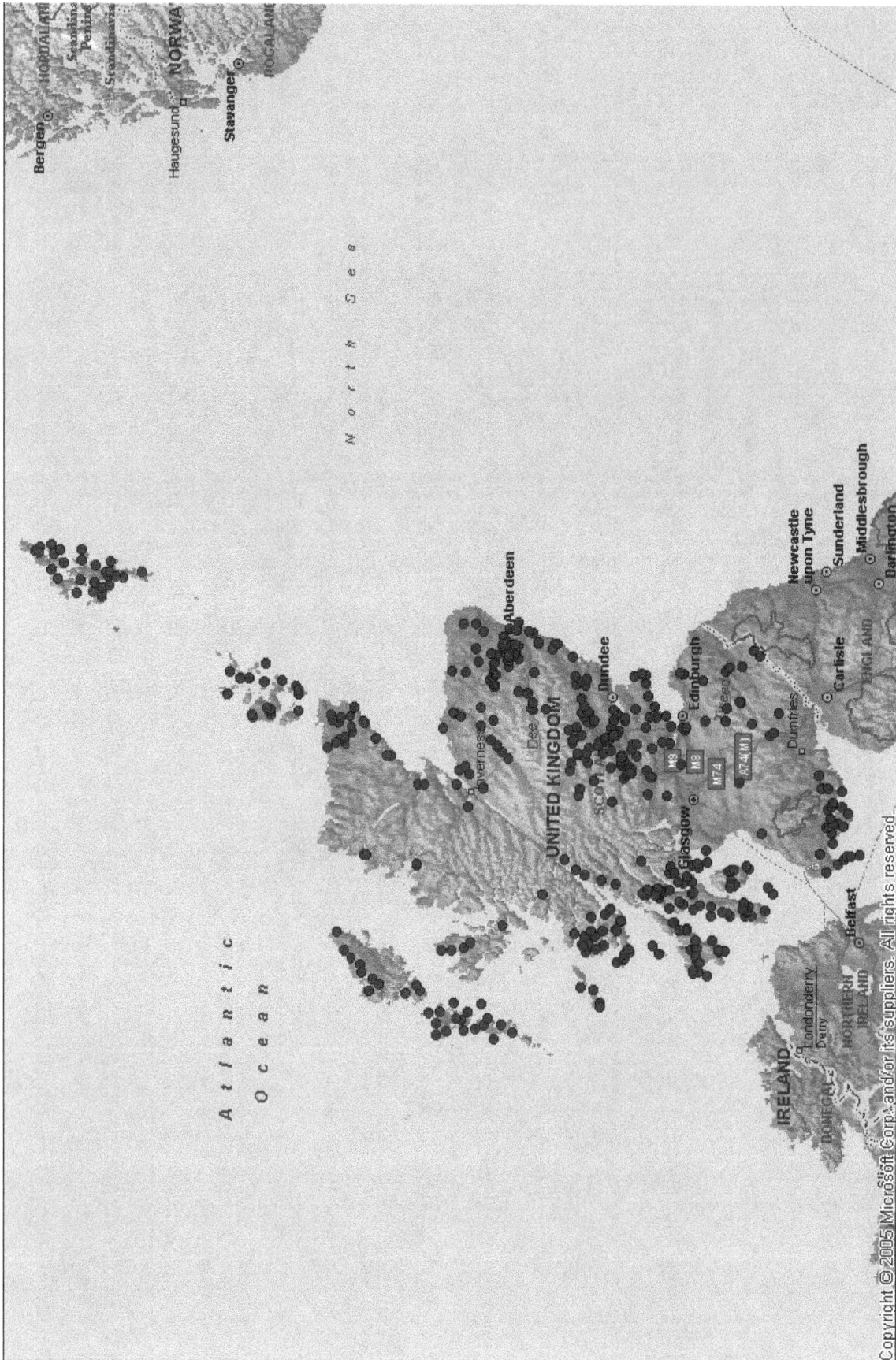

Fig. 2 Distribution of Standing Stones in Scotland

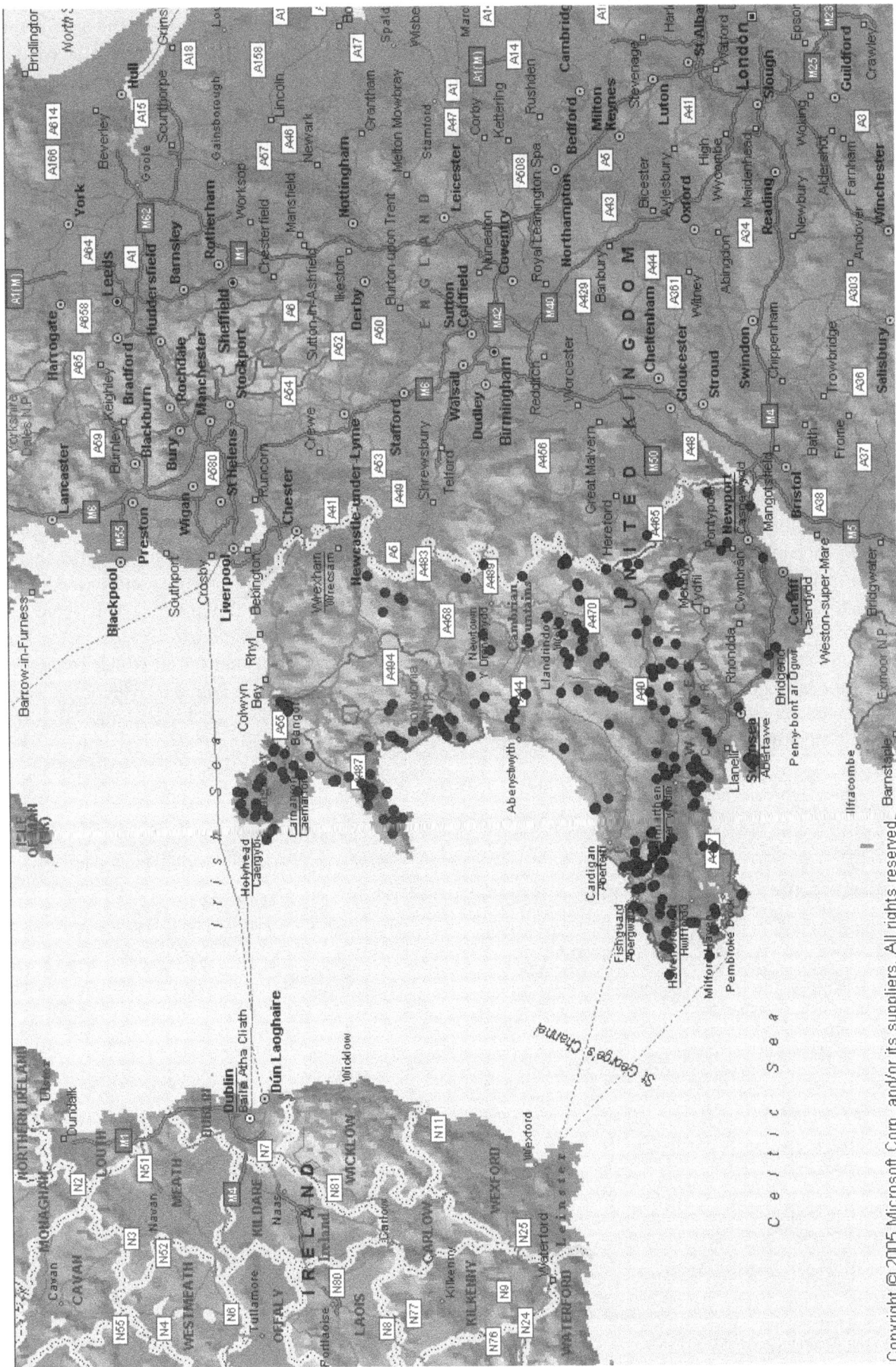

Fig. 3 Distribution of Standing Stones in Wales

none to the north-east of the sites at *(21, Warwick, SP196310 7 and 151, Oxford, SP378238)*. This seems odd, especially as there are many archaeological remains to the northeast of Oxford along this ridge of good quality limestone which continues northeast for a further 200 kilometres. There are three scattered sites in the Derbyshire Peak, only one site on the Pennines *(1138, West Yorkshire, SE207435)* with none along the central Pennine ridge which again seems odd considering the substantial amount of archaeological remains along the Pennines. It is not clear if Stones have been lost in these areas or very few Stones were erected. There are 14 sites around the edges of the Lake District *(one of which, the Shap Alingment, Cumbria 170 to 176 has 12 Standing Stones, and 132 'Long Meg' Cumbria NY570372 photo 4, an outlier who has a stone circle with 69 'daughters')* and 11 sites on the North Yorkshire Moors. In the Highlands of Scotland some isolated sites are found far up the glens at Killin *(651, Perth, NN561316)*, Kinloch Rannoch *(682, Perth, NN670580 and 683, Perth, NN617590)*, Ballater *(787, Aberdeen, NO30011692)*, Boat of Garten *(956, Highland, NH969201)* and Spittal of Glenshee *(761, Perth, NN109703)*. All these Highland sites are in the bottom of the glens and close to rivers. Williams (1988b), quoting Roese, points out that most of the Welsh Standing stones are on relatively low ground, below 250 metres. Fig. 3 shows that most of the inland Welsh Standing Stones are in the southern half of Wales.

Figs. 1, 2, and 3 show that most sites are in the coastal areas and below 200 metres. There are 55 sites *(10.8% of all prehistoric sites)* between 200 metres and 300 metres and a further 61 prehistoric sites *(6.8%)* are above 300 metres as is shown in Table 7. In the Scottish Highlands there are only 5 sites above 300 metres compared with 24 in England and 32 in Wales. As noted above three of these higher Scottish sites are in the bottom of and far up the Highland glens *(752, Perth, NO153607; 753, Perth, NO138670 and 761, Perth, NN109703)*, and the other two are on rolling hills in the Borders *(765, Highland, MM659493 in the west, and 764, Borders, NT519580)*. Most of the Scottish sites above 200 metres are in the bottom of glens, except for 6 sites above 200 metres in the Border uplands one site *(764 Borders NT519580)* being at 370 metres, and one each in Dumfries and Ayrshire. Central Wales has large areas of high rolling hills above 200 metres where there are 55 sites which includes the Harlech Alingment of 8 Standing Stones *(603, Gwynedd SH608322)*. 32 of the Welsh sites are at or above 300 metres on the tops of the central Cambrian Mountains, 6 of which are above 400 metres and have not been visited by me (my hill walking days were over). This contrasts with only 5 sites above 300 metres in the whole of Scotland. A great deal of organisation, engineering skill and manual effort would have been required to move and place these various Stones onto the high hills.

TABLE 7 PREHISTORIC STANDING STONE SITES IN COASTAL COUNTIES

Total number of all prehistoric coastal sites : 698 & prehistoric coastal Standing Stones : 948

West coast with archipelagos & Isle of Man				East Coast with Orkney & Shetland Islands		
	sites	Standing Stones			sites	Standing Stones
Cornwall	45	62	Includes the isles of Scilly	East & North Yorkshire	14	31
Carmarthen	28	42		Northumberland	15	22
Pembroke	58	75		Lothians	9	9
Cardigan	12	13		Fife	17	22
Llyen peninsula	20	20	Part of Gwynedd	Perth (with inland sites)	65	81
Rest of Gweynedd	21	32		Angus	17	22
Anglesey	29	33		Aberdeen (with inland sites)	54	84
Isle of Man	5	5		Highland coastal areas	50	63
Galloway	24	45		Orkney islands	22	27
Argyll mainland	61	92		Shetland Islands	27	40
Argyll islands*	68	90				
Western Isles	28	38				
Totals	399	547			290	401
% of all the prehistoric sites and stones	*44.5%*	*44.5%*			*32.4%*	*32.6%*

TOTAL of all prehistoric sites in coastal counties: 698 – *77.9% of all 897 prehistoric sites*

TOTAL of all prehistoric Standing Stones in coastal counties: 948 – *77.2% of all 1203 Standing Stones*

* includes the islands of the Inner Hebrides & in the Firth of Clyde

There are no sites on the slopes or the tops of the Highland mountains or in the broken mountainous areas of North Wales and the Lake District, which appears to reflect the precipitous topography making these areas unsuitable for habitation and the erection of Standing Stones. The more southern part of the Cambrian mountain area is generally rounded and rolling, as are the hills along the Scottish Borders, Dartmoor, Exmoor, and the North Yorkshire Moors. There are Standing Stone sites within all these latter hill areas. Table 8 also shows that *79%* of all the prehistoric sites and *75.8%* of the prehistoric Stones are on lower ground within littoral counties and that *21%* of all sites are above an altitude of 200 metres. The distribution and concentration of the Stones, except in the chalk areas of the south east of England, may indicate and have been associated with the centres of population during the prehistoric era when the Stones were being raised.

The depth of the Stones within the sockets is recorded from various sources for 30 prehistoric Stones in Table 11, and varies from 0.3 metres up to 2.5 metres in the ground. There is one exceptionally deep socket recorded to be at least 4.8 metres *(the Rudstone Monument, 50, York, TA09867)* which is not typical of the general socket depth. If correct it makes the overall length of the Rudstone Monument to be an incredible 12.8 metres. The Hoar Stone *(152, Gloucester, SP171259)* is thought to have been broken (Corio and Corio 2003) and the suggested socket depth of 2.5 metres *(228% of the current height)* which is clearly unnecessarily deep for a Stone only 0.9 metre high seems to support this suggestion.

TABLE 8 PREHISTORIC STANDING STONE SITES ABOVE 200 METRES

	Total number of prehistoric sites	Sites at 200 to 300 meters	Sites above 300 meters	
ENGLAND	160 *(100%)*	27* *(17%)*	24 *(15%)*	*includes the Shap alignment of 12 Standing Stones as one site
SCOTLAND	484 *(100%)*	57 *(12%)*	5 *(1%)*	
WALES	252 *(100%)*	55** *(22%)*	32 *(13%)*	**includes the Harlech Alignment of 8 Standing stones as one site
TOTAL for Great Britain	896 *(100%)*	139 *(16%)*	61 *(7%)*	

The unusual socket depths of the Rudstone Monument and the Hoar Stone are excluded from analysis of the depths of the sockets. The Stone at Trye *(345 Cornwall SW460350)* is unusual in that it was inserted into a burial chamber and is also excluded. Eleven *(42.3%)* of the recorded sockets are less than 1.0 metre deep, and one is only 0.3 metres. Based on data from the other 28 Stones , the percentage of the Standing Stones within the socket varied from *15% to 36%* of the total length of the Stone and the average insertion is *24.6%*. This seems little enough to support some of the larger Stones as the packing stones within the socket could only have been poorly compacted with wooden rammers. Some Stones lying exposed have a square cut foot *(599, Gwynedd, SH412430)* whereas others have convex ends *(1118, Aberdeen, NJ7101570)* which would further reduce the stability. There is no obvious correlation between between the total length of the Standing Stones and the depth of the sockets even though the prehistoric peoples were well able to undertake deep excavations, as shown by the 9 metre deep and steep-sided ditch at Avebury (Hawkes 1986). There are many examples of tall thin Standing Stones which have a shallow socket and appear inherently unstable (Williams 1988c). Some Stones *(243 Dartmoor Devon SX69665)* are somewhat loose within the socket and should be repacked around the base before they fall. One method of packing and possibly stabilising slabs is clearly shown around the base of a slab 2.25 metres high *(720 Caithness ND33844, sketch 10)*. This Stone is a slab 2.25 metres high, and with the associated packing stones appears to stand almost clear of the ground. The age is not clear and nor is it clear if the Stone and packing stones were always standing almost above ground level. Given the shallow sockets of many stones it is suprising that so many are still standing and vertical.

Leaning , Fallen and Destroyed Stones

265 *(21% of all Stones)* of the prehistoric Standing Stones are now leaning and there are numerous now fallen Stones, both of which appear to reflect the shallow sockets of some Stones (Table 11). The recorded height of the leaning Stones was measured from ground level along the length of the Stone to the summit; the recorded height is thus not the current height of the summit above ground level, but the original height of the Stone had it been vertical (sic). The angles of lean were recorded to the nearest 5° and vary from the vertical by 5° up to 80° (Table 9). Out of 265 leaning Stones 111 Stones *(42% of all leading Stones)* lean to only 5° or 10°. Some large Standing Stones such as *(409, Carmarthen, SN515281)* and *(95 Powys SO124396, photo 21)* both of which have a length of 2.2 metres and lean at 30 ° and are large heavy Stones. *(1098 Glamorgaan SO104034)* leans at 40° but although 2.4 metres long it is a much lighter Stone as is *(804 Aberdeen NJ699066, sketch 4)* Two substantial Stones, one at *(826 Tiree, Highland NM074480)* 2.6 metres long leaning at 50° and another *(671 North Uist, Western Isles)* 3.3 metres long leaning at 30°, both overhang a pool in waterlogged ground and would appear to be quite unstable. At *(247 Powys SO014580)* the angle of lean had recently increased to 30° (personal information from the farmer 1998).

Leaning Stones do not appear to have been noted in the literature. As with other factors associated with the Stones the numbers and percentages of leaning Stones and the angles of lean are generally similar for England, Scotland and Wales. The large angles of lean of over 50° or more generally occur in small short stones. The movements generated by the lean of the larger Stones are obviously substantial and it is difficult to comprehend how these angles of lean are sustained, especially in waterlogged ground. If these now leaning Stones were originally vertical, the sockets of many Stones must somehow have become more stable and secure after the leaning movement commenced, and it seems that some Stones are still moving in their sockets. It may be that some were never raised to be completely vertical.

TABLE 9   LEANING PREHISTORIC STANDING STONES
(WITH % OF LEANING PREHISTORIC STONES IN PARENTHESIS)

	number & % of all GB leaning prehistoric Stones	angles of lean			
		0° to 19°	20° to 39°	> 40°	
ENGLAND	**53** *(22%)*	24 *(45%)*	20 *(37%)*	9 *(17%)*	2 Stones lean at 70° & 75°
SCOTLAND	**146** *(22%)*	87 *(60%)*	51 *(35%)*	8 *(12%)*	4 Stones lean at 50°, 55°, 60 ° & 80°
WALES	**66** *(27%)*	32 *(51%)*	23 *(35%)*	11 *(17%)*	1 Stone leans at 80°
TOTALS for GREAT BRITAIN	**265** *(21%)*	**143** *(60%)*	**94** *(35%)*	**28** *(12%)*	

This work records 49 prehistoric Stones which have fallen, been thrown down or otherwise destroyed. An unknown number of Stones appear to have been lost over the centuries. Numerous fallen Stones which are still visible at the site are recorded in the gazetteer but are excluded from the analyses. There are some sites with a fallen Stone lying at the foot of a still upright Stone *(60, Isle of Wight, SZ407842, photo 22 and 918 Sutherlqnd, NH587968, and 206 Angus NO274564 with 2 prostrate Stones beside a large Stone)*. Some Stones may never have been erected, as has been suggested at the Cultoon circle *(10 and 11, Islay, Argyll islands, NR187560)* (Newton 1995) or some of these Stones may have been thrown down later (Burl 1979) as at *(121 Perth NN946521)* or intentionally destroyed.

There are records that 14 Stones have fallen in recent years and there must be others --

(327 Glamorgan SS462901) fell in 1947 at end of a severe winter (personal information from farmer 1999) and is still lying where it fell
(61 Fife NO1149044) fell in 1972, one of a pair, both of which were then set into concrete.
180 Argyll NM831505) fell in 1978 and was re-erected and set into concrete, but not on the original site (National Monuments Records Scotland 1999).
(710 Western Isles NB11164343) is one Stone on a complex site, 3.1 metres high, which fell in 1910 and was re-erected in concrete in 1998
(545 Mull, Argyll NM545396) which fell in 1999 and was re-erected in the same socket by the farmer (personal information 2004)
(595 Gwynedd SH403525) fell in 2000 and needs to be re-erected
the slab at *(1118 Aberdeenshire NJ710157)* was blown over c. 1995 (information from farmer, 2004) and lies where it fell; the total length on the ground is 3.1 metres.
(599 Lleyn Gwynedd SH412403) fell in about 1938 and still lies in the farmyard
Stone 2 at *(1059 Galloway NX352581)* fell in 1995. It is 1.7 metres on the ground and has spherical ends so may have been unstable.
(1068 Galloway NX) fell 'some years ago' but is still marked on the OS map as a 'Standing Stone'. It is a flat stone 1.7 metres long lying on the ground. There is no sign of the socket or how far it was in the ground.
(790 Grampian NJ314381) fell and was re-erected in 2000.
A Stone at *(187 Aberdeen NJ760243)* is marked on the OS map. It is stated by the farmer (personal information 2004) to have fallen in 1999 and broken into three pieces.
(1118 Aberdeen NJ710157) was 'blown down' in 1985 (farmer communication 2004) and lies on the ground.

11 Stones on seven sites are known to have been intentionally thrown down or destroyed in recent years --

Two large stones at *(121 Perth NN946521)* are stated by the farmer (personal communication 1997) to have been thrown down in 1910 'to improve the field' and they are visible today, partially buried, beside the large Stone which is still standing.
Two Stones were destroyed by the farmer in 1935 *(Stones Not visited or Lost 50 Powys SO094599)* (information from Carregwiber farmer 2000).
A Stone marked on the OS map *(Stones Lost or Destroyed 185 Aberdeen NJ824137)* was removed some twenty years before the current farmer took the farm (information from the farmer 2004). This Stone is still marked on the Ordnance Survey map.
The Giant's Stone *(Bisley Gloucester SO918062)* was removed by the farmer about 1990 (D. Martin personal communication 1997).
Two Stones *(Stones Lost or Destroyed 50 Powys SO084598)* were destroyed by the farmer in 1987.
Two Stones *(Stones Lost or Destroyed 81 Powys SO071594)* are stated by the farmer to have been destroyed in 1985.
The Stone at *(Stones Lost or Destroyed 164 Aberdeenshire NJ984416)* has 'recently disappeared' (information from farmer 2003).

In addition 2 Stones have been destroyed by explosives --

The Stone at *(888 Pembroke SN136379)* was broken in half by explosives in c. 1900 because it was loose in the socket and thought to be dangerous (personal information from the farmer in 2002). The stump is 1.2 metres high and the shot hole is clearly visible What appears to be the top portion of the Stone, which is 1.25 metres long, is visible in the bottom of the nearby hedgerow. It should be replaced onto the stump.
A quartz Stone in Cardigan *(SN382433)* was destroyed by explosives in about 1932 (personal information from the farmer 2006) and some of the resulting quartz rubble is visible where it has been built into the field bank by the farm entrance and also across the road.

15 other Stones *(1.2%)* are now known to be concreted into place, 5 in England, 8 in Scotland and 2 in Wales. Presumably some appeared to be unstable and others were set into concrete when re-erected after falling *(180 Argyll NM831050)* or having been moved *(1007 Aberdeen NJ922083)* may not now be in the original orientation.

It is now easy to remove large Stones with modern excavators and this appears to have occurred all too often after WWII. The Stones were seen as an interference with modern agriculture. Farmers and landowners now (2008) appear to better appreciate and understand the intrinsic value of the Stones on their land and have ceased to destroy them. Relatively few of the extant Stones are currently scheduled as Ancient Monuments and this protection should be rapidly extended to many more Stones., but there appears to be beaurocratic inertia to avoid doing this. There must be numerous other Stones which have been lost over the recent decades. The environmental agencies need to be more vigilant.

963 *(79%)* of all the prehistoric Standing Stones recorded in this gazetteer are still vertical after c. 4000 or more years. It is a great tribute to the engineering skills of our forebears that these Stones, many three, four or more metres high and often weighing many tonnes, were transported, some apparently onto hilltops, erected and stabilised in the sockets without steel rammers or concrete. Packing stones can be readily seen around the base of many Stones and could have been but poorly compacted with wooden rammers. These packing stones are noted in the appendices. There must be many other fallen and destroyed sites and Stones which are unrecorded and lost as shown by the farms called 'Standingstones' or similar names (as at NO740931 and NO845978 in Aberdeen) where no Stone is now present. It seems probable that more Stones will start to lean and may fall in the future.

The Configuration of Multiple Stone Sites

Sites with multiple Standing Stones may be arranged in numerous configurations as indicated in Table 10. Some appear to be quite random *(710 Lewis Western Isles NB164343)* and cannot be easily categorised. Three Stones may appear as triangles *(266, Anglesey, SH364917)*, or as short rows *(392, Monmouth, SO499051)* and some may be the remains of ruined circles *(66 Fife NO405026, photo 23)* (information from Fife County Council 1997). Sites with four Stones may form 'four posters' (Burl 1988) with the four Stones arranged in a square or rectangle (photo 3). The size of 'four posters' can vary from that at *(1078, Galloway, NX531524)* which is 2.7 by 2.4 metres with the highest Stone 0.7 metres to one at *(1140, Mull, NM503462)* with sides up to 40 metres and a Stone of 1.8 metres. Burl (1988) suggests it is not always clear if four posters were intended to be rectangular settings or if some may be basic or ruined circles.

TABLE 10   THE CONFIGURATIONS OF SITES WITH MULTIPLE STANDING STONES (AFTER BURL 1993 B)

A   PAIR of STONES

B   SHORT ROW of 3 *(392 Monmouth SO 499051)* or 4 Stones *(624 Carmarthen SH714717.)* Along the coasts of the Irish Sea these rows are often aligned to the mid-winter sunset.

C   LONG SINGLE ROW, seldom straight, often 180 metres or more *(512 Cornwall SW936676 and as around the Erm valley on 344 Dartmoor).* Some rows on Dartmoor extend for several kilometres or more, but these are not included in this work.

D   DOUBLE ROW of MANY STONES *(653 Dartmoor Devon SX555748)*

E   TANGENTIAL AVENUE associated with Stone Circles

F   TRUE AVENUE double rows, unequivocally attached to a henge or circle *(The West Kennet Avenue at Avebury Wiltshire)*

G   SETTING of MULTIPLE ROWS, complexes of several rows set alongside each other, parallel or splayed; mostly confined to Southern Britain *(on Dartmoor)*, Caithness *(Hill o' Many Stones Caithness ND295384 – not in gazetteer)* and Sutherland *to which can be added (Author's suggestion) --*

'FOUR POSTERS' (Burl 1971)

COMPLEX SITES *(Author's terminology)* comprising numerous Stones in unexplained configurations such as *(344 Cornwall SW426349 and 179 Kilmartin Argyll, NR834964, photo 12)*

The now EXPOSED STONES of BURIAL SITES *(1155 Pembroke SN100370 and 966 Galloway NX517538)*

The PORTAL STONES of some barrows *(985 Wiltshire SU1104978)*

Table 11 The Recorded Depths of the Sockets of 30 Standing Stones

Measurements in metres, 1 - height above ground; 2 - depth of socket; 3 - total length of Stone; 4 - % total length in socket

OS ref	Name	County	1	2	3	4	references & comment
180	KINTRAW	Argyll	4	1	5	20%	Cowie (1980) Glasgow Arch. J. 7 pp 27
345	TRYE	Cornwall	2.5	1.4	3.9	36%	Russell & Pool refs 2; Stone originally in cairn. Excluded
62	ORWELL	Fife	3	0.8	3.8	21%	Buchanan 91979) Kinross antiquarian Soc. no. 6
50	RUDSTONE	Yorks	8	4.8	12.8	38%	Humberside CC. Monuments Record - excluded
14	Lwr. KILCHATTA	Colonsay	3.3	1.2	4.5	27%	RCAHMS pp88 of printout; bottom of Stone not found
336	BLIND FIDDLER	Cornwall	3.3	1.2	4.5	27%	Prehistoric Cornwall, John Barnatt, 1982, pp229
320	PIPERS est Stone	Cornwall	4.3	1.5	5.8	26%	Prehistoric Cornwall, John Barnatt, 1982, pp226
313	LONG STONE	Cornwall	2.9	1.5	4.4	34%	Prehistoric Cornwall, John Barnatt, 1982, pp236
*	MEAN PERHAN	Scilly Isles	7.3	1.3	8.6	15%	lost; Ancient Scilly, P. Ashby, 1974, pp149
474	RHOS-Y-CLEGYM	Pembroke	2.8	0.8	3.6	22%	Sacred Stones of Wales, Terry John, 1994, pp37/38
427	YAHAARWELL	Shetland	2.2	0.6	2.8	23%	fallen; it appears 0.6 metre was in ground – OS record
48	DEVILS ARROWS	Yorks	6.9	1.8	8.7	21%	SE Stone) these are the depths of the sockets given
48	" "	"	6.7	1.5	7.2	21%	Central Stone) by the Scheduling Authority 1997
49	" "	"	5.5	1.4	6.9	19%	NE Stone)
64	EASTER PITORTHIE	Fife	2.4	0.6	3.2	19%	S. Farrell, Fife County Archaeologist 1997, from county records
*	DAME BLANCH	Channel Islands	2.5	1	3.6	28%	Archaeology of Channel Islands, J. Hawkes 1986, pp300
*	LITTLE MENHIR	" "	1.8	0.6	2.4	25%	" " " " " " pp303
*	WHITE MENHIR	" "	1.7	0.3	2	15%	" " " " " " pp306
595	GLASFRYN LLEYN	Gwynedd	1.5	0.4	1.9	22%	fell June 2000; measured by OS 19-4-00
1145	BRIDGEND	Glamorgan	1.8	0.8	2.6	31%	Guide to Ancient Historic Wales – Glamorgan & Gwent, Whittle, 1992, HMSO & CADW pp25
50	ADAM, Avebury	Wilts	3.5	0.8	4.3	19%	Hengeworld, Mike. Pitts, 2001, pp208
*	DRUMFOURS	Aberdeen	1.4	0.4	1.8	22%	Stones lost in 1945
*	NINE STONES	Derbyshire	2	1	3	33%	Shell Guide to British Archaeology, Hawkes 1986, pp174
1097	AVEBURY cove stones	Wilts	4.4	2	6.4	31%	British Archaeology, May 2004, pp6
1113	AUCHRONIE HILL	Aberdeen	1.5	0.25	1.75	14%	1994 & re-erected by farmer
1118	NETHER COULIE	Aberdeen	2	0.7	2.7	26%	OS records – info from farmer after Stone "blown over"
152	HOAR STONE	Wilts	0.9 #	2.5	3.4	36%	Megaliths, Corio, 2003, pp88 – seems unlikely depth? *Excluded*
320	PIPERS est Stone	Cornwall	5	1.5	6.5	23%	Standing Stones in Wales & SW Engand 1988 pp 66
415	QUEEN'S STONE	Hereford	1.75	0.6	2.35	25%	Burl 1993, Carnac to Callanish, Yale university Press pp161
1118	NETHER COULIE	Aberdeen		0.7	3.1	22%	blown down 1985 & lies where it fell (farmer information 2004)

RANGE of SOCKET DEPTH is 0.3 to 2.0 metres, AVERAGE INSERTION is 22% & RANGE is 15% to 37% (with 3 suspect socket depths excluded)
345 TRYE (36%) , 313 RUDSTONE (385) & 152 HOAR STON E (36%) are excluded as the recorded depths are

* these sites are recorded in the literature   # the Hoar Stone may have been much taller & become broken

Some sites with multiple Stones are arranged as simple Stone rows or alignments some of which have two rows of Stones to form an avenue and either may have a blocking Stone at one or both ends *(653 and 654, Dartmoor, SX655748, photo 24 and SX555648)*. The various types of Stone Rows are well discussed by Burl (1993). Included in this gazetteer are the shorter Stone rows or alignments. The Merry Maidens *(512, Cornwall, SW936676)* has nine Standing Stones, the Harlech alignment *(603, Gwynedd, SH599309 and others)* has eight Standing Stones over a distance of 2.2 kilometres and The Shap alignment *(170, Cumbria, NY558152 and others to 175)* has twelve Standing Stones (some no more than small glacial boulders) and is 2.4 kilometres long. Some prehistoric Stone rows on Dartmoor contain hundreds of individual stones and are up to 3.4 km. long (Hansford Worth 1981), but are not included in this work. Kilmartin Glen in Argyll is now effectively one large, varied and very complicated site well described by (Butter 1999) covering an area of about 16 km. by 10 km. within which are several individual complex sites such as Ballymeanoch *(179, Kilmartin, Argyll, NR834964, photo 12)* which covers an area approximately 50 metres square with 6 large Stones up to 4 metres high and two large fallen (?) Stones with a ruined curb cairn 6 metres in diameter. The Templewood Setting *(527,528, and529, Kilmartin, Argyll, NR828976)* has 7 Standing Stones with numerous cup marks together with stone circles and other monuments. The Kilmartin area was developed over centuries. Some of the complex sites with Standing and fallen Stones may be ruined burial chambers or cairns *(924, Sutherland, NC629092)*. There may be no obvious explanations for some of these highly complex sites. The current arrangement of the Stones on multiple Stone sites may be different today from the original grouping for numerous different reasons (Thom and Thom 1990b) as has apparently occurred at Men an Tol *(344 Cornwall SW426349)* (Barnatt 1982b).

The Heights of Prehistoric Stones

The heights of prehistoric Stones above ground vary from 0.3 metres up to 8.2 metres and the average height is 2.0 metres (Table 1 and Figures 4, 5 and 6). The 'height' of all Stones refers to the visible height above ground and not the total length of the Stone. There are no differences in the overall heights between England, Scotland and Wales where the average heights are 2.0 metres, 2.0 metres and 1.9 metres respectively, although the tallest Stones in Wales are somewhat lower than in England and Scotland. The seven tallest Stones in Great Britain are shown in Table 12.

TABLE 12 THE SEVEN TALLEST STANDING STONES IN GREAT BRITAIN

England	Rudstone Monument	50 Yorks TA098677	8.2 metres	Devil's Arrow (south)	48 Yorks. SE392664	6.9 metres
Scotland	Stones of Stenness	976 Orkney HY308126 photo 19	5.5 metres	Balinaby	13 Islay Argyll NR200672 photo 32	5.4 metres
	Clach an Truiseil	679 Lewis NB375537	5.7 metres			
Wales	Fish Stone	71 Powis SO183198	4.5 metres	Llangynidr Bridge	72 Powis SO156203	4.2 metres

There are a few very small Stones, although the provenance of some *(898 Powys SN943699, photo 15)* may be uncertain. This short Stone, 0.4 metres high, may be the summit of a taller Standing Stone now almost buried in the machair. In a row of three Stones *(1072 Dumfries NT083038)* there is a small Stone of 0.4 metres, and at *(651 Perthshire NN561316)* there is a subsidiary Stone 0.25 high which may, however, be unconnected with the main Stone on that site. In Wales an alignment *(624 Conwy SH714717)*, orientated at about 135 degrees, has one larger Standing Stone of 1.8 metres with three smaller Stones two of which are 0.25 and 0.2 metres high and are within 28 metres of the major Stone and may be of equivocal provenance. Another alignment, oriented at c. 40 degrees *(557 Powys SO157569)* is composed of four small glacial boulders, two of 0.7 metres, and the others of 0.4 metres and 0.3 metres, with a large cairn 55 metres to the north-east. The Shap Alignment *(170 to 176 Cumbria NY566143)* orientated at 40 degrees includes, within the line of the alignment, three small uninteresting pink glacial granite boulders each c. 0.4 metres high, Stone numbers 11, 12, and 13, which may or may not be part of the prehistoric alignment.

The Shape of the Stones

The Stones are very varied and highly pleomorphic *(19 Avon 601631, photo 17, 934 Eday, Orkney HY564372, sketch 1 and 992 Aberdeen NJ461047 sketch 2 and 111 Wiltshire SU088963, sketch 5)* with many different shapes, contours, surfaces, cracks and visual impacts. The different shapes are suggested in Table 5 and the numerical distribution of these shapes are shown in Table 13. There is obviously no information whether some shapes may have had a particular significance for the peoples who erected them. Most Stones may have been used because they were immediately available and the shape might not have been considered or have been important, although tall columnar and slab Stones such as An Carra *(669 South Uist, Western Isles NF770320, photo 13, 536 Mull, Argyll NM618251, photo 16,* the Stones of Stenness *942 Orkney HY306126, photo 19 and 339 Cornwall SW442289, photo 39)* and other similar Stones could have been selected for their immediate visual impact like *(185 Argyll NR729864, sketch 3)* which is 3.3 metres high with a thin cross section. The geology of the local rock and the available boulders would determine the shape, outline and the surface of Stones such as The Pipers *(319 Cornwall SW435247, photo 30)* and is well shown by the Stone ploughed up and erected at Garth Farm in 1999 *(601 Gwynedd SH553422, photo 11)*. Some Stones appear to have been dressed because they are smoothed all over and/or shaped, such as the quartz centre Stone at Boscowen Un *(1173 Cornwall SW412273, photo 5)*, the square-cut Strontoiler *(364 Argyll NM908290)*, the phallic symbol (?) at *(15 Islay Argyll NR372457, photo 14)* and the elegant, thin smooth Balinaby Stone *(32 Islay Argyll NR220672, photo 32 a and b)*. One wonders how these tall slim Stones like *(1160 Anglsey SH508702, photo 23)* 2.9 metres high but only 0,7 by 0,3 metre in section and *(804 Aberdeen NJ699066, sketch 4)* 2.8 metres and 0.5 metre square and *(185 Argyll NR729864, sketch 3)* 3.3 metres high and 0.6 by 0.5 metre in section were found, or perhaps quarried. It seems most unlikely that Stones such as *364, 15, and 32* could have been found in their present form and shape after the ice finally thawed in c. 6000 BC.. If correct this supports the opinion

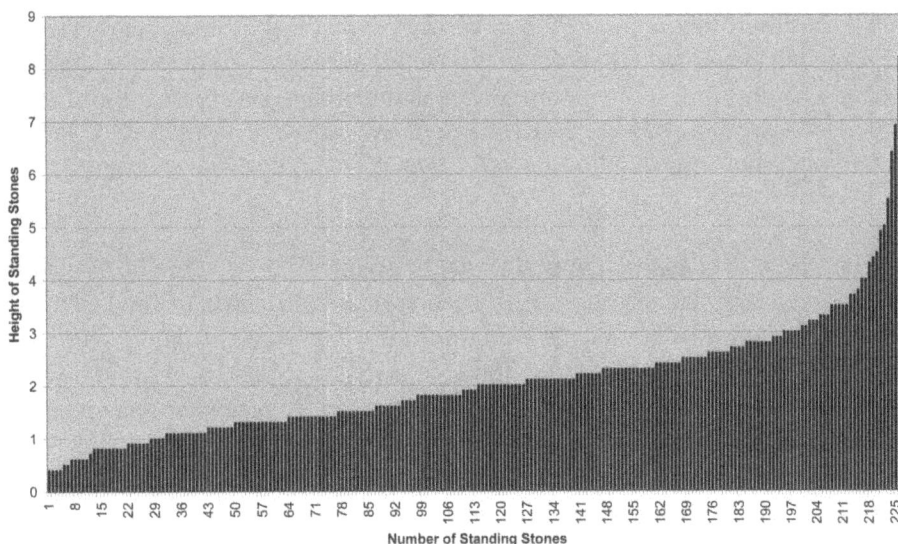

Fig. 4. Heights of Standing Stones in England

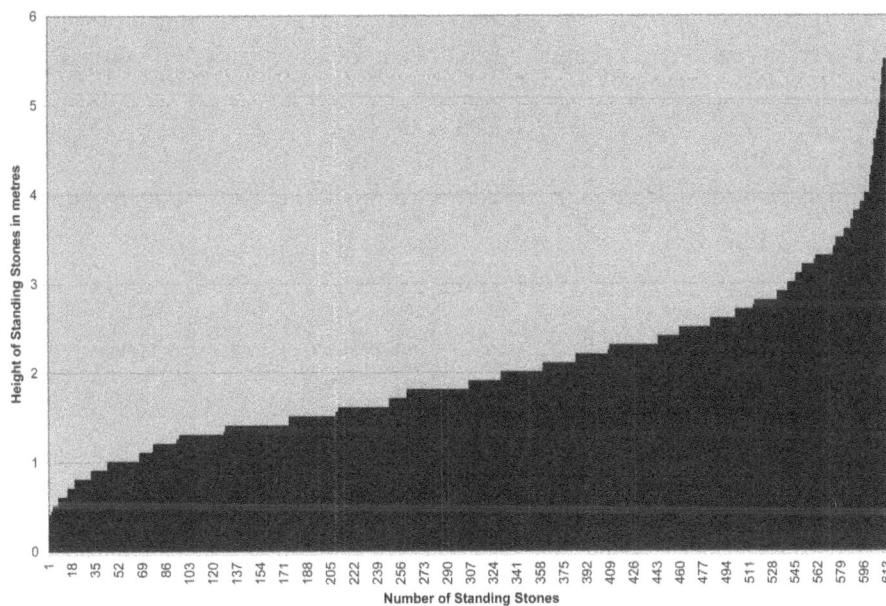

Fig. 5. Heights of Standing Stones in Scotland

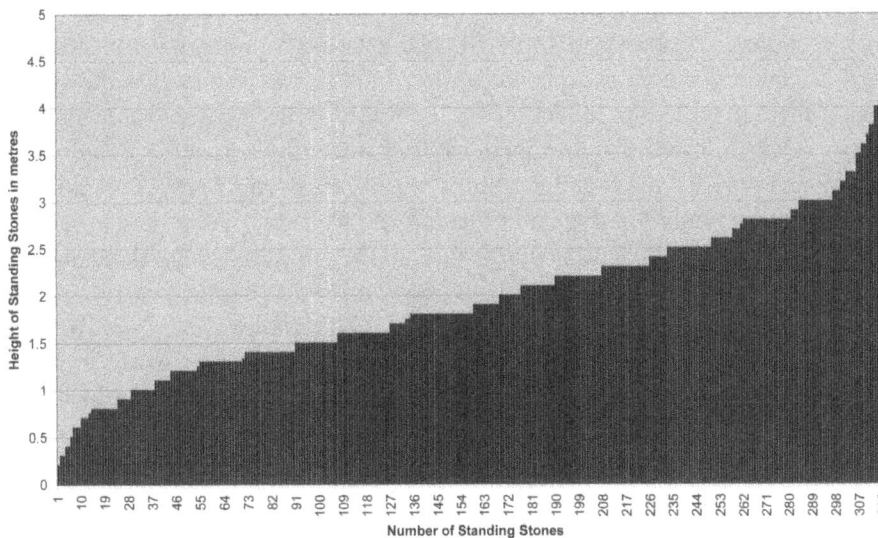

Fig. 6. Heights of Standing Stones in Wales

of the Monuments Protection Programme 1990 (cited above) that some Stones may have been 'sometimes dressed to shape'. Dressing these Stones to produce the shape and smooth surface would have been a laborious and difficult process without metal tools. Some Stones may perhaps have come out of the glaciers already smooth all over *(1108 Aberdeen NJ835152 and 1094 Lothians NT149744, photo 25)*. How the shapes of the three twisted 5 metre high Stones at Lundin Links *(66 Fife NO405026, see frontispiece)* were produced is an unresolved enigma.

The shapes vary from tall pillars and columns such as the southern most Stone of the 'Devil's Arrows' *(48 Yorkshire SE389663)*, which is perhaps not properly representative because of the height of 6.9 metres and the large volume, to other Stones of 3.3 metres *(536 Mull, Argyll NM618251, photo 16)*, a slim leaning stone of 2.7 metres at *(804 Aberdeen NJ699066)* to 'thick columns' *(197 Angus NO070369 and 139 Cumbria NY4863740)*, stumps at *(1183 Exmoor SS465443, photo 2))* and the somewhat rectangular Cat Stone *(1094 Lothians NT149744 photo 25)*. Most stumps are substantially below 2 metres in height. Slabs *(260 Anglesy SH228809, photo 20 and 931 Highland NH679359, photo 27)*, are found everywhere but are especially frequent in the areas of stratified sandstones in Caithness and Orkney *(720 Caithness ND338447)* and slate *(639 Isle of Man SC209683 and 630 Anglesey SH571776)*. Some conical and amorphous Stones are substantial *(58 Northumberland NT930304– 2.0 metres and 111 Wiltshire SU088963 - 3.5 metres high)* but are usually smaller *(253 Shropshire SJ237329 – 1.3 metres)* and some are longer than high *(509 Gloucester SP964065 – 1.2 metres high and 1.8 metres wide)*. *(273 Anglesy SH446843)* of metamorphic rock has an unusual hammer head shape. The numerous astronomical sighting lines suggested by Thom (1990a), would require tall thin Stones.

TABLE 13 THE NUMERICAL DISTRIBUTION OF THE SHAPES OF THE PREHISTORIC STANDING STONES

Stone shape (table 5, page 8)		1	2	3	4	5	6	7	8	9&10 together
	total prehistoric Stones	the numbers of stones exhibiting each shape								
ENGLAND	239	45	43	38	55	11	32	12	3	0
% distribution	*100%*	*19.1%*	*18.3%*	*16%*	*23%*	*5%*	*13%*	*5%*	*1%*	-
SCOTLAND	668	149	153	148	141	23	15	29	2	8
% distribution	*100%*	*22%*	*23%*	*23%*	*21%*	*4%*	*2%*	*4%*	*0.5%*	*1%*
WALES	322	42	91	51	66	29	25	18	0	0
% distribution	*100%*	*13%*	*28%*	*16%*	*20%*	*9%*	*8%*	*6%*	-	-
Total for GB	1224	236	282	237	262	63	72	59	5	8
% distribution	*100%*	*19%*	*24%*	*19%*	*21%*	*5%*	*6%*	*5%*	*0.4%*	*0.6%*

There are 275 Stone 'slabs' *(21% of all the prehistoric stones)*. The numbers of 'slabs' and the true compass orientations, where recorded, are shown in Table 14. The bearings were taken from the western edge of the Stone to within +/- 5° and are shown in Appendices 1, 2 and 3. This shows that the slabs have no obvious orientation, although there may be a predilection for the north/south bearing. Some slabs are proportionally very thin; *(91 Powys SO236328) is* 1.2 metres long and 0.15 metre thick and *(79 Pembroke SM828076)* is 3.1 metres high, 2.0 long and only 0.3 thick and the Stone at *(927 Highland NH679359, photos. 26a and 26b)* is 3.1 metres high, 3.0 wide and only 0.2 thick and that at *(720 Caithness ND338447, sketch 10)* is 2.3 metres high 1.1 long and 0.2 thick. Slabs are a particular feature of the northeast of Scotland and Orkney which is an area of narrowly but strongly bedded sandstones with very narrow strata which easily produce tall thin tabular blocks, some of which form spectacular tall and thin Stones *(937 Orkney HY312122, 3.5 metres high and 0.3 metres thick, photo 27, and 942 Orkney HY306126 5.5 metres photo 19)*. One would expect that these tall and thin Stones and those at *(79 Pembroke SH828076 and 927 Highland NH679359)* would be easily broken during transport, particularly if this was by glaciation. They could, in the sandstone areas of Northeast Scotland, have been easily and locally quarried. There are also slabs of igneous rock, such as the Balinaby Stone *(13 Islay, Argyll NR220672, photos 32 a and b)* which is 5.4 metres high, 0.9 metre wide and only 0.3 metre thick, and two igneous slab Stones *(260 Anglesy SH228809)* which are 2.85 metres high. And 0.35 and 0.2 metre thick.

TABLE 14 THE NUMBER OF 'SLABS' AND THE COMPASS ORIENTATIONS WHERE RECORDED

compass orientation		+/- 10°	10° to 33°	to 56°	to 79°	80° to 99°	100° to 123°	to 146°	to 170°
	total no. of slabs		north/south			east/west			
ENGLAND	33	6	4	4	4	5	4	4	2
SCOTLAND	177	29	10	24	20	25	26	32	11
WALES	65	11	11	12	11	5	9	2	4
Total GB	275	46	24	40	35	35	39	38	17

Substantial cracks

There are substantial fractures or cracks in many Stones, especially in the well defined strata of the sandstones of northeast Scotland. In some of the cracked Stones there have been attempts to fill and alleviate the resulting cracks with cement, which is well seen in *(928 Rousay Orkney HX404275, sketch 9)*. This does not effectively prevent further ingress of water which, subsequent upon freezing, is followed by further enlargement of the crack. Stones may thus be effectively split from top to bottom, as has happened with *(780 Caithness Highland ND199338, photo 28)* , and an early fracture in *(1084 Westray Orkney HY442472)* which, running from top to bottom of this 3.4 metre Stone, may eventually split the Stone. The Stone *(357 Argyll NM860016, photo 29)* is now reduced to a stump 1.8 metres high with a flat piece of Stone 4.0 metres long and 1.0 wide and 0.4 thick lying on the ground at the foot of the stump. This clearly fits neatly onto the stump from where it was 'blown down' in 1879 (RCAHM Scotland 1999), so it seems possible that there was then a significant fracture in the Stone which must originally have been almost 5 metres high and very impressive. Considerable fractures also occur in granite Stones. A granite Stone 4.0 metres high *(319 Cornwall SW435247, photo 30)* has two deep fractures visible on the northwest and east, and *(339 Cornwall SW442289)* has a well marked fracture running from the top to the ground which is visible from both the west and east. The pillar Stone, 2.7 metres high, at *(261 Anglesey SH341832, photo 31)* which was beginning to break up has been stabilised with two embracing bronze bands together with through bolts from west to east. The small Stone at *(1013 Aberdeenshire NJ610303)* which was broken is now riveted together with steel straps. It is probable that these fractured Stones will eventually be further split by ice and that many others will be damaged or destroyed. This appears to be a particular risk with the sandstone Stones.

Research is needed now on how to conserve these cracked Stones before they disintegrate, possibly by filling the fractures with modern pliable waterproof plastics. This would need to be done after a period of prolonged dry weather.

The Movement and Transport of Stones

Some large Stones have been moved substantial distances. Taking the specific gravity of stone to be about 2.6 it is possible to calculate the approximate weight of the visible portion of Stones. The weights of Stones as indicated here refer to the estimated weight of the portion of the Stone above ground, without accounting for the portion in the socket. Browne (1963) had served in the Royal Artillery and in an article titled 'Neolithic Engineering' described how it is possible to move heavy weights considerable distances using wooden rollers, sledges and man-power alone. It is possible using hardwood wedges and a heavy mallet to split fir tree trunks into semi-cylinders which can make a trackway for rollers (Swarbrick J. T. personal communication 2008). The prehistoric quarry extraction and transport of large pieces of stone is described in some detail by Mohen (1989 a). Thom (1984), who was an engineer, discussed the handling, moving and erection of 'large menhirs', and calculating the stresses involved, suggests that Stones could have been moved by levering the menhirs sideways or even rolling long menhirs along the ground. Thom concludes that our forebears were skilled engineers but that it is not possible to determine how these tasks, including the erection of the large menhirs, were accomplished. This skill and effort is demonstrated by the movement over c. 35 kilometres of the Stonehenge sarsens, the erection of the capstone at Tinkinswood *(333 Glamorgan ST092732)* which weighs about 40 tons (Whittle 1992) and the largest 'Devil's Arrow' *(48 Yorkshire SE3989663)* which weighs about 80 tonnes together with the apparent movement of large Stones onto the top of some Welsh hills *(899 Powys SN863620, photo 16)* which weighs c. 5.6 tonnes to an altitude of 545 metres. There is a Stone, 1.9 metres of height, on the side of a steep valley *(497 SN855215 Powys)* which weighs about 7.25 tonnes at an altitude of 500 metres and some 55 metres above the bottom of the valley and a smaller Stone somewhat over 1.0 metres of height on a steep hill side at an altitude of 260 metres *(Other Stones 124 Caithness ND0605500)*. It is not clear why Stones should be placed in these somewhat difficult hillside positions and whether the Stones were found *in situ* or were transported to their present positions. The movements and sites of many Stones, together with the construction of the Maes Howe chambered barrow in Orkney *(Ordnance Survey Laandranger map 6, HY317127)* with large slabs of rock accurately dressed, levelled and plumbed (Hawkes 1986 b) all demonstrate the engineering abilities, the perseverance and hard physical work of our forebears.

There was clearly skill in collecting suitable candidate standing stones, and most were found in the area local to the site of a Stone and were probably transported for only one to five kilometres (Thorpe and Williams-Thorpe 1991). In the areas subject to earlier glaciation it seems probable that some candidate standing stones were glacial boulders. Even today suitable boulders to produce Standing Stones of varying shapes may be seen in many areas *(Other Stones 102 Wester Ross NG702571 and Other Stones 1330 Pembroke SN038364)*. As discussed above it seems unlikely that some individual Stones would have been found in their present form in the environment. The tall thin Stone at Balinaby *(13 Islay Argyll NR202672, photo 32 a and b)* is 5.4 metres high, 0.9 m. wide but only 0.35 thick and weighs c. 4.25 tonnes without allowing for the portion underground is a very obvious example. It is a magnificent sight, and is probably the most elegant of all the Standing Stones in GB. It is composed of black igneous rock and seems to have been polished smooth on all sides with almost straight and smoothly rounded edges and it thus appears to have been dressed. How was this achieved? It must have been a difficult and potentially fragile Stone to handle, possibly to transport and then to erect and one which seems unlikely to have survived glacial transport and then to have been found locally after the last ice had thawed. Similar comments appear to apply to the Rudstone Monument *(50 Yorkshire TA098677)* which is 8.2 metres long with several metres underground and 1.8 metres but only 0.7 metre thick. It would have been easily broken within a glacier.

Some large and heavy Stones have been moved considerable distances from the area or outcrop where they apparently originated. The seventy-seven sarsens used at Stonehenge, averaging twenty-six dragging tons, were brought about 35 kilometres from the Marlborough Downs (Burl 1979). This journey would presumably have been over the dry chalk downs around the headwaters of the River Kennett. The Rudstone Monument *(50 Yorkshire TA098677)*, weighs up to 27 tonnes and is 8.2 metres high, without allowing for the large portion in the socket.. It is composed of a gritstone of which the nearest outcrops of this are c. 15 kilometres away at Cayton and Cornelian Bays (record of National Monument no. 26515 in County of Humberside, file reference AA 20090/1) who suggest movement by glaciation. The transport of this Stone by human agency would have been a substantial engineering feat (Evans D. H., Humberside Archaeology Partnership, personal communication

1997) and the ordnance survey map shows this would have involved crossing much low lying land associated with the rivers Derwent and Hertford which was probably swamp in prehistoric eras. This seems to be almost inconceivable, which suggests glacial movement. This Stone would probably have been easily damaged or broken in a glacier. The three extant Devil's Arrows *(48 and 49 Yorkshire SE389663)* which weigh c. 80, 46 and 32 tones above ground are of Millstone Grit, were possibly brought from Plumpton Rocks some 14 kilometres to the SW (Burl 1990) which would have involved crossing the River Nidd but Thorpe and Williams-Thorpe (1991) suggest the 'Arrows' came by glacial action from another outcrop 15 to 20 kilometres to the northwest, arguing that the movement of the ice sheet was from that direction. Transport of these large Stones over land by human agency would have involved a difficult river crossing from either possible source area. Clach an Truiseil *(679 Lewis Western Isles NB375537)* is a massive pillar 5.7 metres high and the portion above the ground weighs about 30 tonnes. There are no similar stones in that area of Lewis so it appears that this too may have been transported some distance, but there is no suggestion as to the possible source. It is suggested by Thorpe and Williams-Thorpe (as above 1991) that the movement of these large Stones over substantial distances must have been due to glaciation. It seems unlikely, however, that tall Stones with relatively square-cut upper ends like the Devil's Arrows *(48 and 49 Yorkshire SE389663)* or long fragile Stones such as Balinaby *(13 Islay Argyll NR202672, photo 32 a and b)* and the Rudstone *(50 Yorkshire TA098677)* could have survived the stresses inside a glacier for several kilometres without some evidence of glaciation. The movement of the Preselli bluestones over 300 kilometres to Stonehenge currently has no satisfactory explanation because convincing evidence for glacial movements or human transport by sea and land are considered by some people to be equivocal. The Fish Stone *(161 Powys SO183198),* which stands in the bottom of the narrow gorge of the River Usk, is suggested by Barber and Williams (1989) to have come from a quarry on the opposite side of the gorge and thus across the deep bed of the River Usk. This would have been a difficult undertaking. This Stone weighs some three tonnes (without the volume underground) and it must have a deep and secure socket to have withstood the numerous floods during the last three to four millennia.

Apart from moving Stones on reasonably level ground some appear to have been moved up hills. As discussed above there are numerous Stones which may have been transported onto the summit of hills up to 545 metres high and this is particularly evident in central Wales. Moving heavy stones over dry land would been difficult enough but moving stones uphill would be very laborious and crossing rivers and swamps would have been much more difficult and seemingly impossible. Much of this thus seems to argue for the long distance movement of some Stones by glaciation. The explanations for the movement and transport of large and potentially fragile Stones, whether by human or glacial agency, for substantial distances and often across what is now difficult terrain are thus not clear. Both human movement and glaciation appear to be incompatible with some aspects of the movement of some Stones so that there often seems to be no basis for any particular conclusion. As Thom pointed out some of our forebears were skilled engineers but after four millennia we seem unlikely to find the correct explanations for the transport of many of these Stones.

'Grooves'

Obvious 'grooves' due to weathering, some large, are now a significant feature on 32 Stones *(2.5% of all prehistoric Stones)* (Table 15). There is very little comment about grooves in the literature. 'Grooved' Stones are found in GB in the areas of calcareous sandstone. The grooves are considered to result from erosion along the joint planes when the calcareous material cementing these sandstones is eroded by acid rain (Dr. R. Ixer, personal communication 2009) which produces weathered grooves along both the joint planes in the strata and along the cross-bedding joints. This results in one, or more frequently two or more multiple grooves being formed along the joint planes on one, two three or all four sides of some Stones. The Stones with weathered joints are generally rectangular and this suggests that, having been erected with more or less flat sides, the grooves developed after erection of the Stone and are still continuing to be enlarged. The grooves thus have no archaeological significance, but they are now significant and obvious features on many Stones which cannot be ignored.

The grooves along the weathered joints are generally straight with perpendicular and well defined straight sides and clear-cut bevelled edges and the groove is usually smooth inside. Some are open and shallow and others deep and narrow. A marked feature is that most grooves are wider and deeper at the top and taper as they descend towards the ground becoming shallower and narrower, but some have parallel sides as on the north side of *(48 Yorkshire SE392664)*. Many Stones have multiple grooves, some as many as 13 on all four sides *(415 Hereford SO561181, photo 34)*. Depending on the height of the Stone the grooves vary in length from 0.5 metre up to 6.9 metres *(48 Yorkshire SU128715)* and may stretch from the summit to ground level. These weathered grooves are easily differentiated from the cracks and fissures resulting from other natural environmental effects and which usually have irregular sides, shapes and outlines. O'Toole (1939) described many 'grooves' in granite Standing Stones in Co. Carlow in Eire, noting that straight grooves do not occur 'on unworked granite stone'. Some of his Stones were "channelled from the tops to the middle" on all sides, the grooves being up to 180mm. wide and 150 mm. deep and some were up to 1.5 metres long. Mitchell (1940) describes and illustrates a 'grooved' Irish Stone, seven feet high, which has three well defined grooves which he considers were man-made. The illustrations suggest that the grooves described by O'Toole and Mitchell are different to the weathered joints in the GB. sandstone Stones. O'Toole suggests these grooves were man-made by rubbing with a stout pole and quartz sand, supporting this argument that the grooves are straight and that some are undercut and he points out the great effort and time this would require when working with granite. Such 'grooves' are not seen in the granite Stones in GB although some natural weathering is present on the summit of some granite Stones *(284 Cornwall SW453254, photo 37)* and there are wide shallow grooves on *(1120 Aberdeen NJ641149)*. A square dressed granite Stone *(82 Northumberland NZ034842, photo 33)*, possibly medieval, has a wide groove incorporating a right-angle corner cut into the flat summit and continued down one side which has no obvious explanation. It was clearly man-made and is different from the grooves in the Irish granite Stones. Mohen (1989b) illustrates a large Standing Stone in the Cotes-du-Nord which has seven long straight 'natural' grooves but ten years later Mohen (1999) stated that they were carved 'on one side *(of the Stone)* with long folds'. The geology of this Stone is not stated and this illustrates the difficulty in assessing some of these various grooves.

32 sandstone Stones with grooves, more correctly described as weathered joints, are indicated in Table 15. These Stones are found in the areas of calcareous sandstones and are particularly obvious in Arran where there are 9 grooved Stones, including one on Great Cumbrae which is considered to be part of the Arran group of islands. 5 are present in Yorkshire three of which are on one site, 4 in Northumberland, 3 in Fife and 3 in Carmarthen with isolated Stones in other areas. Siliceous sandstones which have well defined bedding planes cover much of the north-east of Scotland and the Orkney Islands and do not have grooves. The sarsens on the chalk Downs are composed of quartzite sandstone and also do not have grooves. The siliceous and quartzite sandstones are not subject to acid rain erosion which explains the differential distribution of grooved Stones around GB.

One of the best examples of a multiple grooved Stone is that at *(415 Hereford SO561181, photo 34)*. This is a striking Stone of red sandstone 1.8 metres high which contains quartz pebbles. It has 13 large and deep and obvious grooves which reach from the summit to the ground and are up to 20 cms. deep on the south-east, the north-east and on the north-west. The grooves on the south-east and north-west are straight with well defined square edges. Burl (1993) suggests that the grooves are 'natural' and records that this Stone was excavated in 1926 with a photograph in his text showing that the grooves stop abruptly at ground level where the Stone has a well marked ridge around the rectangular base. There are 5 other Stones with similar grooves to those on *(415 Hereford SO561181)* on a square base. On Arran a Stone 4.2 metres high has seven grooves 3 metres above ground level which are confined to the top one third of the height *(840 Arran Argyll NR910325, photo 35)*.

The Stone at *(113 Fife NT159844, photo 36)* is 2.0 metres high and is orientated with the bedding planes at 20°. There are 12 grooves, distributed on every side, which are up to 1.4 metres long and 25 cms wide ad deep, together with cup marks and later graffiti. All are quite straight and on the west stretch from summit to the ground. This Stone has a well marked 'neck' and square base and the grooves display varying degrees of weathering. Near Penicuik the Stone *(865 Lothians NT204567, photo 44)* is 1.8 metres high and photo 44 shows the well marked and square base. The Stone has deep grooves on three sides, but none on the flat south-west face exposed to most of the weather. Two other Stones *(55 Northumberland NZ033704 and 1189 Northumberland NZ046829)* are similar. There appear to be differential weathering effects, which do not always appear on the side of maximum weather exposure. Some weathered sandstone Stones may have rough uneven grooves and surfaces as in the pair of Stones at *(838 Arran, Argyll NS053243, photo 41)*. Other interesting and significant grooved Stones are the three 'Devil's Arrows' *(48 and 49 Yorkshire SE392664')* composed of Millstone Grit. The southernmost Stone is a particular example. It is 6.9 metres high and has significant long straight grooves on all four faces , some of which reach from the top to the ground. The limestone Stones in this gazetteer show significant random weathering effects *(21 Warwick SP196310, 25 Somerset ST390578 photo 42, and 125 Oxford SP297210)* and *(136 Gloucester ST884999, photo 48)* with two penetrating holes which are quite different to any of the grooves in calcareous sandstone.

Some granite Stones in GB have substantial fissures and cracks as in *(76 Carmarthen SN675244 photo 38)* which is 2.5 metres high and has a deep fissure down the north-east side and the substantial cracks in *(319 Cornwall SW435247, photo 30)* which is 4.0 metres high and has a 'natural' hole perforating the Stone. The granite Tresvennack Pillar *(339 Cornwall SW442289, photo 39)* is 3.7 metres high and has a large crack extending through the Stone from east to west and is another large aesthetically satisfying Stone in need of conservation before it becomes split apart. In GB none of the granite Stones have grooves similar to the putative man-made grooves found in Ireland. A granite Stone 2.4 metres high at *(1168 Isles of Scilly Cornwall SV891084 photo 56)* has, however, two well marked grooves on the west side One terminates after c.0.8 metres and the other then becomes less distinct and descends to the ground. Between these two grooves there is a third much less obvious groove also about 0.8 metre long. This feature does not appear on other granite stones in GB.

There are six stones with man-made grooves (Table 16) which are clearly different from the effects of weathering along the joint planes of the other Stones. They are clearly not standing stones. One is a sarsen stone, 2.1 metres long, lying flat on Fyfield Down *(1187 Wiltshire SU128715, photo. 46)*. Sarsen stones are composed of hard siliceous sandstone. This Stone is illustrated by Mohen (1989c), who with Lacaille (1963), describes it as a 'polishing stone . It has five well marked parallel grooves running across the width, not the length, of the Stone, which are c. 25 cms. long, 5 cms. to 10 cms. wide and 5 cms. deep together with, and immediately beside, an elliptical and smooth polished area c. 45 by 20 cms.. Mohen (1989b) also described a vertical Standing Stone with grooves in Northern France, suggesting it was used to sharpen or polish stone axes but it is not clear how it could have been used for this purpose. Beside a Standing Stone on Machrie Moor *(840 Arran Argyll NR910325, photo 47)* is a recumbent Stone, about 2.0 metres long and 0.6 metre wide lying partially buried. This stone has five well marked and prominent large grooves and a 'polishing area' all of which are similar to those on the grooved 'polishing' stone on Fyfield Down *(1187 Wiltshire SU128715, photo 46)*. The grooves on *840* are straight, extend across the entire width of the Stone and vary in width from c. 0.25 to 0.10 metres and are polished smooth. This stone does not appear to have been previously recorded. Another nearby Stone some three metres to the northeast has a single large deep wide furrow *(which can be seen in photo 47)* across the width of the Stone ; this stone and the furrow, which is substantially larger than the grooves in stones *1187* and *840*, needs to be properly assessed. The fourth Stone is a sandstone glacial boulder at *(145 Northumberland NU130104, photo 43)* 1.0 metres long, 0.6 metres high and 0.65 metres wide which has a single deep narrow and straight groove running over the convex south-east face and has already been noted above. This Stone is listed by the Northumberland County Archaeologist (Caroline Hardy, personal communication 1997) as a prehistoric Standing Stone. The straight neatly cut groove is clearly not the result of 'natural' forces and displays no weathering and is somewhat different from the grooves on *1187* and *840*. The grooves on Stones *1187, 840* and *145* are clearly man-made and different to all the grooves along the bedding planes of the calcareous sandstone Stones discussed above. It is suggested these grooves could have been used to sharpen spears, arrow heads or cutting tools. It is not clear if these tools were stone, bronze or iron; perhaps over many centuries it was all three. The flat elliptical polished areas on stones *1187 and 840* could well have been used to grind and polish axes. The real use or uses of these 'grinding stones' and when and how they were developed may not have been properly determined. It seems possible that there may be other unrecorded 'polishing' stones in GB.

Two other Stones with grooves are recorded here. One Stone 500 metres to the south-west of Stone 1187 on Fyfield Down is at *(1188 Wiltshire SU127713)* and is a much smaller sarsen Stone 0.8 metres long which lies on the east side of the Ridgeway. It has three narrow, shallow but well marked parallel markings, which are not really grooves, and which run along the length of the Stone. There are small pits along two of these markings. The provenance and association of this Stone and the marks thereon, which I do not consider to be ploughshare marks, are not clear. It does not appear to have been recorded before and is noted here to complete the record..

TABLE 15 THE 31 STANDING STONES WITH SUBSTANTIAL 'GROOVES' IN CALCAREOUS SANDSTONES

(2.5 % of all Standing Stones)

identification of Stone	rock type	height of Stone	number of grooves	length of grooves	comments
ENGLAND 13 Stones – 5.7% of 226 English Stones					
415 Hereford SO561181	sandstone	1.45	11	c. 1.5	very deep grooves, present on all four faces; best example
55 Northumberland NZ033704	sandstone	2.25	4	Over 2.0	also has cup marks
56 Northumberland NZ043746	sandstone	2.0	2	c. 0.75	much weathered
145 Northumberland NU130104	sandstone	recumbent	1	c. 0.5	1 groove curves over surface of recumbent Stone
146 Northumberland NU157168	sandstone	1.6	3	c. 0.4	2 grooves, c. 0.45 metres, on north face
1189 Northumberland NZ046829	sandstone	1.5			
178 Stafford SJ717378	sandstone	2.0	5	c. 1.2	this stone has been moved
1187 Wiltshire SU128715	sarsen	1.0	5	c. 0.5	recumbent with axe 'polishing' area
48 Yorkshire SE392664	gritstone	6.9			SE Stone) 'Devil's Arrows' alignment
	gritstone	6.4			central Stone) alignment
	gritstone	5.5			NE Stone) 170 metres long
348 Yorkshire SE766992	sandstone	1.8	5	up to c. 1.1	grooves & weathering
1138 Yorkshire SE207435	sandstone	1.8	8	c. 1.0	Grooves c. 13 cm deep; 2 on S; 3 on E; 3 on W
SCOTLAND 15 Stones – 2.3% of Scottish Stones					
1005 Angus NO717627	sandstone	3.7	3	up to c. 3.0	long shallow groove & one short
831 Arran Argyll NS017355	sandstone	3.2	2	3.0	one long groove on east, south and west faces
976 Arran Argyll NS005375	sandstone	3.4	3	up to 2.0	on south, west & north
978 Arran Argyll NR894337	sandstone	1.4	6	up to 1.25	on south across strata; possibly 2 on west along strata
840 Arran Argyll NR910325	sandstone	4.0	5	1.5	grooves run across the width of the Stone & are quite different to any other grooves
840 Arran Argyll NR910325	sandstone		lies flat	4	
840 Arran Argyll NR911324	sandstone	3.5	5	up to 1.5	3 on east across strata; 2 on south along strata
842 Arran Argyll NR907326	sandstone	1.4	4	up to 1.0	2 grooves on south (both slightly bent) & 2 on west
843 Arran Argyll NR906324	sandstone	1.5	5	up to 0.8	3 slightly bent grooves on east & 2 on west along strata
1052 Cumbrae Argyll NS175564	sandstone	1.9	1	0.3	short groove on east; possible groove on west
113 Fife NT159844	sandstone	2.0	14	up to 1.0	grooves on all faces up to 0.15m wide & 0.25m deep
116 Fife NT028855	sandstone	2.5	11	up to 1.6	grooves c. 0.25m deep, 7 on E & 4 on W; & weathering
981 Fife NO571047	sandstone	0.9	3	c. 0.35	poor grooves on north; wheel motive on south (a later feature?)
1044 Grampian NJ152684	conglomerate	2.2	4	0.6	grooves on north; ring mark; large crack
865 Lothian NT204576	sandstone	1.8	6	up to 1.4	deep grooves on SE across strata & on NE along strata
WALES 3 Stones – 0.9% of Welsh Stones					
400 Carmarthen SN432101	not recorded	2.4	2	c. 1.5	wide shallow bent grooves on southeast corner
406 Carmarthen SN455151	sandstone	1.6	4	0.75	grooves on southwest & northwest; needs re-examining
575 Carmarthen SN381112	sandstone	2.25	8?	1.4	3 well marked grooves on southeast face & on top
Groove in Granite Stone on Isles of Scilly					
1168 Cornwall SV891084	granite	2.4	3	0.8 to 2.0	

A sixth Stone with another quite different groove is at *(735 Perth NN930124 photo 45)*. This leaning gneiss Stone has a bold continuous groove clearly cut into the circumference on all four faces. It is one of a group of three Stones and this groove was clearly man-made. The origins, date and significance of this Stone and the groove therein are uncertain (Timoney S., Perth and Kinross Heritage Trust, personal communication 2008).

All these six Stones should receive further careful assessment and be properly recorded.

TABLE 16 SIX STONES WITH MAN-MADE GROOVES

1187	Wiltshire SU128715	Fyfield Down	sarsen	5 parallel grooves	elliptical 'polishing' area	photo 46
840	Arran Argyll NR91032	Machrie Moor	sandstone	5 shallow polished grooves	elliptical 'polishing' area	photo 46
	"	"	"	one deep V-shaped groove		photo 47
145	Northumberland NU310104	on Corby's Crags	sandstone	1 thin long narrow groove		photo 43
1188	Wiltshire SU127713	beside the Ridgway	sarsen	3 parallel markings		
735	Perth NN930124	Auchterarder	gneiss	horizontal groove around circumference		photo 45

Carvings on Stones

Some prehistoric Stones have carvings and other human stone workings which may be from the prehistoric or post AD 1 eras. Prehistoric stone carvings include the enigmatic 'cup marks' which are small circular depressions of unknown significance carved into some Stones (Mohen 1989 d) which often appear in groups and rings or spirals all of which may occur on several Stones in a locality and there may be spirals and rings. The distribution and other features of these carvings have been well described by Hadingham (1977) and Service and Bradbery (1993 b) and are more usually present on rock faces than on Standing Stones. Cup marks are usually about 5cms. in diameter but smaller cups do occur. The number of cup marks on a Stone varies from just one *(149 Perth NO050344)* up to 33 cups on the massive Stone 2.3 metres high *(64 Fife NO500040, sketch 7)* and 16 cups on the flat top of Stone 2 at *(855 Perth NN 754004)*. Cup marked Stones are especially frequent in the east of Scotland *(1005, Angus, NO775795)* and also at Kilmartin *(528 Kilmartin Argyll NR828976)* and in Northumberland *(55, Northumberland, NZ033704)*. A few cup marks are seen in Wales *(264, Anglesey, SH333900)* but are not mentioned in Wales by Barber and Williams (1989a).

In this gazetteer cup marks are recorded on 37 Stones in GB *(3.1% of all Stones)* --

5 Stones in England	*(2.2% of English Stones)*
27 Stones in Scotland	*(4.1% of Scottish Stones)*
5 Stones in Wales	*(1.5% of Welsh Stones).*

The higher number and percentage of cup marked Stones in Scotland *(2.2% of all the Standing Stones in GB)* is obvious. Cup marked Stones are not recorded from Cornwall, Devon, Exmoor, Dorset, Gloucestershire (where any cups are likely to have become obscured by weathering of the soft limestone), Wiltshire (in the sarsens), Caithness, Sutherland, Western Isles, Orkney and Shetland. The cup marks in Northumberland may suggest an association with those in Scotland. Except for the cup marks, spirals and rings on some Stones carvings are not a feature of prehistoric Stones, although there is a spiral on Long Meg *(132 Cumbria NY507372, photo 4)*. This contrasts with the numerous, varied and different medieval carvings placed onto some prehistoric Stones and onto Stones raised after AD 1.

Pictish, Ogham, Christian and other symbols have been carved onto numerous prehistoric Stones in Scotland and onto other Stones erected after AD 1. Most of the carvings are early medieval and include Pictish 'symbols' on a prehistoric pillar Stone 3.3 metres high *(908 Ross and Cromarty, NH709851, photo 49)* which has a salmon inscribed onto the North side and Stones 'Christianised' by the addition of a Cross *(1042 Moray NJ325393 and 1135, Sutherland, NJ63789)*. There are also 'Christianised' Standing Stones in Wales *(895, Pembroke, SN177421)* which, unusually also has both Ogham and cup marks. Ogham marks are present on *(209 Gigha, Argyll NR642482)*. Most of the Pictish symbols, ogam marks and Crosses appear to have been carved onto Stones which were set up for the purpose. A sandstone Stone 0.9 metre high *(981 Fife NO571047, photo 54)* has numerous small cup marks, a wheel type carving on the south face (probably of later date) and three, or perhaps four, substantial grooves on the north with a large groove within the strata on the east end. It is an interesting and unusual Stone of unknown provenance. Pictish Symbol Stones have been extensively studied and some publications with photographs and diagrams of many are listed in the bibliography.

Fourteen Stones have holes which perforate the Stone and which do not appear to have been recorded or studied. They are of some interest. Soft oolitic limestone is easily worked, but drilling holes through granite without steel tools would be difficult and it is not clear how the holes were made and whether this was before, at the time of or after the Stones were erected. In many Stones it appears the holes possibly were made centuries later. Assuming that some of the holes are prehistoric it is suggested (Hartgroves S., Principal Archaeologist, Cornwall County Council, personal communication 2008), that these holes were made by 'pecking' with another hard stone, such as fine grained greenstone or a sharp flint as was used by Neolithic man to produce perforated stone axe hammers, and that maybe stones were selected which already had a 'natural rock basin cut into them by weathering processes'. The Wardens at the model crannog on Loch Tay demonstrate drilling holes through flat stones about 2.5 cms. thick using a bow drill to drive a rotating hardwood stick with water and coarse sand in the drill hole. To make the much larger and longer holes, some of narrow bore, through thick granite Stones would have been a different and more difficult and prolonged undertaking.

The Stone at *(136 Gloucester ST884999, photo 48)* of soft oolitic limestone is 2.4 metres high and has two holes, each about 0.5 metre in diameter, and the significant and uneven weathering which is found on the oolitic limestone Stones of Cotswold. It is not clear if the two holes in this Stone are man made or the result of weathering. At *(116 Fife NT028855)*, sandstone, 2.5 metres high and 0.5 metre thick, there are two substantial elliptical holes, one each on the east and west sides, which are directly opposite each other and are about 20 cms. wide and 10 cms. deep, but they do not perforate the Stone. This may have been an unfinished attempt to make a perforating hole. These two partially made holes in the same Stone, if that is what they are, appear to support the working method suggested above by Hartgroves S. An obvious difficulty, however, is the reduced working space inside the hole as it becomes deeper and narrower and it is difficult to conceive how this technique could produce a hole of 8 cms. diameter through a Stone of 20 cms. thickness *(1085 Orkney HY752529)*; a metal tool appears more likely. The triangular granite Tolvan Stone *(501 Cornwall SW706277, photo 52)* has a circular hole 0.25 metre in diameter through a Stone 0.3 metre thick and this appears to be a more feasible, but nevertheless, substantial achievement. The surface inside this hole is very smooth. A probable Bronze Age Stone, now used as a gatepost, *(1172 Cornwall SW432246, photo 57 a and b)* has a neat hole c. 8 cms. diameter with clean cut edges and a smooth internal surface through granite 0.25 metre thick. This seems to argue that the hole was made with a metal drill The holes in Stones *344, 501* (photo 52) *and (970 Galloway NX365557, sketch 8)* are made through thick granite. In *344* and *501* the holes are circular with bevelled edges but in *970* the entrance hole on the southwest is c. 0.22 metre in diameter and somewhat elliptical with sharp edges and it is reduced to 0.1 metre on the northeast exit; it was made through 0.7 metre of granite. The Stone at *178* (Table 17) which has been moved is of sandstone with a large hole of 0.45 metre which has smooth bevelled edges. A row of three small granite Stones in West Cornwall *(1186 Cornwall SW389325)* has, in each Stone., a perforating hole with bevelled edges. The holes have a maximum diameter of 20 cms. and one emerges at only 7.5 cms diameter. They are described by (Sykes 1993) who erroneously indicates that the hole in one Stone has a sharply drilled edge, but this is not correct. The Stone *(1169 Isles of Scilly, Cornwall SV910110)* has a penetrating hole only c. 4 cms. in diameter through c. 0.3 metres of granite with each entrance bevelled. At *(1123 Lewis Western Isles NB282192)* the Stone, of uncertain provenance but possibly mediaeval, has a hole 5 cms. diameter through 0.5 metres of granite with sharp cut edges at each end and a smooth bore as though it has been mechanically drilled. The two holes in *(820 Highland NN025613)*

Table 17 Fourteen Stones have holes which perforate through the body of the Stone

Stone identification & County	rock type	height of Stone metres	thickness of Stone metre	diameter of hole metre
136 Gloucester ST884999	ooltic limestone	2.4	0.4	2 eliptical holes – both c. 0.4, these holes may not be man-made, photo 48
178 Stafford SJ776376)	sandstone	1.8	0.6	0.45 has been moved
344 Cornwall SW426349 stone 2	granite	1.0	0.2	0.4
1169 Cornwall SW910110	granite	2.6	0.3	0.04
501 Cornwall SW706277	granite	2.0	0.3	minimum diameter 0.25 photo 52
1186 Cornwall SW389325	granite	0.7	0.2	minimum diameter 0.10
"	"	0.8	0.4	" 0.075
"	"	1.2	0.25	" 0.10
1172 Cornwall SW432246	granite	1.7	0.25	Bronze Age Stone, photo 57 modern drill hole*
820 Highland NN025613	sandstone	2.0	0.3	2 holes – 0.08 & 0.1
970 Galloway NX365557	granite	1.4	0.7	0.22 reducing to 0.1, sketch 8 modern drill hole*
1085 Orkney HY752529	sandstone	3.8	0.2	
1123 Western Isle NB282192	granite	1.6	0.5	modern drill hole*
1156 Pen Feidr Coedan outlier	dolerite	2.2	0.5	two holes 0.1

*modern drill holes indicated by Dr. R. Ixer – personal communication 2010

are neatly drilled in sandstone and have sharp edges and diameters of 10.5 cms. and 8 cms.. and also appear to have been neatly drilled. It seems improbable that holes only 8 cms. in diameter through 0.25 metre or more of granite could have been made by 'pecking' with another stone. There are illustrations of different penetrating holes in *photos. 48, 52 and 57, and sketch 6.*

Three small Stones have the remains of bore holes for shot blasting. Shot holes will post date the introduction of gunpowder for quarrying or maybe later of power drills after about 1840. Two are at *(586 Cardigan SN685837)* and *(371 Pembroke SM885299)*, The third Stone is 1.6 metres high and forms part of the circle at *(1134 Aberdeen NO19651)* which is a scheduled ancient monument (MRS card no. NO99NW003), but the shot hole indicates that Stone, at least, may not be that old.

It is thus uncertain whether some holes were made before or after the Stones were erected and how some of the holes were made.. Some holes were made after suitable metal tools and drills became available and like the Christian Crosses, Pictish symbols and ogam were added onto prehistoric Stones. Even using steel tools substantial time and effort would have been required. These holes must have been important to those who made them, but their rational and use cannot now be envisaged and may have been quite different in prehistoric and medieval eras.

Other Features associated with some Stones

Some Stones are now found in apparently unusual positions in beside houses and other buildings, in gardens and in housing estates and urban areas which have been developed around extant Stones, with the Stones left in situ -

England - 3 in gardens, one set into a garden wall at *(234 Oxfordshire SP359221)* is a Scheduled Ancient Monument
       1 in the bar wall inside the Oxenham Arms *(652 Dartmoor Devon SX5567530)*; it is a Scheduled Ancient Monument
       1 3.3 metres high on a school playing field *(496 Cornwall SX029521)* in a dangerous position by the touchline.

Scotland - 8 in gardens, one is 3.8 metres high *(803 Aberdeen NJ7231449)*, one set into a garden wall *(277 Argyll NR761254)*,
       and one is c. 1.0 metre from the house *(863 Borders NT355278)*.
       5 Stones in a row c. 4.0 metres from a farmhouse *(845 and 846 Argyll NR46668)*
       6 in farmyards, one Stone is 3.7 metres high *(1005 Angus NO717627)*
       within housing estates, one in rural housing area *(711 Lewis Western Isles NB215349* and one in a residential urban area *(1007 Aberdenn NJ922083)*. Both of these Stones have been moved and are now set in concrete .
       2 in schools grounds. One in the playground wall of a now closed school *(721 Caithness ND 324416)* and one beside a modern school (389 Argyll NM906387)
       1 is incorporated into the wall of a building in the city *(983 Aberdeen NJ9830559)*
       1 is on the public roadside beside a croft house *(928 Rousay Orkney HX404275, sketch 9)*

Wales   2 in gardens. *(334 Glamorgan ST242834)* was moved c. 1910
     1 in the village street beside a garden wall, 2.6 metres, set in concrete *(1127 Powys SJ125260)*
     2 in urban areas *(525 Glamorgan SS676953 and 1145 Glamorgan SS902795 which has been moved)*
     1 with a church yard wall built around it, is 3.4 metres high *(561 Cardigan SN7522791)*
     1 in school playground now set in concrete *(567 Glamorgan SN744953)*. It has been moved.
     1 a scheduled monument *(880 Glamorgan ST444878)* is now incorporated into and partially obscured by an earth bank thrown up when a large farm building was recently erected. This vandalism of a scheduled monument has not been corrected CADW.
     1 incorporated into a wall when a road was widened *(296 Anglesea SH461833)* ; this was also official vandalism.

Some Stones have other interesting features. There are cobbled pavements around some sites -

                2 sites in England
               11 sites in Scotland
                0 sites in Wales.

At the start of this work cobbles were not specifically observed and it may be that there are more than are here recorded. These were presumably a significant part of the original site and it is suprising that these cobbles have survived for so many centuries. There are proportionally more in Scotland. Lightning strike severely damaged the quartz Stone at *(190 Exmoor SS601439)* in 1996 reducing the height to 2.5 metres. The farmer said it was originally about 3.75 metres high and it must have been a fine sight. The Stone at *(992 Aberdeen NJ46104, sketch 2)* has been broken possibly by lightning strike and now stands 1.4 metres high. One of the Stones at the Ring of Brodgar, Orkney was also destroyed by lightning in 1980 (Rideout RCAHMS personal communication 2008). Explosives were used to destroy two Stones, as noted above. Personal information from the farmer (2002) was that *(888 Pembroke SN136379)* was broken in half by explosives in c. 1900 because it was loose in the socket and thought to be dangerous. The stump is 1.2 metres high and the shot hole is clearly visible What appears that the top portion of the Stone lies in the bottom of the nearby hedgerow covered in tree roots. It should be replaced onto the stump and would make a Stone over 3 metres high. A quartz Stone in Cardigan at *SN382433* was destroyed by explosives (personal information from the farmer 2006) and some of the resulting quartz rubble is visible where it was built into the field bank by the farm entrance and on the opposite side of the road. Two Stones have been moved from their original sites for use as War Memorials in the centre of villages. One of quartz is now at *(1101 Gwynedd SN661856)* and the other is *(829 Coll, Highland NM171560)*. There are Stones in roadside walls at *(234 Oxfordshire SP359221, Galloway, 1057 NX467398 and 1058 NX423542), (227 Argyll NR761254)* and at *(296 Anglsey SH461833 photo 50)* which is 3.0 metres high was incorporated into a wall when the road was widened. This was and is official vandalism.

Scheduled Ancient Monuments

Many of the Standing Stones are Scheduled Ancient Monuments in the care of the Royal Commissions for Ancient Monuments, English Heritage and County Councils. All these Stones, and many others which are not scheduled need to be conserved, but this is not happening. There are young trees growing at the base of the Wimblestone *(24 Somerset ST434585 photo 1)* which is a Scheduled Ancient Monument. This was reported to the County Archaeological Office in 1997; they need removing but by 2005 they were still there. The scheduled beautiful small Nine Stones Circle at *(33 Dorset SY922805)* has mature beech trees growing beside the Stones and beginning to upset the Stones. Once again I informed the County archaeologist. It will be necessary to fell the trees to prevent destruction of the circle; trees are expendable and others will grow again. As pointed out above numerous Stones have been intentionally or wantonly destroyed since the last War and some at least of the more important and spectacular Stones need to be scheduled for future preservation. I am critical of the bureauratic inertia to prevent this and to conserve many Stones and other monuments. A clear area around Ancient Monuments needs to be left in new planted forestry.

Stones not Visited

Thirty-three other pre-historic sites with thirty-four extant Standing Stones have not been visited (Appendix 4). There must be other extant Stones not yet recorded. Most of the extant Stones listed in Appendix 4 are marked on the Ordnance Survey maps and are listed here as extant because they can be seen from a distance, are recorded in recent publications or local people know them to be still present. These Stones were not visited because of inaccessibility over high hills (my hill walking days are over), across abandoned water-logged peat cuttings (too dangerous), hidden in impenetrable growths of gorse and other undergrowth, could not found within forestry (usually impossible) or are on islands which I failed to visit. There is thus no specific site information available about these particular Stones and although they represent only 3% of the surviving Stones recorded in this work they still form a part of any overall gazetteer of prehistoric Stones in GB.. Appendix 4 also lists 61 Stones marked on the Ordnance Survey maps or listed by the County Archaeological Officers or recorded elsewhere which could not be found at the site and are lost. The lists received from County Archaeological Officers often document the sites of lost Standing Stones and the Ordnance Survey continues to mark Stones which have disappeared some years ago. One wonders how this inefficiency arises.

'Other Stones'

The 'Other Stones' in Appendix 5 include many diverse and interesting stone monuments of both prehistoric and of post AD 1 origin. These include chambered tombs *(36 Ardmamurchan Scotland NM5690619)*, the enigmatic and complex setting of c. 200 small Stones *(Other Stones 27 Caithness ND394383)*, flagstone field boundaries *(Other Stones 57 Caithness ND218648)*, several mediaeval Crosses *(Other Stones 25 Caithness NC959645)* most of which are damaged, the memorial Stone to the French landing at Strumble Head in 1787 *(Other Stones 136 Pembroke SM9264050)* which commemorates the last 'invasion' of GB, a modern 'Curse Stone' considered to be a work of art *(Other Stones 114 Cumbria NY397562)*, 28 stepping stones of probable medieval origin *(Other Stones 137 Anglsey SH441648, photo 51)* each of which is a cube of about 1.25 metres and probably dressed more or less to shape, the 1820 Haytor mineral tramway on Dartmoor *(Other Stones 142 Devon SX769776)*, the Dun Telve broch *(Other Stones 144 NH834173)* which is clearly not a Standing Stone, a glacial boulder incorrectly marked on the Ordnance Survey map as a Standing Stone *(Other Stones 92 SO 167573)*, pillars of dry-stone work up to 3.0 metres high in Orkney *(Other Stones 82 Orkney HY750530)* of unknown use, 'grey wether' sarsens scattered in situ on Marlborough Downs *(Other Stones 65 Wiltshire SU141686)*, a setting of 40 small square dressed Stones of unknown date, origin and use *(Other Stones 20 Exmoor SS649458, photo 55)* and some 'millenium' Stones *(Other Stones 66 NO597940)*. These and many other different and unusual monuments and Stones are listed in Appendix 5. Apart from the very numerous Christian Crosses, there are a large number of different, interesting and varied post AD 1 stone monuments scattered all over GB which need to be properly recorded in a gazetteer and conserved.

Conclusions

Eight enigmatic features of the Prehistoric Standing Stones may never have satisfactory explanations –

- Quartz Stones (especially in Wales) and quartz veins and crystals in other Stones. What, if any, was the significance of these quartz Stones?
- The transport of heavy Stones over several kilometres from the probable outcrops of origin. Was this human agency or glacial action?
- How were potentially fragile Stones *(79 Pembroke SM828076)* transported without becoming broken? Maybe many were broken in transit.
- How was the smooth polished surface of the Ballinaby Stone *(13 Islay Argyll NR220672 photo 32 and b)* produced?
- How were large and heavy Stones like the south-most Devil's Arrow *(48 Yorkshire SE392664)* erected?
- What is the significance of the 'cup marks', rings and spirals? This question has a much wider general application.
- Perforating holes through 14 Stones. Assuming the holes are man-made and some pre-date steel tools, why was this done, especially in thick granite?
- The astronomical observations of Thom and Thom (1990) and other suggestions put forward need further investigation and assessment.

Some relevant conclusions can be drawn and some required actions determined from this field assessment of our extant prehistoric Stones -

- Many Stones have intrinsic aesthetic attributes which need to be recognised., but this has not so far been considered.
- Some of our forebears were clearly skilled engineers who were able to transport, manoeuver and erect large and heavy Stones.
- The erection of these Stones would have involved continued laborious effort suggesting that the Stones were very important to these people..
- It is not known how or when perforating holes were drilled through 14 Stones. This would have involved substantial effort and must have been important.
- Many holes appear to have been made long after some Stones were erected. The significance of the holes is totally unknown.
- Many prehistoric Standing Stones have been lost or intentionally destroyed over the centuries and more recently. Nevertheless 933 sites with 1257 prehistoric Stones have survived down the centuries. More sites should be Scheduled and conserved to avoid further loss and damage to Stones..
- Some Scheduled Stones have been moved, built over or incorporated into road works and industrial and residential sites or are lost in forestry. This is official vandalism and must be rectified where possible and prevented in the future.
- Some Scheduled Stones, and other Stones, need immediate conservation actions to prevent damage and eventual destruction by large trees and forestry, ground erosion and splitting due to the weather and ice. The County archaeologists and others involved seem unwilling or unable to do this necessary work for which they have a legal obligation.
- Most Stones are still vertical although 264 *(21%)* are leaning and given that many Stones have relatively shallow sockets this is not suprising.
- There is an obvious concentration of prehistoric Stones along the Western seaboard of GB *(43.7% of all Stones)* including the western peninsulae and archipelagoes with most of the Stones relatively close to the coast and below 200 metres altitude. There are only 61 Stones *(5% of all Stones)* above 300 metres.

- Some investigative work to determine how to conserve splitting and cracked Stones is required.. Without this many Stones will be broken and destroyed.
- Many of the sites have cobbled areas. These were not at first recognised in this work, but clearly require attention and recording.
- There are numerous interesting Stones which post-date AD 1 which are not a properly catalogued or recorded on a national basis.
- Further study and assessment of the extant prehistoric Standing Stones may elucidate some of the enigmatic features of these Monuments.

REFERENCES

Barber Chris and Williams J. G. 1989 *The Ancient Stones of Wales* Blorenge Books, Abergavenny, 78 page 1165

Barnatt J (1982a) *Prehistoric Cornwall*, Turnstone Press Wellingborough, page 95.

Barnatt J. (1982b) as above page 95

Brennand M. (2004), *British Archaeology* issue 78 September 2004, page 24.

Browne F. S. A. (1963) *Antiquity* vol. 37, pages 140.

Burl A. (1971) *Arch. Ael.* 49, pages 37-51.

Burl A. (1979) *The Stone Circles of the British Isles*, Yale University Press, page 41.

Burl A. (1979) as above page 312

Burl A. (1979) as above, page 150

Burl A. (1988) *Four Posters* BAR British series 195, published BAR Oxford, page 6

Burl A. 1990 in Thom A. and Thom A. S., 1990, *Stone Rows and Standing Stones* parts 1 and 2. edited A. R. Hands and D. R. Walker, BAR Oxford, page 43.

Burl A. (1993 a), *From Carnac to Callanish*, Yale University Press, page 18 et seq..

Burl A. (1993 b), as above, page 3.

Burl A. (1993 c), as above, pages 231 and 233.

Burl A. (1993 d), as above, page 218.

Butter Rachael 1999, *Kilmartin*, published Kilmartin House Trust, Kilmartin, Argyll

Childe V. G.(1940) *The Prehistoric Communities of the British Isles*, and R Chambers Ltd., London page 246

Cope J. (2004) *The Megalithic European*, Element an imprint of Harper Collins, London

Corio D. and Corio N. L. (2003) *Megaliths*, Jonathan Cape, page 88

Daniels G. (1958) *The Megalitic Builders of Western Europe*, Hutchinson of London page 15 et seq.

English Heritage (1990) *Monuments Protection Programme 'Standing Stones'*

Heggie D. C. (1981) *Megalithic Science, mathematics and astronomy*, Thames and Hudson London.Heggie

Hadingham E. (1993) *Circles and Standing Stones*, William Heinemann Ltd., pages 136-151

Fife County Council, Records and Monument Office 1997, Kirkaldy Fife.

Hallendy N. (2000) *Inuksuit – silent messengers of the Arctic*, Douglas and McIntyre Ltd, pages 30 and 31.

Hawkes J., (1986a) *Shell Guide to British Archaeology*, 1986, Michael Joseph, page 19.

Hawkes J., (1986a) *Shell Guide to British Archaeology*, 1986, Michael Joseph, page 100.

Hawkes J., (1986b) *Shell Guide to British Archaeology*, 1986, Michael Joseph, page 258.

Humberside County Council County Architects Department, Sites and Monuments Records no. 6335, County Hall, Hull.

Lacaille A. D., (1963) Antiquities Journal vol. 43 page 190

Mitchell G. F., (1940) *Journal of the Royal Society of Antiquaries of Ireland* vol 70 page 164

Mohen Jean-Pierre (1989 a), *The World of Megaliths*, Cassell Publishers Ltd, page 165 et seq..

Mohen Jean-Pierre (1989 b), as above, page 14.

Mohen Jean-Pierre (1989 c), as above , page 208 and page 87.

Mohen Jean-Pierre (1989 d), as above, page 292.

Mohen Jean-Pierre (1989 e), as above, page 208.

Mohen Jean-Pierre, *Standing Stones*, English translation (1999), Thames and Hudson Ltd., page 20.

Newton N. (1995) David and Charles plc.,page 73

O'Toole E. (1939) *Journal of the Royal Society of Antiquaries of Ireland* vol. LXIX page 99

RCAHM Scotland (1999), *Kilmartin – Prehistory and Early History*, page 74

Ritchie G, editor (1997) *The Archaeology of Argyll* (1997), RCAHM Scotland, Edinburgh University Press, page 87

Ritchie Graham and Anna, (1991), *Scotland Archaeology and Early History*, Edinburgh University Press, page 105.

Service A. and Bradbery J. (1979) *Megaliths and their Mystery*, George Weidenfield and Noccholson, London, page 10.

Service A. and Bradbery J. (1993a) *The Standing Stones of Europe*, Orion Publishing Group London, page 10.

Service and Bradbery (1993 b), as above, page 38 – 41.

Swarbrick O, (2005), *British Archaeology*, Nov/Dec 2005, pages 30 and 31.

Sykes H., *Mysterious Britain* (1993), George Weidenfield and Nicholson Ltd., London, page 48

Thom A., (1984) *Proceedings of the Prehistory Society* vol. 50 page 382.

Thom A. and Thom A. S., (1990 a) *Stone Rows and Standing Stones* parts 1 and 2. edited A. R. Hands and D. R. Walker, BAR Oxford

Thom A., and Thom A. S., (1990 b) as above, Part I page 4.

Thorpe R. S. and Williams-Thorpe O. (1991) *Antiquity* vol 65 page 64-73.

Williams 1988a, in the *Standing Stones of Wales and South-West England*, page 1, BAR

Williams 1988b, ibid, page 5.

Williams 1988c, ibid, page 124.

Whittle E., (1992) *A Guide to Ancient and Historic Wales* CADW Cardiff , page 10

Worth's Dartmoor, R Hansford Worth, edition of 1981 published by Peninsula Press Newton Abbot page 202 et seq..

BIBLIOGRAPHY where not already mentioned in list of references

Kilmartin – Introduction and Guide, Rachael Butter, published Kilmartin House Trust, Kilmartin, Lochgilphead, Argyll 1999

Lithic Monuments within the Exmoor National Park, Quinnell and Dunn 1992, a survey for the RCAHM England, unpublished, obtained from English Heritage, National Monuments Records Centre, Kemble, Swindon

Magic Stones by Jan Pohribny 2007, published by Merrell Publishers Ltd, 81 Soutwark Street, London

The Standing Stones of Wales and South-West England, George Williams 1988, BAR series 197, 1 Oxford

Bibliography of Pictish Symbol Stones

The Sculptured Stones of Caithness, by Tim Blackie and Colin MacCauly 1998

The Symbol Stones of Scotland, Anthony Jackson, The Orkney Press.

The Sculptured Stones of Caithness, Tim Blackie and Colin Macaulay 1998, The Pinkfoot Press, Balgavies, Angus

Field Guide to Pictish Symbol Stones, Alan Mack 1997, Pinkfoot Press, Balgavies Angus

Pictish Symbol Stones, an illustrated gazetteer, RCAHMS 1999

Pictish Trail (traveller's guide) Anthony Jackson 1989, Orkney Press

The Pictish Stones of Easter Ross, Ellen MacNamara 1999

GAZETTEER

APPENDIX 1   THE STANDING STONES of ENGLAND from field work between 1997 and 2009

The Isle of Wight and Isle of Man are listed as separate counties, as is Exmoor (including Brendon Hill) which lies within both Devon and Somerset.
All measurments are in metres, and compass bearings and angle of lean are given to the nearest 5   degrees
Leaning Stones are measured along the length from ground level to the summit. This thus represents the height had the Stone been vertical.
Excluded from the analyses are the Stones lying flat, medieval and later Stones, dolmens and circles but outliers and centre Stones of circles are included.

SUMMARY of English prehistoric sites and Standing Stones

COUNTY	total number of all sites	of all Stones	sites (Stones)	leaning	average height	height range of Stones	1	2	3	>3	notes
AVON	2	4	1 (3)	1	1.8	1.1 to 2.8			1		
CAMBRIDGE	1	2	0								
CORNWALL	57	76	42 (59)	14	2.2	0.4 to 4.3	37	5	2	1	
CUMBRIA	16	32	14 (30)		2.2	0.4 to 4.3	9	3	1	1	
DERBYSHIRE	2	2	2 (2)	1	1.4	0.4 to 2.3	2				
DEVON	2	4	0								
Dartmoor	21	25	15 (18)	4	2.1	0.8 to 4	13	2			
DORSET	5	5	2 (2)	4	2.4	2.3 to 2.5	2				
EXMOOR	14	16	11 (16)	3	1.5	0.4 to 2.8	9	1			
GLOUCESTER	11	13	9 (11)		1.6	0.6 to 2.6	8	2			
HEREFORD	5	5	4 (5)		2.1	1.5 to 2.7	5				
ISLE of MAN	8	13	5 (5)	2	2.1	1.5 to 2.7	5				
KENT	1									1	excluded - burial chamber
LANCASHIRE	3	3									
NORTHUMB'LND	29	29	14 (20)	3	1.5	0.6 to 3.2	12	1		2	
OXFORD	6	13	5 (8)	2	2.1	1.6 to 3.2	4			1	
SHROPSHIRE	3	3	3 (3)	2	1.9	1.6 to 3.2	3				
SOMERSET	11	13	3 (3)		1.6	0.8 to 2.2					
STAFFORD	2	5	1 (2)	2	1.9	1.8 to 2	1	1			
SUSSEX east	1	1	1 (1)	2	2.3		1				has been moved
WARWICK	1	1	1 (1)		2.3		1				
WILTSHIRE	11	20	9 (15)	1	2.1	0.4 to 4.9	5	2			
YORKSHIRE	18	36	19 (30)	13	2.1	0.4 to 8.2	9	1	1	3	
ENGLAND total	**230**	**321**	**161 (234)**	**54**	**2**	**0.4 to 8.2**	**126**	**18**	**5**	**9**	

prehistoric sites as a % of all sites — 70%
prehistoric Standing Stones as a % of all Stones — 73%
percent of prehistoric Standing Stones which are leaning — 23%
percent of prehistoric sites with 1, 2, 3 or >3 Standing Stones — 78 11 3 6 %

Column key:

- A — number of drawing & Stone
- B — date
- C — name of Stone &/or site
- D — national grid reference
- E — altitude of Stone
- F — total Stones on site
- G — number of each Stone
- H — shape
- I — compass orientation
- J — height
- K — width
- L — thickness
- M — Vertical Leaning Fallen
- O — angle of lean in degrees
- P — Natural or Dressed Stone
- Q — geology
- R — age
- S — special features of Stone &/or site

AVON

A	B	C	D	E	F	G	H	I	J	K	L	M	O	P	Q	R	S
(19	22/09/1996	STANTON DREW cove Sts	ST601631	50	3	1	4		3	1.1	0.3	L	5	N	9	PH	) Stanton Drew circles nearby
(	"	"				2	5		1.6	1.6	0.5	V		N	9	PH	) see Other Stones 124;
(	"	"				3	7		5	2.8		F		N	9	PH	) age 2500 to 2000 BC
20	22/09/1996	STANTON DREW CIRCLE	ST601633												6	PH	excluded; see Other Stones 124
26	29/01/1997	CANNAWAYS Farm Banwell	ST387613	5	1		3		1.2	1	0.3	V		N	6	Pnk	on flood plain

CAMBRIDGE & Peterborough

A	B	C	D	E	F	G	H	I	J	K	L	M	O	P	Q	R	S
(649	15/10/2000	ROBIN HOOD) Castor, nr	TL139984		2	1	3		0.8	0.3	0.3	L	45	D		M	) may be difficult to find
(		LITTLE JOHN) Peterborough				2	3		0.6	0.3	0.3	L	45	D		M	)

CORNWALL   with 3 Stones on Isles of Scilly shown separately, but included in the analysis

A	B	C	D	E	F	G	H	I	J	K	L	M	O	P	Q	R	S
278	14/10/1998	SENNEN	SW355255	115	1		1		3	0.8	0.8	V		D	2	M?	now in wall/bank; squared all round & top
279	15/10/1998	BOSCOWEN ROSE west	SW427259	105	1		2		1.9	0.8	0.5	V		N	2	PH	now in wall/bank; see 322 for East St
(280	21/02/1999	GIANT`S ROCK Zennor	SW453388	110	2	1	6		2	1.3	0.7	V		N	2	PH	) packing stones
(		& smaller Stone				2	6							N	2	PnK	) small stone beside larger one
281	21/10/1998	BOSULLOW COMMON	SW414343	180	1		2		2.1	0.7	?	V		N	2	PnK	in hedge/bank; typical of PH Stone
282	21/02/1999	WHITE DOWNS common	SW420356	250	1		1		1.8	0.6	0.3	L		N	2	PH	surrounding cairns & mine workings
283	22/02/1999	CASTALLACK 1 WEST	SW447255	100	1		2		1.5	0.4	0.4	V		N	2	PH	will soon be lost in undergrowth
284	22/02/1999	CASTALLACK 2 EAST	SW453254	110	1		3		1.3	1.1	0.8	L	10	D ?	2	PH	squared? Weather-worn furrows on summit
(285	22/02/1999	KEYMEL FARM, Paul	SW458253	100	3	1	2		1.4	0.6	0.5	V		D		PnK	)are Stones 1 & 3 rubbing posts or PH Stones?
(		"				2	6		1	1.5	0.7	V		N		PnK	) long low lying stone
(		"				3	2		1.6	0.5	0.5	V		N ?		PnK	) Stones 1 & 3 look like prehistoric Stones
286	23/02/1999	BOSCOWEN St 2 nr Drift	SW416277	115	1		4	95	2.3	2.8	5	V		N	2	PnK	large triangular Stone now in field bank see340

No.	Date	Name	Grid ref	Ht	a	b	c	Brg	D1	D2	D3	Or	Dist	Type	Notes
287	23/02/2000	"HEATHER BRAE"	SW451362	190	1		4	110	2.1	1.4	0.6	V	N	LL	modern name stone
288	24/02/2000	MEN SERYFA, W Penn'th	SW426353	210	1		1		1.6	0.4	0.3	V	D	2 PnK	boundary mark? Stone 282 intervisible
316	14/10/1998	TREVORGANS St Buryan	SW404261	125	1		1		2.3	0.8	0.7	L	150 N	2 PH	
317	14/10/1998	PRIDDEN St Buryan	SW417267	105	1		4	80	2.6	1.8	0.5	L	40o N	2 PH	massive; stated attempts to throw down
318	14/10/1998	TRELEW Farm St Buryan	SW421269	115	1		1		3.2	1	0.5	L	10o N	2 PH	square section
(320	15/10/1998	The PIPERS EAST St	SW543524	95	2	1	1		4.3	1.4	0.7	V	N	2 PH	) 3 flat stones & boulder in hedge
(319		" "				2	1		4	0.9	0.9	V	N	2 PH	) deep cracks on S & W; irregular shape
321	15/10/1998	GOON RITH St, St Buryan's	SW429245	95	1		1		3.3	0.6	0.6	V	D	2 PH	stones at base;now in hedge
322	15/10/1998	BOSCAWEN ROSE east	SW428239	105	1		1		2.4	0.6	0.4	V	D	2 PH	square dressed; may be medieval?
323	15/10/1998	CHYANHALL FARM	SW451275	110	1		1		2.6	0.8	0.6	V	N	2 PH	
324	15/10/1998	BEERSHEBA FARM	SW625371	115	1		1		3.2	1.1	0.8	V	N	2 PH	
335	21/02/1999	PORTHMEOR	SW453388	120	1		1		2.1	0.7	0.7	V	N	2 PH	packing stones
336	22/02/1999	BLIND FIDDLER Catchall	SW282425	100	1		4	0	3.3	1.8	0.4	V	N	2 PH	
337	22/02/1999	KERRIS, SW of Newlyn	SW443274	105	1		4	0	2.1	2.6	0.6	V	N	2 PH	
338	22/02/1999	TREVERN HOUSE	SW408240	90	1		2		1.9	0.7	0.7	V	N	2 PH	packing stones
339	23/02/1999	TRESVENNACK PILLAR	SW442289	95	1		1		3.7	0.8	0.6	V	N	2 PH	packing stones; long crack on SW side
340	23/02/1999	BOSCAWEN St 1, nr Drift	SW415276	125	1		1		2.6	1.3	0.9	V	N	2 PH	see 286
341	23/02/1999	WHEAL BULLER St Just	SW4023`8	185	1		1		3	0.8	0.9	V	N	2 PH	not marked; in wall; erectedd 1989
342	232-2-99	Rosemergy engine house	SW364241												Cornish engine house
343	23-22-99	BOSWENS COMMON	SW400329	210	1		1		2.4	0.9	0.8	V	N	2 PH	on top of moor
(344	24/02/1999	MEN-an-TOL	SW426349	190	3	1	2		1.1	0.7	0.4	V	?	2 PH	) historic era not certain
(		" "				2	8	160	1	1.2	0.2	V	D	2 PH	) this Stone has 0.4 metre hole
(		" "				3	2		1.1	0.3	0.3	V	?	2 PH	) see178 & 501 for similar Stones
345	24/02/1999	TRYE FARM Gulval	SW460350	150	1		1		2.5	0.6	0.6	V	D?	2 PH	burial chamber now excavated & lost
346	24/02/1999	PROSPIDNICK nr Helston	SW659315	165	1		1		2.8	0.8	0.5	V	N	2 PH	Stone measured from roadside
(379	13/11/1999	LANTGLOSS NORTH St	SX137511	100	2	1	5		1.1	0.7	0.4	V	N	8 PH	)
(		" "				2	7					F	N	8 PH	)fallen Stone at base; see 379 at 160m.
380	13/11/1999	LANTGLOSS SOUTH St	SX137510	100	1		4	100	1.3	1	0.4	V	N	8 PH	packing stones; Stone 379 at 160 metres
381	13/11/1999	TREMENHERE Farm	SX749368	155	1		1		2.3	0.5	0.5	V	D	2 PnK	square Stone; iron ring on NW face
382	13/11/1999	DRY TREE STONE	SW728210	105	1		1		2.8	0.8	0.8	V	N	2 PH	concreted in place
496	13/11/1999	LONG STONE St Austell	SX029521	70	1		1		3.3	1.1	0.5	V	N	2 PH	on college playing field
499	13/10/1999	BURRAS, Lezern Farm	SW680344	160	1		1		3.5	0.8	0.5	V	N	2 PkN	set into flat granite flagstone 1.8by1.4 m
500	14/11/1999	LONG STONE St Keverne	SW778211	100	1		3		2.6	1.2	0.7	V	N	2 PH	
501	14/11/1999	TOLVAN CROSS stone	SW706277	20	1		8		1.6	2.5	0.3	V	N	2 PH	large through hole, minimum diameter 0.25m
(502	14/11/1999	at DRIFT near Newlyn	SW438283	100	2	1	2		2.3	1	0.5	V	N	2 PH	)
(		" "				2	2		2	1	0.5	V	N	2 PH	)
503	15/11/1999	TRISTAN ST, nr Fowey	SX112521	75	1		1		2.5	0.4	0.4	V	D	2 M	moved, concreted in place; 6th. Century
504	15/11/1999	SYBLYBACK fm St Clears	SX241739	290	1		2		2.3	0.9	0.7	V	N	2 PH	packing stones
(505	15/11/1999	The HURLERS Minions	SX256714	290	2	1	2		1.5	0.5	0.4	V	D	2 PH	) outliers to the Hurlers Circles
(		"				2	2		1.4	0.4	0.4	V	D	2 PH	)
(506	30/03/2000	The HURLERS Minions	SX256714	290	2	1	1		1.3	0.8	0.4	L	10 N	2 PH	) other outliers
(		"				2	3		1.4	0.8	0.5	V	N	2 PH	)
385	30/03/2000	SPETTAGUE fm gatepost	SX209791	275	1		5		1	0.6	0.3	V	N	2 PnK	gatepost? Or similar? In field bank
507	30/03/2000	SPETTAGUE Farm	SX213796	265	1		2		2.4	1	0.6	V	N	2 PH	packing stones
510	30/03/2000	KING DONIERT'S STONE	SX236688	210	2							V	D	2 M	2 broken carved crosses 9th. Century
511	30/03/2000	LONG STONE in Roche	SW987601	165	1		4	80	2.8	1.3	0.3	V	N	2 PH	moved; cemented into stone plinth
(512	30/03/2000	NINE MAIDENS	SW936676	165	9	1	2		1.5	0.7	0.3	V	N	8 PH	) all with prominent viens of quartz
(		" near St. Columb Major				2	1		1.5	0.5	0.3	V	N	8 PH	)
(		"				3	1		2.1	0.6	0.4	L	20 N	8 PH	)
(		"				4	2		0.9	0.5	0.4	V	N	8 PH	)
(		"				5	3		1.7	0.8	0.4	L	10 N	8 PH	)
(		"				6	7		0.4	0.7	0.3	V	N	8 PH	)
(		"				7	7		1.4	0.8	0.3	L	75 N	8 PH	)
(		"					2								) this is a field stone placed here
(		"				8	2		1.4	0.6	0.4	L	5 N	8 PH	)
(		"				9	7					F	N	8 PH	)
313	30/03/2000	ST BREOCK'S DOWN	SW973682	200	1		4	30	2.2	1.7	0.5	L	20 N	8 PH	through crack whichmay split the Stone
314	30/03/2000	LONG STONE St Breock's	SW968693	215	1		3		2.9	1.5	0.9	V	N	8 PH	packing stones; on mound; quartz veins
515	01/04/2000	LONG Stone at Camelford	SX114820	250	1		2		2.8	1	0.6	V	N	2 PH	packing stones; stonefield c.25 metres N
1172	15/09/2006	MERRY MAIDENS St Buryan	SW432246	120	1		8	130	1.7	0.7	0.3	V	N	2 PnK	now used as gatepost in field bank
1173	15/09/2006	BOSCOWEN UN St Buryan	SW412273	115	1		1		2.7	1	0.5	L	20 N	2 PH	stands in centre of circle of 23 stones
(1186	24/09/2008	TREGASEAL West Penwith	SW389325	120	3	1	4	45	0.7	1.2	0.2	V	N	2 PH	) hole 20cms by 10cms.
(		"				2	4	20	0.8	1.2	0.4	V	N	2 PH	) hole 15cms by 7.5cms.
(		"				3	4	40	1.2	1.3	0.3	V	N	2 PH	) hole 20cms by 10cms.

ISLES of SCILLY

No.	Date	Name	Grid ref	Ht	a	b	c	Brg	D1	D2	D3	Or	Dist	Type	Notes
1168	10/09/2006	OLD MAN of GUGH St Agnes	SV891084	20	1		1		2.4	0.8	0.7	L	20 N	2 PH	packing stones; 2 fissuress on west side
1169	10/09/2006	HARRY'S WALLS St Mary's	SV910110	30	1		1		2.6	0.7	0.3	V	N	2 PH	concreted onto plinth
1170	11/09/2006	LONG ROCK, St Mary's	SV913124	40	1		2		2.8	0.7	0.7	L	20 N	2 PH	fisssures on west

CUMBRIA, The Shap alingment of 12 Stones is shown separately and is included in the Cumbrian analysis.

No.	Date	Name	Grid ref	Ht	a	b	c	Brg	D1	D2	D3	Or	Dist	Type	Notes
(130	12/10/1997	MOUNT CLIFTON Farm	NY534259	180	3	1	3		1.1	1	0.6	L	20 N	8 PH	) moved; now set in concrete
(		" "				2	3		1.9	1.4		1 L		PH	) Stone 2 is 3 metres away at 320o
(		& third Stone lies flat				3	7					F	40 N	8 PH	) bears 320o at 120 metres
131	11--10-97	MAYBURGH HENGE	NV534296	145	1		2		2.9	1.4	1.3	V	N	PH	packing stones; 8 other stones lost; impressive
132	12/10/1997	LONG MEG & her daughters	NY570372	160	1		1		3.7	1.2	1.1	L	10 D?	1 PH	2 large ring marks; circle of 69 'daughters'
138	05/02/1998	HOLME HEAD Stone	NY496343	135	1		2		2.4	1.8	1	V	N	2 PH	411
139	05/02/1998	MONKS HOUSE Farm	NY486374	130	1		2		2.1	1	0.8	V	N	2 PH	not marked on OS map; packing stones
(169	06/02/1998	SEWBORWENS, Penrith	NY488300	170	1		6		1.9	1	0.8	V	N	2 PH	see 368 - 2 small Stones c. 120 metres at 280o
(368	03/07/1999	SEWBORWENS small Sts	NY488301	1`70	2	1	4	140	1	0.8	0.3	V	N	PH	) both now in hedge; may have been moved?
(		"				2	3		0.8	0.8	0.4	V	N	PH	) connection with 169 not known

No	Date	Name / Site	Grid Ref												Notes
410	03/07/1999	SKIRGILL industrial estate	NY509288	140	1		5		1.8	1.5	1 V		N	1	PH	probably glacial boulder
(411	03/07/1999	HIGHGATE fm Penruddock	NY443273	250	2	1	1		2	0.8	0.4 V		D	9	PnK	) moved -ref farmer; 2 holes - gatepost?
(		"				2	1		1.6		V			1	PnK	) gatepost?
412	03/07/1999	LITTLE MEG StSt & circle	NY577375	170	1				1.3	1	1 V		D	2	PH	glacial boulder with circle of 10 squat stones
413	03/07/1999	The COP STONE Helton	NY497217	315	1				1.5	1.4	1 V			8	PH	packing stones;glacial boulder with ruined circle
(1089	16/08/2003	KIRKSTANTON, nr Millom	SD137811	10	2	1	1		3.1	1	0.4 V		N	8	PH	) large field stones at base
(		"				2	1		2.3	0.9	0.6 V			8	PH	) of both Stones
1090	17/08/2003	WHITESTOCK HALLRusland	SD331888	20	1		5		1.4	1.2	0.7 V		D?	2	PH	packing stones; stands on drumlin
(1096	07/09/2003	ASH HOUSE Duddon Bridge	SD193872	125	2	1	3		1.4	1.4	1.1 V	20 N		8	PH	) glacial boulders? Marked on OS map
(		" "				2	5		0.8	1.7	0.7 L		N	8	PH	) as Standing Stones
1122	28/04/2004	GOSFORTH CROSS	NY072036	60	1		1		4.5	0.3	0.3 V		D	1	M	highly carvbed; cemented onto plinth

The SHAP ∕ ALINGMENT of 12 STONES.   . Included as one site. The Stones are numbered in the archaeological record from the north but are shown here in the chronological order in which I visited them; the archaeological number is shown beside the name or site.
All are porphyritic granite.   The Shap circle was ruined by the railway & is not included in the analysis.

No	Date	Name / Site	Grid Ref												Notes
170	07/02/1998		NY558152	245	13	5	6		3	1.8	1.3 L	50 N		2	PH	possible cobbled pavement 10metres at 320o
171	07/02/1998	06-GOGGLEBY STONE	NY559150	270		6	3		2.1	1.4	1.1 V			8	PH	massive dumbell-shaped Stone
172	07/02/1998	07-	NY560149	260		7	4		1.4	2.4	0.7 V				PH	) large Stone in wall visible both sides
		07a-					7		0.5	1.8	?		N	2	PH	) smaller Stone visible on west side of wall
173	07/02/1998	03-	NY555152	280		3	6		1.1	2.3	1.6 V		N	2	PH	) in north-east face of wall
		04-				4	5		0.9	1.1	F		N	2	PH	) 12 metres to south-east
174	07/02/1998	02-THUNDER STONE	NY551157	260		2	6		2.4	3.6	1.7 V		N	2	PH	glacial erratic in original site
174a	07/02/1998	01-LITTLE THUNDER St	NY551592	270		1	7				F		N	2	PH	lies flat with surface 2.5 by 2.2 metres
175	03/07/1999	11- all theses 3 Stones are	NY566143	270		11	6						N	2	PH	) these three Stones appear to be
		12 - in the gardens of				12	6						N	2	PH	) glacial boulders and all
		13- Carleton Terrace				13	6						N	2	PH	) individually uninteresting
176	03/07/1998	10- beside GREEN FARM	NY565145	260		10	6		O.6	1.5	1.5 V		N	2	PH	small boulder
176a	03/07/1998	SHAP SOUTH circle	NY567133	260			9				V		N	2	PH	ruined circle 6 glacial boulders - Other Stones 84

DERBYSHIRE

No	Date	Name / Site	Grid Ref												Notes
41	21/02/1997	CORK STONE	SK245626	310										7		excluded; wind eroded natural outcrop
1180	20/04/2007	outlier to NINE LADIES circle	SK249633	320	1		3		0.4	0.6	0.3 V		N	1	PH	
1181	20/04/2007	near WIRKSWORTH	SK274292	250	1		4	195	2.3	1.4	0.4 L	15 N		9	PH	large crack; little weathering - unusual

DEVON with the Dartmoor Stones & Drizzlecombe Rows .
The Stones on Dartmoor including the Drizzlecombe Rows appear to form a separate population and are shown separately.
See EXMOOR for the Stones within Devon which are on Exmoor

No	Date	Name / Site	Grid Ref												Notes
46	30/03/1997	LONG STONE E Worlington	SS774158	210	1		1		2.3	0.3	0.3 V	40o D		L	?	squared & flat top; provenance uncertain
(240	08/08/1998	TAVISTOCK RECTORY	SX474739	150	3	1	4	40	2.1	0.7	0.3 V		D	2	M	) ogam sts late late 5 to 7 C AD; all
(241		" "				2	2		1.5	0.4	0.3 V		D	2	M	) inscribed
(		" "					3		1.8	0.5	0.4 V		D	2	M	) hole on W side & embedde gate hinges

Dartmoor Stones & Drizzlecombe Rows together.

No	Date	Name / Site	Grid Ref												Notes
28	05/03/1997	HEATH STONE Fernworthy	SX671838	370	1		3		1.3	0.8	0.3 V		N?		PH	part of wall? 17C ? Inscription
29	05/03/1997	FERNWORTHY CIRCLE	SX655832	380		transferred to Other Stones 126										small circle & stone row
224	08/08/1998	PETERTAVY boundary St	SX577794	450	1		2		1.3	0.5	0.4 V		D	2	M	packing stones; boundary mark?see 242 c. 300m
225	08/08/1998	MERRIVALE boundary St	SX556748	350	1		1		2	0.4	0.4 V		D	2	M	packing stones; boundary mark set in cobbles
226	06/06/1998	MERRIVALE Standing St	SX553746	330	1		1		3	0.6	0.6 V		D	2	PH	Merrivale Row & circle nearby
242	08/08/1998	PETERTAVY Standing St	SX550788	330	1		1		3	0.6	0.3 V		N	2	PH	irregular shape; see 224 300m at 40o
243	09/08/1998	HARBOURNE HEAD	SX696651	340	1		4	140	2.2	1	0.3 L	10o N		2	PH	packing stones; needs repacking before it falls
244	09/08/1998	MERRIVALE NEWTAKE	SX556753	375	1		4	50	2	2.3	0.3 V		N	2	PH	packing stones; set in hut system
652	15/11/2000	OXENHAM Arms,South Zeals	SX650936	200	1		1		2.2 ?	?	?	V		N	2	PH	scheduled monument; inside bar parlour
685	16/11/2000	LEEDEN TOR, south slope	SX 650712	360	1		4	60	1.2	0.9	0.3 V		N	2	PH	packing stones; stands on small flattened platform
(653	16/11/2000	MERRIVALE S row west st	SX555748	350	2	1	3		0.8	0.5	0.3 V		N	2	PH	) stone at east end of Row, 175 metres long
(		S " east st				2	4	60	1.4	1.3	0.3 V		N	2	PH	) Blocking Stone at east end of South Row
(654	16/11/2000	MERRIVALE N row west st	SX555748	350	2	1	3		0.8	0.8	0.3 V		N	2	PH	) small Stone at east end of North Row
(		" N " east st				2	2		1.3	0.8	0.4 V		N	2	PH	) Blocking Stone at east end of North Row
655	17/11/2000	CHALLACOMBE Down row	SX690798	490	1		4	60	1.8	1.5	0.4 V		N	2	PH	Blocking Stone at south end of Row
866	13/10/2001	HANGING STONE LeeMoor	SX584688	340	1		4	170	2.3	1.3	0.5 L	20o N		2	PH	large stones at base;may be boundary stone
867	13/10/2001	LONG STONE Shovel Down	SX660857	420	1		1		2.9	0.8	0.6 L	10o N		2	PH	boundary mark with large packing stones
774	04/03/2002	nr HEALE FARM M`tn Hpsd	SX721850	240	1		2		1.5	0.7	0.7 V		N	2	PnK	rubbing post?- looks prehistoric
1000	22/09/2003	WHITE MOOR St Dartmoor	SX643896	470	1		2		1.8	1	0.7 L	25o N		2	PNK	PH Stone?; now inscribed as boundary mark
1001	22/09/2003	KENNON HILL St Dartmoor	SX639895	460	1		4	220	1.4	0.6	0.2 V		D?	2	M?	packing stones; medieval boundary mark?

Drizzlecombe menhirs & rows are analysed with the other Dartmoor Stones

No	Date	Name / Site	Grid Ref												Notes
875	04/03/2002	boundary post 1	SX589670	330	3	1	1		1.8	0.6	0.3 V		D	2	LL?	civil or stannary boundary?
		" " 2				2			1.2				N	2	PnK	not clear what this small Stone was/is
		" " 3, 4 & 5	SX587665			3	1						D	2	LL?	individual Stones not recorded
876	04/03/2002	MENHIR A	SX590668	320	1		4	60	3.1	1.7	0.3 V		N	2	PH	re-erected; fissures; row to north-east
877	04/03/2002	" C	SX592670	330	1		4	140	4	1.3	0.4 V		N	2	PH	re-erected; row to north-east
878	04/03/2002	" B	SX592671	330	1		4	50	2.2	1	0.3 L	10o N		2	PH	re-erected; row to north-east runs for 150 metres

DORSET

No	Date	Name / Site	Grid Ref												Notes
33	15/03/1957	HARP or HARD STONE	SY922805	55	1		2		2.3	0.8	0.5 V		N	9	PH	
44	19/03/1997	Nine Stones circle	SY610904													transferred to OTHER STONES 122
45	15/03/1997	in LONG BREDY parish	SY357914	160	1		6		2.5	2.5	0.8 V		N	9	PH	much eroded
85	05/06/1997	PORTSHAM FARM	SY615866	155	1		7				F		N	9	PnK	listed by CC., but looks questionable
86	05/06/1997	CROSCOMBE Stone	ST520069	110	1		7				V		N		PnK	Listed by CountyCC

No	Date	Name	Grid ref	Alt	N	g	sd	az	H	W	D	sec	dist	D/N	#	Type	Notes
158	08/12/1997	STINSFORD CROSS	SY708913	45	1		2		0.9	0.4	0.4	V		D	9	M	moved; allegedly Roman milestone

EXMOOR from Baggy Point east to A383 (Taunton to Minehead road) & north of the M5 & A361 (Tiverton to Barnstaple)
Exmoor includes Stones in Devon and Somerset

No	Date	Name	Grid ref	Alt	N	g	sd	az	H	W	D	sec	dist	D/N	#	Type	Notes
(34	29/03/1997	WITHERIDGE MOOR	SS859151	230	2	1	7					F		N		PnK	now fallen; provenance uncertain
(	" "		SS856153			2	7					F				PnK	lies beside tumulus; no drawing/photo
35	29/03/1997	KNOWSTONE Beeple Hill	SS205825	230	1		2		1.4	0.4		V		D		PnK	moved for new road; circular section
36	29/03/1997	CARACTACUS STONE	SS890335	370	1		2		1.1	0.5	0.2	V		D		M	c. 6C?; inscribed; inside shelter
37	30/09/1997	CODSEND MOOR	SS863411	580	1		6		0.4	0.5	0.3	L	30o	N		PH	uninteresting; another st near not found
47	30/03/1997	SWAP HILL on south slope	SS820411	430	1		2		1.7	0.4	0.3	V		N	8	PH	square section; quartz vein
144	07/05/1998	above KNAPP DOWN	SS603469	260	1		4	60	1.3	0.8	0.4	V		N	4	PH	another St (SS601439) 3.2km at 185o
(211	07/05/1998	KENTISBURY DOWN	SS640441	315	1		5		0.9	0.8	0.3	V		N		PH	) nearby small stone
(	" "						7					F				PH	) small prostrate St lies 20m at 100o
212	07/05/1998	BULL POINT SOUTH ST	SS470462	80	1		5		0.9	0.9	0.6	V		N	3	PH	see 213 for Bull Point North Stone
213	07/05/1998	BULL POINT NORTH ST	SS472466	100	1		3		1.3	0.7	0.5	V		N	4	PH	see 212 for Bull Point South Stone
190	07/05/1998	MATTACK DOWN	SS601439	220	1		2		2.5	1.6	1.3	V		N	4	PH	broken by lightning Oct 1996
516	01/04/2000	CHALLACOMBE LONG ST	SS705431	460	1		4	20	2.8	0.8	0.3	V		N		PH	stands in water over a spring
353	03/03/1999	DUNS ST on Brendon Hill	ST018331	380	1		6		1.8	2	2	L	40	N	4	M	thought to be medieval boundary stone
354	03/03/1999	NAKED BOY Brendon Hill	ST015345	400	1		5		1.2	1.3	0.7	L	30	N		M	probably medieval boundary mark
(1144	19/06/2006	LONG STONE on Lyn Down	SS727475	330	2	1	4	0	2.1	0.8	0.3	V	180	N	3	PH	)
(	" "					2	2		1	0.4	0.2	V		N	3	PH	)

GLOUCESTER   includes Forest of Dean

No	Date	Name	Grid ref	Alt	N	g	sd	az	H	W	D	sec	dist	D/N	#	Type	Notes
152	02/09/1997	LOWER SWELL Stow-o-W	SP171250	190	1		6	70	0.9	1.9	0.8	V		N	9	PH	long low lying stone; uninteresting
(136	21/10/1997	LONG STONE Minchinh'tn	ST884999	180	2	1	4	135	2.4	1.7	0.4	V		N	9	PH	)2 holes c 0.5m; part of a dolmen?
(	" "					2	3		0.8						9	PH	)bears 90o & 10o metres built in wall
(137	21/10/1997	TINGLE STONE in	ST883988	165	1		4	0	1.7	2.2	0.3	V		N	9	PH	) packing stones; much weathered; stands at
(347	15/10/1999	Gatcombe Park															) north end of long barrow; may be dolmen?
(352	29/03/1999	WICK Burial chamber	ST706719	60	2	1	6		1.4	1.3	0.8	V		N	6	PH	) packing stones & 4 other large stones around
(	" "					2	6		1.4	1.4	0.4	L	15	N	6	PH	) base;both much weathered
383	15/03/2000	WHITTLESTONE Lwr Swell	SP174256	160	1		7		0.6	1.3	1	F		N	9	PH	has been moved
384	15/03/2000	KIFTSGATE St Chipping C.	SP135389	155	1		7		0.9	0.8	0.2	V		N	9	PkN	very little weathering
508	15/03/2000	BOURTON HILL HOUSE	SP144319	235	1		1		1.7	0.5	0.3	V		N	9	LL	marker &/or gatepost
509	15/03/2000	HOAR STONE D Abbots	SP964065	200	1		6		1.2	1.8	1	V		N	9	PH	remains of dolmen? On long barrow
648	07/10/2000	BOXWELL MANOR Tetbury	ST820924	190	1		4	40	2.1	1.3	0.3	V		N	9	PH	on mound; oolitic stone much weathered

Forest of Dean

No	Date	Name	Grid ref	Alt	N	g	sd	az	H	W	D	sec	dist	D/N	#	Type	Notes
393	27/04/1999	LONG STONE, Staunton	SO550120	210	1				2.3	1.1	1.1	L	15	N		PH	fissures
465	29/08/1999	BROADSTONE Stroat	ST578972	5	1		4	40	2.6	1.5	0.4	L		N	1	PH	beside shore; 3 large flat stones 200 metres north

HAMPSHIRE

No	Date	Name	Grid ref											D/N	#	Type	Notes
191	09/05/1998	BRAMDEAN memorial sts	SU6330271			transferred to OTHER STONES 132									N	10	LL	late 19 C memorial; circle of trilthons

HEREFORD

No	Date	Name	Grid ref	Alt	N	g	sd	az	H	W	D	sec	dist	D/N	#	Type	Notes
67	02/07/1997	LOWER KINGSHAM	SO358641	125	1		7					F		N	2	PH	large recumbent stone with cupmarks
(68	03/07/1997	KING STONE Michaelchurch	SO303372	320	1		1		2.7	0.8	0.6	V		N	1	PH	) large elegant Stone
(1141	16/09/1997	" "															) second visit
88	02/07/1997	WIRGINS STONE Sutton	SO529439	55	1		2		1.5	0.3	0.3	V		N	1	PH	stand in circular plinth
415	27/08/1999	QUEEN'S ST near Goodrich	SO561181	20	1		3		1.8	1.4	0.9	V		N	1	PH	packing stones; spectacular fissures; on mound
1141	16/09/2005	BOOBY DINGLE Peterchurch	SO303372	320	1		2		2.3	0.8	0.5	V		N	1	PH	

ISLE of MAN

No	Date	Name	Grid ref	Alt	N	g	sd	az	H	W	D	sec	dist	D/N	#	Type	Notes
632	16/08/2000	near ORRISDALE	SC933335	50	1		1		2.5	1	0.6	L	20	N	8	PH	
633	17/08/2000	KING ORRY'S GRAVE	SC438844	50	1		1	120	2.5	0.8	0.2	V		D		PH	C. 3000 BC; part of burial chamber
634	17/03/2000	SPIRAL STONE, Ballaragh	SC451857	255	1		3		2.5 ?	?		V		N		PH	now in bank -- features not visible
635	17/08/2000	CASHEL yn ARD nr Laxey	SC892462	150										N		PH	burial chamber complex; many stones
(636	18/08/2000	BALLAHOTT Fm, Ballasalla	SC273702	40	2	1	1		2	0.6	0.3	L	10	N	9	Pkn	) sparse lichen - "rubbing post"? Both
(						2	3		1.2	0.4	0.3	V		N	2	Pkn	) " " ; probably modern
637	18/08/2000	BALLAHENNEY, nr Colby	SC221717	135	1		2		2	0.8	0.8	V		N	3	PH	quartz on summit
638	18/08/2000	BALLAQUEENEY CROSS	SC206689	20	1		4	40	2.5	0.7	0.2	V		D	3	M	moved; now on plinth; 2 holes drilled later
639	18/08/2000	GIANT'S QUOIT	SC209683	20	1		4	60	3.5	11	0.5	L	10	N	3	PH	massive stone
(640	19/08/2000	ST. PATRICK'S CHAIR	SC318780	100	3	1	2		1	0.4	0.3	V		N	3	PnK	) pile of field Stones (?) around all three
(						2	4		1.3	0.6	0.2	V		N	2	PnK	) Christianised cross) this site probably
(						3	2		0.7	0.3	0.2	V		N	2	PnK	) " ") a hoax

ISLE of WIGHT

No	Date	Name	Grid ref	Alt	N	g	sd	az	H	W	D	sec	dist	D/N	#	Type	Notes
(60	03/06/1997	MOTISTONE LONG Stone	SZ407842	140	2	1			3.8	2	1.8	V		N	1	PH	) large greensand Stone
(	"					2						F		N			) lies at foot of standing stone

KENT

No	Date	Name	Grid ref	Alt	N	g	sd	az	H	W	D	sec	dist	D/N	#	Type	Notes
(732	21/06/2001	COLDRUM burial Trottiscliffe	TQ654607	80	5	1	4	90	2.5	3.5		V		N	10	PH	) large burial chamber
(	"					2	3		0.5	1		V		N	10	PH	) with interesting Stones
(	"					3	3		1.4	1.3		V		N	10	PH	) all are excluded from the
(	"					4	4	80	1.1	1.7		V		N	10	PH	) analysis

No	Date	Name	Location	Grid	Alt	n	s	a	Az	W	B	H	Sh	d	N/D	No.	Type	Notes
(		"				5	2			2	2.5		V		N	10	PH	)

LANCASHIRE

No	Date	Name	Location	Grid	Alt	n	s	a	Az	W	B	H	Sh	d	N/D	No.	Type	Notes
109	16/08/1997	GREAT STONE	Lunesdale	SD671663	280	1	1	6		5	12	4.5	V		N	1		glacial boulder excluded; Other Stones121
110	16/08/1997	BIRK`S FARM	Lunsedale	SD633667	210	1	1	1		2.3	0.6	0.4	V		N	1	PnK	not recorded or marked on OS map
(879	18/03/2002	LANGTHWAITE WEST ST		SD498606	120	2	1	1		1.4	0.4	0.2	V		N?	2	PnK	) probably 'rubbing posts'
(		"	EAST ST				2	1		1.1	0.4	0.2	V		N?	2	PnK	) excluded

NORTHUMBERLAND

No	Date	Name	Location	Grid	Alt	n	s	a	Az	W	B	H	Sh	d	N/D	No.	Type	Notes
55	20/05/1997	STOB STONE	Matfen	NZ033704	160	1		2		2.3	1.3	0.4	V		N		PH	cup marks & grooves
56	20/05/1997	WARRIOR STONE	Matfen	NZ043746	205	1		1		2	0.6	0.5	L	15	N		PH	cups & fissures
57	20/05/1997	The POIND & his MAN		NZ065821	160	1		4		2	1.5	0.7	V		N	1	PH	stones around base; originally 2 Stones
58	21/05/1997	BATTLE STONE,	Akeld	NT930304	50	1		6		2	1.8	1.1	V		N		PH	now set in concrete
59	21/05/1997	HURL or BURL STONE		NU039247	85	1		1		4	0.5	0.4	V		D	1	M	set on stone plinth
82	20/05/1997	nr WALLINGTON PARK		NZ034842	140	1		1		2	0.6	0.4	L	15	D	1	PnK	deep grove on top & side
83	21/05/1997	NEWTON MILL	Lilburn	NU043242	60	1		1		1.3	0.7	0.4	V		N	1	PH	cup marks & shallow grooves
84	22/05/1997	NEWBIGGIN Caravan Park		NZ304859	10	1		2		1.6	0.4	0.4	V		D	1	M	marker post?
87	09/06/1997	WETWOOD MOOR	Wooler	NT014278	160	1		7		1.5	1.3	0.6	F		N		PnK	
112	25/08/1997	BATTLE STONE 2,	Akeld	NT696295	45	1		3		1.8	0.8	1.1	V		N	2	PH	
(133	13/10/1997	WHEATHILL Fm	Colwell	NY938746	120	1		1		3.5	1.2	0.6	L	10	N		PH	) possible cupmarks on South
(134		"	"															
(135	13/10/1997	MARE & FOAL,	Haltwhistle	NY725664	230	2	1	3		1	1	0.4	V		D		PH	) both stand on a raised cobbled area
(		"	"				2	2		1.6	0.8	0.5	V		D		PH	)
145	25/08/1997	CORBY`S CRAGS	Alnwick	NU130104	230	1		6		0.5	1	0.5	V		N	1	PH	recumbent; deep groove over surface
146	25/08/1997	HULNE PARK	Alnwick	NU157168	55	1		2		1.6	1.7	1.6	L	20	N		PH	2 deep grooves
771	03/10/2001	KETTLEY STONE	Chatton	NU072298	90	1		4	160	1.5	2.5	0.7	V		N	1	PnK	not clear if this is the Ketley Stone
861	03/10/2001	KING`S STONE	Cornhill-o-T	NT884385	60	1		2		2.2	1.5	1.2	V		N	1	PH	much weathered on North
781	28/05/2002	HANGING STONE	Hexham	NY881618	230	1		2		1.4	0.8	0.5	V		N		PnK	
(782	29/05/2002	BIDDLE STONES,Netherton		NT956082	210	2	1	3		0.4	0.7	0.6	V		N	1	PnK	)
(		"	"				2	3		0.3	0.7	0.6	V		N	1	PnK	)Stone 2 has depression cut in top
783	29/05/2002	ROTHBURY 1		NU051023	210	1		3		0.8	0.6	0.6	V		N	1	PH	small uninteresting Stone
784	29/05/2002	ROTHBURY 2		NU056030	180	1		3		1.2	1.1	0.7	V		N	1	PH	packing stones; much weathered summit
(1091	29/05/2002	GOAT STONES	nr Wark	NY829748	245	4	1	3		0.6	0.7	0.4	V		N	1	PH	) FOUR POSTER
(	04/09/2003	"	"				2	3		0.6	0.7	0.3	V		N	1	PH	)
(		"	"				3	3		0.6	0.8	0.5	V		N	1	PH	) 12 deep cup markson flat top
(		"	"				4	5		1.2	0.8	0.6	V		N	1	PH	)
(1092	04/09/2003	FIVE KINGS Dueshill Hepple		NT957002	230	4	1	2		2.1	1.4	0.7	V		N	1	PH	) square section; ROW of 4 Stones
(		"	"				2	3	120	1.6	2.3	0.7	V		N	1	PH	)
(		"	"				3	4	70	1.4	1.5	0.6	V		N	1	PH	) grooves on summit
(		"	"				4	4	190	2.1	2.1	0.7	V		N	1	PH	)
1189																		

OXFORDSHIRE

No	Date	Name	Location	Grid	Alt	n	s	a	Az	W	B	H	Sh	d	N/D	No.	Type	Notes
124	02/09/1997	HAWK STONE,	Spelsbury	SP339235	170	1		2		2	1	0.8	V		N	9	PH	much weathered
125	02/09/1997	LYNHAM LONG BARROW		SP297210	190	1		4	60	1.6	1.6	0.6	L	10	N	9	PH	
151	02/09/1997	HOAR STONE,	Enstone	SP378238	165	1		2	80	2.7	1.8	1.2	L	5	N	9	PH	) 2 leaning onto main upright & 2 lying flat
		"	"										F			9	PH	)
234	24/06/1998	TASTON ST	Taston	SP359221	145	1		4	90	2.1	0.8	0.4	V		N	9	PH	now in garden wall; scheduled
762	15/07/2001	BLOWING STONE		SU324871	120	1		3		0.8	1	0.7	V		N	10	PnK	moved;age uncertain
(756	15/07/2001	WAYLAND`S SMITHY		SU281854	135	4	1	4		2.3	2	0.6	V		N	10	PH	) large sarsen slabs at entrance
(		"	"				2	4		2.8	2	0.6	V		N	10	PH	) to burial chamber in long
(		"	"				3	4		3.2	2	0.5	V		N	10	PH	) barrow; these stones are not free
(		"	"				4	4		2.1	1.3	0.3	V		N	10	PH	) standing stones but are included as such
1179	03/04/2007	STONE HOUSE		SP356194	105	1		2		1.1	0.7	0.6	V		N	9	PH	much weathered; in garden

SHROPSHIRE

No	Date	Name	Location	Grid	Alt	n	s	a	Az	W	B	H	Sh	d	N/D	No.	Type	Notes
235	03/07/1998	CROWN HOUSE,Pant-Glas		SJ237329	320	1		5		2	1.3	1.2	L	30	N	8	PH	
236	03/07/1998	CYNINIONst Rhydycroesau		SJ243304	285	1		2		2.1	0.8	0.7	L	10	N		PH	
1126	07/07/2004	MITCHELLS FOLD		SK305948	350	1				1.6	0.7	0.7	V		N		PH	east Stone in stone

SOMERSET   see EXMOOR for Stones on Exmoor & Brendon Hill

No	Date	Name	Location	Grid	Alt	n	s	a	Az	W	B	H	Sh	d	N/D	No.	Type	Notes
24	21/01/1997	WIMBLESTONE	Mendip	ST434585	75	1		4	90	1.7	1.7	0.3	V		N	6	PH	packing stones
25	21/01/1997	YARBERRY Farm	Mendip	ST390578	5	1		4	90	2.2	1.2	0.3	V		N	9	PH	weathered and cracked
26	29/01/1997	CANNAWAYS	Banwell	ST387613	5	1		4	135	1.2	1	0.3	V		N	6	PnK	
(30	10/03/1997	ORCHARDLEIGH	Frome	ST	95	2	1	1		4	1.5	0.8	V		N	9	PnK	)large Stone inside circular bank
(42		"					2						L		N	9		) leans against larger upright stome
31	10/03/1997	HURDLESTONE	Mendip	ST676480	200	1		7		0.6	1.6	0.6	F		N	9	PH	recumbent
32	10/03/1997	PRIORS HILL	Wells	ST564479	235	1	3			0.8	0.7	0.4	V		N	6	PH	
(43	10/03/1997	nr EBBOR GORGE	Wells	ST517487	210	2	1	3		0.7	0.6	0.4	V		N		PnK	)
(		"	"				2	3		0.8	0.7	0.5	V		N		PnK	)
81	29/04/1997	nr CROSS Bridge	Axbridge	ST409548	5	1		5		1.4	0.8	0.3	V		N	9	PH	
275	09/09/1998	at WELLS MUSEUM		ST551460	45	1		1		1.7	0.7	0.6	V		D	9	PnK	moved;has 2 holes;gatepost or marker?
292	29/03/1999	BUTESTONE	Banwell	ST399592	20	1		6		0.4	1.3	0.5	V		N	6	PnK	in main street; mounting block?
293	29/03/1999	TRISCOMBE ST	Quantock	ST163359	310	1		3		0.8	0.8	0.5	V		N	1	PnK	on ridge of Quantock

STAFFORD

Ref	Date	Name	Grid	Elev	N	St	Ct	Az	H	W	D	O	Deg/DN	Type	Remarks
221	02/07/1998		SJ776376	135											error - excluded
(178	04/07/1999	DEVIL`s RING Mucklestone	SJ717378	115	2	1	8		1.8	1.5	0.6	L	25 D	1 PH	) central hole 0.3 metres diameter; moved
(		& FINGER				2	1		2	0.8	0.6	L	25 D	1 PH	)moved; 5 deep straight grooves
(1159	31/08/2006	in CHECKLEY Churchyard			3	1	1		1.6	0.5	0.3	V	D	1 M	) all 3 set in concrete; Saxon
(		"				2	1		1.3	0.5	0.3	V	D	1 M	) pillars with Celtic designs on
(		"				3	1		1.4	0.4	0.3	V	D	1 M	)2 & 3

SUFFOLK

Ref	Date	Name	Grid	Elev	N	St	Ct	Az	H	W	D	O	Deg/DN	Type	Remarks
40	21/04/1997	OAKLEY CHURCH	TM157773	40	1		1		1.5	0.3	0.3	V	D	1 PnK	dressed square; bolt hole

EAST SUSSEX

Ref	Date	Name	Grid	Elev	N	St	Ct	Az	H	W	D	O	Deg/DN	Type	Remarks
414	06/07/1999	GOLD STONE Hove Park	TQ288060	30	1		6		2.3 N	3	1.5	V	N	10 PH	moved; sarsen with embedded flints

YORKSHIRE   includes North Yorkshire Moors

Ref	Date	Name	Grid	Elev	N	St	Ct	Az	H	W	D	O	Deg/DN	Type	Remarks
38	30/03/1997	St CATHERINES Church	SE776489		1		2		1.4	0.5	0.2	V	D	1 M	moved; flat stone nearby not seen
39	10/04/1997	SPEETON Church	SE151748	120	1		1		1.4	0.3	0.2	V	D	M	medieval; see 40 & 1159 for two similar Stone
(48	09/04/1997	DEVIL`S ARROWS	SE392664	20	3	3	1		6.9	1.5	1.5	V	N	7 PH	) all 3 Stoneshave deep fissures on
(49		" Boroughbridge	SE391665			2	1		6.4	1.6	1.6	V	N	7 PH	) summits, which extend c. quarter
(		"	SE390666			1	2		5.5	2.3	1.3	V	N	7 PH	) of way down the sides
50	10/04/1997	RUDSTON MONUMENT	TA098677	30	1		1		8.2	1.8	0.7	V	D	7 PH	tallest Stone in Great Britain
(140	31/03/1998	on SIMON HOWE	SE830982	260	4	1	4	90	1.1	0.8	0.3	V	D ?	PH	Stones lie at a tangent to the curb Stone
(		North Yorks Moors				2	2		1.4	0.7	0.4	L	350 D ?	PH	) circle & cairn; complex site
(		"				3	7					F	N ?	PH	)
(		"				4	3		1.1	).8		L	70o D ?	PH	)
(141	31/03/1998	HIGH BRIDE STONES	NZ850046	275	5	1	3		0.6	0.4		L	80o N	1 PH	) alingment of 5 Stones
(		North Yorks Moors				2	1		2.2	0.4	0.3	L	15o N	1 PH	) alingment of 5 Stones
(		"				3	2		1.2	0.4	0.3	L	`5o N	1 PH	) 3 fallen? Stones near Stone 2
(		"				4	4	105	0.8	0.5	0.1	V	N	1 PH	)
(		"				5	4	30	1.3	0.8	0.2	L	30o N	1 PH	)
142	01/04/1998	BOG HOUSE Fm N Yorks	SE654933	250	1		4	90	2.3	1.2	0.6	V	N	PH	packing stones; 2 recumbent Stones near
143	01/04/1998	CAMMON St N York Moors	SE626999	400	1		3		1.5	0.7	0.4	L	15o N	PH	deep grooves on NE & SE sides
(160	31/03/1998	NEWGATE FOOT Farm	SE872924	205	5	1	6		1.3	1	0.8	L	20o N	1 PH	) complex site
(161		North Yorks Moors				2	3		1.1	0.7	0.4	V	N	1 PH	) see plan
("		" "				3	7					F		PH	)
(162		" "				4	4	135	1.8	0.7	0.3	L	10o N	1 PH	)
(163		" "				5	3		0.9	0.7	0.4	V	N	1 PH	)
164	02/04/1998	MARGERY BRADLEY	NZ675013	415	1		2		1.9	0.9	0.4	V	N 1	1 PnK	not clear if prehistoric &/or medieval marker
289	17/03/1999	SPIERS HOUSE N Y moor	SE754910	105	1		4	85	1.2	1	0.4	V	N	1 PH	
(290	18/03/1999	MURK MIRE Moor south st	SE803033	210	2	1	1		1.8	0.4	0.2	V	D	1 M	) square hole at top of each; probably
(		" " " north st				2	1		1.9	0.4	0.2	V	D	1 M	) medieval or later boundary marks
(291	19/03/1999	GREY HORSE St, NY moor	SE953009	225	2	1	4	115	1.3	1.3	0.4	V	N	1 PH	) weathered; bench & boundry mark
(		& nearby small stone				2	6		0.4			V	N	1 PH	) small outlier st; & remains of circle?
348	19/03/1999	BLUE MAN i` the MOSS	SE766992	315	1		2	90	1.8	1	0.5	V	N	1 PH	deep flutes on all sides; deep cups? on S
(349	19/03/1999	ST ST RIGG N York Moor	NZ921038	195	3	1	3		1.1	0.9	0.4	L	20o N	1 PH	) deep weathered top; remains of circle ?
(		" "				2	3		0.7	1.3	0.4	V	N	1 PH	) tumulus at 200o nearby
(		" "				3	6		1.5			L	50o N	1 PH	) has subsided more in last 5 years
350	19/03/1999	WADES STONE - SOUTH	NZ830130	195	1		2		1.8	0.8	0.4	L	10o N	8 PH	weathered top; vertical cracks; see 351
351	19/03/1999	WADES STONE - NORTH	NZ830144	180	1		2		1.5	0.7	0.6	L	10o D ?	1 PH	deep flutes on top & s & E sides.; square
1138	10/03/2005	BULL ST, nr Guisley W York	SE207435	230	1		3		1.8	0.8	0.7	V	N	1 PH	deep flutes on S, E & W; probable Cps

WARWICK

Ref	Date	Name	Grid	Elev	N	St	Ct	Az	H	W	D	O	Deg/DN	Type	Remarks
(21	15/12/1996	KING'S STONE Rollright	SP196310	200	1		6		2.3			V	N	9 PH	)impressive, weathered & unusual Stone
(22	"	KING'S STONE "											N	9 PH	)
(23	"	" " "													) circle Stones

WILTSHIRE   all the Stones in Wiltshire are sarsens

Ref	Date	Name	Grid	Elev	N	St	Ct	Az	H	W	D	O	Deg/DN	Type	Remarks
(51	16/04/1997	DOWNS BARN W Overton	SU129696	190	2	1	6		1.8	0.9	1	V	N	10 PH	) two sarsen boulders in hedge
(		" " "				2	6		1.3	1	0.8	V	N	10 PH	)
52	16/02/1997	LONG TOM at Menton Ho	SU144712	230	1		1		2.5	0.4	0.3	V	D	10 PnK	medieval obelisk?
(53	16/04/1997	MENTON GALLOPS	SU143712	220	3	1	3		1	0.4	0.4	V	D	10 PnK	) small stones which appear to
(		" "				2	6		0.9	0.9	0.9	V	N	10 PnK	) have been set up
(		" "				3	6		1	1.5	1.1	V	N	10 PnK	)
(54	21/08/1997	The 2 LONG STONES at	SU088693	175	2										) two massive sarsens; outliers to
(111	22/08/1997	BECKHAMPTON SW st				1	4	119	3.5	3	1.2	V	N	10 PH	) Avebury Circle) see 54 for photos
(114	"	" NE st				2	6		3.5	2	1.4	V	N	10 PH	) and references
(104	22/08/1997	BERWICK St JAMES	SU071392	75	2	1	4	120	1.5	0.8	0.2	V	N	10 PH	) small st in village street
(		" "				2	6		0.8	0.4	0.3	V	N	10 PH	) may have been milestone?
157	21/10/1997	FIDDLERS Fm Broad Hint`n	SU118757	175	1		6		1.9	1.6	0.8	V	N	10 PnK	not recorded; may be field stone?
159	11/01/1998	HANGING STONE Pewsey	SU099605	105	1		6		1.2	2.1	1	V	N	10 PH ?	recumbent; 2 similar sts nearby
860	18/09/2001	HEEL STONE Stonehenge	ST122422	100	1		2		4.5	2.6	2.2	L	30 N	10 PH	Outlier to Stonehenge circle
(985	21/08/2002	WEST KENNET long barrow	SU104978	180	4	1	4	90	3.5	3.5	0.4	V	N	10 PH	) the four portal stones
(		" "				2	4	90	2.7	2.2	0.6	V	N	10 PH	) these Stones re-erected by Min
(		" "				3	2	90	2.1	1.7	0.8	V	N	10 PH	) of Works 1956-8
(		" "				4	4	90	1.8	2.4	0.7	V	N	10 PH	)
(												V	N	10 PH	) six smaller stones at North end
(1097	13/09/2003	COVE STONES at Avebury	SU102700	150	2	1	4	150	4.9	2.5	0.8	V	N	10 PH	) both returned to vertical 2003
(		" "				2	4	60	4.4	4.3	1.4	V	N	10 PH	) St2 wieghs c. 100t.
1106	30/09/2003	AVEBURY West Kennet Ave	SU109603	190	1		6		2.6	2.8	1.8	V	N	10 PH	typical stone in the East Kennet avenue
															transferred to Other Stones 128
1187	08/10/2008	FYFIELD DOWN Marlborough	SU128715	240	1							F	N	10 PH	recumbent grinding and polishing Stone
1188	08/10/2008	FYFIELD DOWN Marlborough	SU127713	230	1							F	N	10 PnK	small Stone with 3 parallell lines

APPENDIX 2   **THE STANDING STONES of SCOTLAND**   from field work between 1997 & 2008

Cowal and Kilmartn shown as separate areas of Argyll. The islands of Argyll are shown as a separate area and include Arran and Bute, the Inner Hebrides, the
Cowal and Kilmartin are shown as separate areas within Argyll. The Islands of Argyll are shown (incorrectly) within a separate area of Argyll and include
Canna, Colonsay, Gigha, Islay, Jura, Mull, Skye, and Tiree.
All measurements are in metres & compass bearings are given to the nearest 5°
Leaning Stones are measured along the length from ground level at mid point to the summit. This thus represents the height of the Stone had it been
vertical, and NOT the current height of the summit above ground level.
Excluded from the analyses are Stones lying flat, medieval and later Stones, dolmens and circles but outliers and centre Stones of circles are included

SUMMARY of Scottish prehistoric sites & Standing Stones

COUNTY	total number of all sites	of all Stones	numbers of prehistoric sites & prehistoric Standing Stones					leaning Stones	number of sites with			
			sites	Stones	average height	range of height of Stones			1	2	3	>3 Stones
ABERDEEN	64	92	54	84	2	1 to	3.8	15	37	8	7	2
ANGUS	23	31	17	22	2	0.8 to	3.7	6	12	2	1	2
ARGYLL mainland	60	93	61	92	2.8	0.5 to	4.6	28	43	11	5	1
ARGYLL islands	83	109	68	90	2.2	0.5 to	8.8	29	53	10	4	1
AYRSHIRE	5	5	3	3	2.2	1 to	2.1		3			
BORDERS	11	13	11	13	1.6	1.2 to	2.4	2	9	2		
DUMFRIES	5	8	5	8	1.1	0.4 to	1.8		3	1	1	
FIFE	18	23	17	22	1.7	0.9 to	5.5	5	13	3	1	
GALLOWAY	29	51	24	45	1.6	0.5 to	3.2	7	16	3	1	4
GRAMPIAN	12	15	9	12	1.7	1.3 to	1.6	2	6	3		
HIGHLAND	60	74	50	63	1.8	0.4 to	3.6	10	39	9	2	
LOTHIANS	10	10	9	9	2	1.1 to	2.7		9			
ORKNEY	22	27	22	27	2.8	0.7 to	5.5	6	18	3	1	
PERTH	67	83	65	81	1.8	0.6 to	3.6	22	52	10	3	
SHETLAND	29	43	27	40	1.7	0.9 to	3.8	3	18	7	1	1
STIRLING	6	10	6	10	1.7	1 to	2.4	3	4		3	
TAYSIDE	8	9	8	9	2	0.9 to	2.3	7	7	1		
WESTERN ISLES	36	50	29	39	1.2	0.3 to	5.7	12	23	4	1	1
SCOTLAND total	548	746	456	670	2	0.3 to	5.7	150	366	77	31	12
prehistoric sites as a percent of all sites			88%									
prehistoric Standing Stones as a percent of all Stones					90%							
percent of prehistoric Standing Stones which are leaning								22%				
percent of prehistoric sites									75%	16%	7%	2%

ABERDEEN

number of site	date visited	name of Stone &/or site	national grid reference	altitude	total stones on each site	number of each stone	shape	compass orientation in o	height	width	thickness	Vertical Leaning Fallen	angle of lean o	Natural or Dressed stone	geology	era/age	special features of Stone or site
987	25/07/2001	RINABAICH Ballater	NO301962	260	1		4	70	1.3	0.8	0.3	V		N	2	PH	on flat area on hillside on mound
788	25/07/2001	DALLIEFOUR Ballater	NO359950	220	1		2		1.9	0.8	0.5	V		N		PH	rectangular section
795	27/07/2001	GAVAL Old Deer	NJ981517	100	1		3		1.5	0.8	0.8	V		N	2	PH	stones around base make a small mound
796	27/07/2001	CANDLE STONE Ellon	NJ921349	55	1		2		3.1	1.7	1.7	V		N		PH	packing stones & also modern stones
(797	28/07/2001	NEW CRAIG Old Meldrum	NJ745289	150	4	1			1.4			V		N		PH	) these 4 Standing Stones are the
(		" "				2			2.8			V		N		PH	) entrance Stones of a recumbent
(		" "				3			1.8			V		N		PH	) circle with stones in wood to west;
(		" "				4			2.9			V		N		PH	) measurements estimated
798	28/07/2001	GROANING ST Old Meldrum	NJ821276	130	1		3		1.7	2.2	1.7	V		N	2	PKn	provenance as prehistoric Stone not clear
799	28/07/2001	FULLERTON Inverurie	NJ784180	60	1		2		1.8	1	0.8	V		N	2	PH	stands on edge of ruined curb cairn
800	29/07/2001	PEATHILL Inverurie	NJ821191	90	1		2		2.1	0.9	0.8	V		N	2	PH	
801	29/01/2001	MUNDERNO Old Machar	NJ940131	55	1		2		1.8	1.3	0.6	V		N	2	PH	
(802	29/07/2001	LEYLODGE Stone A Kintore	NJ767132	100	1		2		1	0.6	0.6	V		N	2	PH	) may not be connected with 802B
("		" 3 Stones B "			3	1	3		1.7			V		N		PH	) excluded; 3 stones seen across standing corn
("		" "				2	7		2.8			F		N		PH	) are part of ruined recumbent circle and
("		" "				3	4		2			V		N		PH	) now appear as Standing Stones
803	29/07/2001	LANG STANE o' CRAIGEARN	NJ723149	90	1		1		3.8	1.3	0.7	L	20	N	8	PH	in garden
804	29/07/2001	MIDMAR KIRK Echt	NJ699066	220	1		1		2.7	0.5	0.5	L	20	N		PH	on small mound; recumbent circle nearby
(805	29/07/2001	SPRINGHILL A Kirton of Skene	NJ803064	110	2	1	2		2.2	1.5	0.7	V		N	2	PH	) the 2 Stones in 805 now have a wall behind
(		" B				2	2		1.8	1	0.8	V		N	2	PH	) them; with Stone 806 these 3 Stones form
(806	29/07/2001	" East Stone	"	110	1		2		2	0.9	0.8	V		N	2	PH	) close group
807	29/07/2001	HILTON FARM Muchalls	NO906953	80	1		4	110	1.9	1.4	0.5	V		N	8	PH	) quartz veins; beside a ruined curb cairn
808	29/07/2001	LANG STANE Stonehaven	NO823908	140	1		1		2.6	0.9	0.6	V		N	2	PH	many large quartz crystals
809	30/07/2001	MILLPLOUGH WEST stone	NO817755	90	1		3		1.4	1.3	0.7	V		N	8	PH	packing stones
810	30/07/2001	MILLPLOUGH EAST stone	NO820755	100	1		4	90	2	3	0.8	L	10	N	6	PH	
983	22/07/2002	LANGSTANE in Aberdeen city	NJ983059	30	1		1		1.2	0.6	0.3	V		N	2	PH	set in wall in Langstane Place
990	03/09/2002	LOCH KINORD cross nr Aboyne	NO430999	180	1		4	80	1.2	0.6	0.2	V		N	2	PH	prehistoric Stone with Celtic Christian cross
991	03/09/2002	MIGVIE churchyard	NJ436068	250	1		2		1.8	0.8	0.4	V		N	2	PH	prehistoric Stone with Celtic Christian cross
(998	04/09/2002	RYNIE North end of village	NJ503278	170	2	1	2		1.8	0.7	0.4	V		N		PH	) packing stones
(		"				2	2		1.9	0.8	0.8	V		N		PH	) packing stones
999	04/09/2002	Nether WHEELDMONT Rhynie	NJ480266	230	1		4	60	2.9	1.3	0.6	V		N		PH	
1004	01/10/2002	MURRAY STONE nr Inverbervie	NO820779	120	1		3		1.6	1.1	0.7	V		N	2	PH	with quartz veins
1006	02/10/2002	COURT STONE nr Drumlithie	NO775795	110	1		2		2.1	1.4	0.7	L	10	N	2	PH	on mound with field stones; painted white
1007	02/10/2002	HILTON COURT Aberdeen city	NJ922083	40	1		2	100	2.9	1.1	1.1	V		N	2	PH	moved; crack on east side
(1008	02/10/2002	NETHER CORSKIE Dunecht	NJ749096	110	2	1	2	100	2.7	1.5	1	V		N	2	PH	) many field stones; ruined
(		" "				2	4		2.1	1.7	0.7	V		N	2	PH	) recumbent circle?
(1009a	2-10-02	WEST MAINS South Kenmay	NJ718125	130	2	1	2		1.8	0.7	0.7	V		N	2	PH	)
(1009b	2-10-02	" "				2	4	70	2.1	1.8	0.5	V		N	2	PH	)
1010	03/10/2002	GOWK STONE Oyne	NJ676258	145	1		2		2.1	1	0.9	V		N		PH	packing stones
(1012	03/10/2002	UPPER BUCHANSTONE Oyne	NJ660268	200	3	1	1		2.7	0.7	0.5	L	10	N	2	PH	) ruined recumbent circle with
(		" "				2	2		1.8	0.8	0.6	L	10	N	2	PH	) curb cairn & 2 other extant .
(		" "				5	4	160	1.6	2.6	0.4	L	15	N	2	PH	) small standing stones; cup marks on Stone 5
1013	03/10/2002	PICARDY pictish STONE, Insch	NJ610303	180	1		2		2	1	0.7	V		N		M	packing stones; in metal surround
1014	03/10/2002	JOHNSTON nr Auchleven	NJ579252	225	1		1		2	0.8	0.5	V		N		PH	packing stones; 6? probable cup marks
(1015a	3-10-02	ARDLAIR WEST St Kenethmont	NJ555279	240	2	1	4	80	1.2	1	0.3	V		N	2	PH	) on small mound; see 105B
(1015b	3-10-02	" EAST St "	NJ555279	240		2	6	160	1.1	1.2	0.5	V		N	2	PH	)

ID	Date	Site	Grid	Brg	a	b	n	dist	H	W	D	Q	num	N/D	Class	Notes
1016	03/10/2002	JELDAH (pvt house)Kenethmont	NJ533304	230	1		2		1.3	0.9	0.9	V		N	2 PH	
(1017	03/10/2002	UPPER THIRD,Kirkton Auchter`	NJ677394	150	2	1	3		2	1.6	1.2	V		N	2 PH	) field stones around bases &
(	"	"				2	6		1.2	2		1	V		N	2 PH	) between
(1018	04/01/2002	ST. BRENDAN`S Sts nrPortsoy	NJ608610	110	2	1	4	130	1.8	1.6	0.6	L	10	N	2 PH	) uninteresting; fieild stones;
(	"	"				2	2	110	1.9	1.7	0.8	L	10	N	2 PH	) ruined recumbent circle?
1023	05/10/2002	NETHER MAINS nr Blackburn	NJ827107	60	1		2		1.5	0.6	0.4	V		N	2 PNK	maybe rubbing post
1031	09/04/2003	HOWE nr Stuartfield	NJ982418	140	1		1		2			V		N	PH	not seen close - electric fence
....	10/04/2003	INVERURIE Henge - OUTLIER	NJ799196	60	1		3		1.7	1.3	0.9	V		N	2 PH	) outlier on small mound c. 100 m. from henge
(1033	10/04/2003	" " central St 1	NJ799196	60	3	1	4	80	1.4	1.1	0.4	V		N	2 PH	) ceremonial circle & henge
(	"	" " central St 2	"	60		2	3		1.3	1.1	1.1	V		N	8 PH	)
(	"	" " " St 3	"	60		3	4	130	1.4	1.6	0.4	V		N	2 PH	) packing stones on south side
1034	10/04/2003	CONGLASS EAST Inverurie	NJ753229	70	1		3		1.3	0.6	0.6	V		N	2 PNK	prehistoric or rubbing post?
1035	10/04/2003	CONGLASS WEST Inverurie	NJ745232	85	1		3		1.4	1.4	0.8	V		N	2 PNK	prehistoric or rubbing post?
1036	10/04/2003	MAIDEN Stone Chapel Garioch	NJ703248	150	1		1	25	3.1	0.9	0.3	V		D	2 M	packing stones; carved on east & west
(1037	10/04/2003	NEWTON HOUSE Old Rayne	NJ662297	110	2	1	1		2	0.8	0.8	V		D	2 PNK	) moved; ogham & other script
(	"	"				2	1		2.1	0.7	0.4	V		D	2 PNK	) packing stones on south side
(1039	11/04/2003	MONYMUSK	NJ684157	110	3	1	5		1.5	1	0.7	L	15	N	2 PH	) all stand on small mound
(	"					2	2		1.3	0.7	0.5	V		N	2 PH	) under trees
(	"					3	5		1.5	1	0.7	V		N	2 PH	)
1040	11/04/2003	CRAW STANE, Rynie	NJ497264	210	1		2		1.8	0.8	0.4	V		N	2 PH	now in concrete; Pictish symbols on south
(1041	11/04/2003	TEMPLAND, Rynie	NJ482270	230	2	1	2	60	1.8	1.5	0.7	V		N	2 PH	) remains of circle? (OS map)
(	"					2	5		1.2	1.3	0.4	V		N	2 PH	) packing stones
1108	19/04/2004	GOWK STONE Hatton of Findray	NJ835152	75	1		2		3.2	1.3	1.3	V		N	2 PH	phallic symbol?
1109	19/04/2004	nr LAIRSHILL nr Newmachar	NJ871183	95	1		1		1.8	0.5	0.5	V		N	2 PH	on large mound of field stones
1110	19/04/2004	CHAPEL of ELRICK, Newmachar	NJ878182	75	1		1		1.3	0.5	0.5	V		N	PnK	moved; rubbing post
1111	19/04/2004	TOFTHILLS, Kintore	NJ802146	70	1		3		1	0.9	0.7	V		N	PH	
1112	19/04/2004	MIANS of BALQUAIN nr Inverurie	NJ735241	100	1		1		3.3	1.4	0.8	V		N	4 PH	outlier to reccumbent circle
1113	20/04/2004	AUCHRONIE Hill Kirton of Skene	NJ809091	190	1		4	160	1.5	0.9	0.3	V		N	2 PH	fell & re-erected;
(1114	20/04/2004	NEW WESTER ECHT Dunecht	NJ739084	165	3	1	4	100	2.5	1.5	0.4	V		N	2 PH	) has fallen stone at base
(	"	" " "				2	3		2.2	1.1	0.8	L	40	N	2 PH	) glacial boulder
(	"	" " "				3	2		3.5	1.4	1.2	V		N	2 PH	) packing stones; fallen stone at base
1115	20/04/2004	WOODEND nr Kemnay	NJ711134	70	1				3.3	1.3	1.1	V		N	PH	packing stones; large ruined circle
1116	20/04/2004	TOMBEG nr Monymusk	NJ679143	120	1		4	100	1.4	0.9	0.3	V		N	2 PH	packing stones
1117	20/04/2004	above PETMATHEN Oyne	NJ664266	160	1		2		3.3	1.4	1.2	V		N	PH	massive square Stone
1118	20/04/2004	NETHER COULIE nr Kenmay	NJ710157	85	1		7		2	1.5	0.3	F		N	PH	packing stones; fell 1985, 22% in ground
(1119	21/01/1900	WHITEBROW nr Insch	NJ601273	215	3	1	4	130	2.8	1.3	0.4	L	10	N	PH	) ruined recumbent circle
(	"					2	4	130	2.3	3.9	0.4	L	10	N	PH	) recumbent Stone
(	"					3	2		2.6	1.4	0.5	L	10	N	PH	)
1120	21/04/2004	LUATH`S St Whitehouse Alford	NJ641149	355	1	1	1		2.9	0.7	0.4	V		N	2 PH	packing stones; grooves top to ground; huge Stone
(1121	22/04/2004	WEST RAEDYKES,Stonehaven	NO831907	190	3	1	2		1.3	0.5	0.5	V		N	PH	) portal sts to ruined ring cairn
(						2	2		1.5	1	0.4	V		N	PH	) 3 sts standing, other curb sts
(						3	4	120	1.1	1.5	0.4	V		N	PH	) fallen around edge
(1134	29/09/2004	CRAIGHEAD circle Portlethen	NO911978	110	4	1	2		1.6	0.6	0.3	V		N	2 PnK	) bore hole for blasting on east
(		"				2	3		1.2	0.4	0.3	V		N	2 PnK	) all 4 have iron hitching rings
(		"				3	2		2.1	1	0.4	V		N	2 PnK	) at base facing into the circle
(		"				4	2		1.6	1	0.4	V		N	2 Pnk	) with mortar in surrounding wall
1174	14/10/2006	DARDANUS STONE nr Aboyne	NO596940	230	1		4	160	1.1	0.4	0.2	L	10	N	2 PH	moved; broken with iron band repairs

ANGUS

ID	Date	Site	Grid	Brg	a	b	n	dist	H	W	D	Q	num	N/D	Class	Notes
216	21/06/1998	SHANZIE on hill above town	NO280507	140	1		4	60	1.4	1.4	0.3	L	10	N	PH	inacessible due to electric fence
(193	21-66-98	DRYLOCH STONES - East	NO301499	80	2	1	5		1.4	1.3	0.8	V		N	PnK	) this st clearly set upright; both look
(	"	" " - West				2	5		1.6	1.9	1.3	V		N	PnK	) like glacial boulders; uninteresting
194	21/06/1998	AIRLIE, W Of Kerrimuir	NO321502	85	1		2		2.2	1.1	0.4	L	10	D	PnK	Mnd; 3m D; square dressed
195	21/06/1998	ALYTH GOLF COURSE	NO265498	85	1		3		2.1	2.2	1	V		N	4 PH	on mound;quartz veins; small fissures
196	21/06/1998	Nth LITTLETON FARM	NO203459	85	1		3		1.5	0.8	0.8	V		N	2 PH	Mnd & PSts; quartz veins; fissures
197	22/06/1998	MURTHLY CASTLE	NO070369	110	1		2		2.3	1.9	1.3	V		N	1 PH	
(203	23/06/1998	COURTHILL Stone Blairgowrie	NO185483	205	1		3		2.8	2	1.8	V		N	PH	) deep cup marks;field stones at base
(203b	23/06/1998	COURTHILL FOUR POSTER	NO184481	190	4		7					F		N	PH	) ruined Four Poster 200 metres south of 203
(204	22/06/1998	PARKNEUK,Mains of Creuchies	NO196515	235	4	1	3		1.3			V		N	PH	) Four Poster; 3 standing & 1 fallen Stones
(		"				2	3		1.2			V		N	PH	) ruined circle of 7 fallen Stones
(		"				3	7					F		N	PH	) 110 meters South
(		"				4	5		1.3			V		N	PH	)
205	22/06/1998	STANDING ST. Cottage	NO243545	185	1		2		2.3	1.3	0.8	V		N	PH	Stone in garden
(206	23/06/1998	PITMUDIE	NO274564	255	3	1	1		3.3	0.8	0.8	V		D	PH	) graffiti; being covered by undergrowth
(		"				2	7					F			PH	) 2 large recumbent Stones 3 metres NE
(		"				3	7					F			PH	) may not have been erected
(757	25/07/2001	KNOWHEAD of AULDALLAN	NO299852	250	2	1	4	20	2.2	1.3	0.4	V		N	PH	)
(		" "				2	7		2.1	1	0.3	F				) 2.I m on ground
834	30/07/2001	CADDAM Kerriemuir	NO385563	165	1		3		1.5	1.3	0.8	L	25	N	PH	
(811	29/07/2001	811A- BLACKGATE WEST St	NO485529	90	2	1	3		3	2	1.1	V		N	6 PH	) S; these 2 Stones stand in the garden
(		811B- " EAST St				2	2		2.3	1.2	0.6	V		N	1 PH	) S
812	29/07/2001	WESTERTON Forfar	NO536521	90	1		4	160	1.4	1.4	0.5	L	20	N	1 PH	
773	23/11/2001	VAYNE Careston	NO497601	105	1		3		0.8	0.6	0.5	V		N	2 PH	field sts at base; quartz veins
984	22/07/2002	ARBIRLOT, in manse garden	N0602402	45	1		4	170	1.6	0.8	0.3	V		N	1 M	in concrete
989	02/09/2002	St. ORLAND`S STONE Forfar	NO401500	60	1		4	170	2.3	0.8	0.2	V		D	1 M	broken & repaired; in concrete with modern cobbles
1005	01/10/2002	Stone of MORPHIE Montrose	NO717627	40	1		1		3.7	1	0.7	V		N	1 PH	cup marks; grooves - weathering?; in farmyard
(1028	09/04/2003	ABERLEMNO 1 Forfar	NO522559	130	4	1	1	190	3.1	1	0.3	L	10	N	1 PH	) southwest Stone; Pictish symbols
(1029a	09/04/2003	ABERLEMNO 2 Forfar	NO522559	130		2	2	30	1.7	0.7	0.3	V		D	1 PH	) central Stone; " "
(1029b	09/04/2003	ABERLEMNO 3 "	NO522559	130		3	4	80	2	0.9	0.2	L	20	N	1 PH	) northeast Stone; " "
(		" 4 "	NO522557	130		4									1 M	) in churchyard; early Cross
1030	09/04/2003	KILLIEVAR ST near Brechin	NO561609	110	1		3		1.7	0.7	0.5	L	40	N	8 PH	on mound; field stones
1142	24/06/1998	KIRKTON of KINGOLDRUM	NO317541	240	1				1.3	1	0.8	V		N	2 PH	no drawing

ARGYLL MAINLAND with Cowal and Kilmartin areas shown seperately   but are included in the analysis of the Argyll Mainland

The Islands of Arran, Bute, Colonsay, Gigha, Islay, Jura & Mull are shown & analysed below as a sepatate area as the `Argyll Islands'

ID	Date	Site	Grid	Brg	a	b	n	dist	H	W	D	Q	num	N/D	Class	Notes
(17	27/09/1996	near CARSE HOUSE	NR743616	<5	2	1	1		3.2	0.6	0.4	V		N -	8 PH	) packing stones; appears to stand
(		" "				2	4	45	2.3	1.1	0.4	V		N	8 PH	) on slight mound c. 7 metres diameter
18	29/09/1996	LOCH HEAD	NR777780	10	1		4	45	2	1.1	0.4	V		N	PH	hidden in rhododendron under growth
129	19/09/1997	BENDERLOCH	NM830883	5	1		2		2.2	1.2	0.6	V		N	3 PH	much weathered shale material
180	12/04/1998	aboveKINTRAW HOUSE	NM831050	45	1		1		3.9	1	0.5	V		N	2 PH	in concrete; cairns nearby
208	15/04/1998	UPPER FERNOCK st 1	NR728861	50	1		4	40	2.4	0.4	0.2	L	25	D ?	PH	another Stone350 metres northeast; see 185

277	23/09/1998	GLENLUSSA LODGE		NR761254	5	1		4	120	2.2	1.1	0.4 V	N	PH	in garden wall
299	18/09/1998	AVINAGILLAN Tarbert		NR839674	5	1		4	0	1.7	1.1	0.2 V	N	PH	on summit of mound of stones 6 metres diameter
(182	14/04/1998	BARBRECK HOUSE		NM832064	15	2 1		4	10	2.4	1.4	0.3 V	N	PH	) small supporting stone at northeast corner
(		"				2		4	0	1.4	1.4	0.2 V	N	PH	)
(363	08/04/1999	BARBRECK HOUSE		NM832064	15	1		4	0	2.5	1.8	0.4 L	10 N	3 PH	) 4 small satellite stones
184	15/04/1998	BARSLOISNOCH		NR821959	25	1		1		2.8	1	0.5 V	N	PH	
185	15/04/1998	UPPER FERNOCH St 2		NR729864	55	1		1		3.3	0.6	0.5 V	N	PH	see 208 350 m to south east
186	14/04/1998	TURNALT FARM		NM841076	25	1		4	10	2.7	0.9	0.3 V	N	PH	packing stones
187	15/04/1998	LECKUARY		NR876955	55	1		1		3.4	0.9	0.4 V	N	PH	on mound; many stones around base
303	22/09/1998	LOCH CIARN on North side		NR548781	130	1		1		2	0.7	0.4 V	N	4 PH	inscribed boundry mark; quartz veins
(304	22/09/1998	BALLOCHORY		NR731524	35	3 1		1		3.2	0.6	0.6 V	N	PH	) cist c. 100m to SW
(		"				2		4	140	2.6	1.5	0.3 L	10 N	PH	) packing stones between Stones 2 & 3
(		"				3		4	140	1.9	1	0.3 V	N	PH	) which may be field stones
305	22/09/1998	BEACHARRS		NR692433	85	1		1		4.6	1.3	0.8 L	10 N	PH	packing stones; on cairn; quartz veins
306	22/09/1998	SOUTH MUASDALE		NR679392	75	1		2		2.9	0.9	0.5 V	N	PH	wall now built around it
307	23/09/1998	BARLEA FARM,		NR661371	40	1		4	180	1.9	1.2	0.3 L	20 N	PH	packing stones
308	23/09/1998	CRAIGS, Campbelltown		NR690236	25	1		4	130	2.3	1.6	0.3 V	N	PH	now in wall; covered in fencing wire!
309	23/09/1998	GLENCRAIGS FARM		NR693235	35	1		4	325	2	1.1	0.4 V	N	PH	packing stones
(310	23/09/1998	MACHRIHANISH LINKS		NR657245	10	2 1		3		2	1.3	0.6 L	N	PH	) in machair & difficult to find; there are
(						2		3		1.4	0.7	0.5 V	N	PH	) other rock outcrops on these links
(311	23/09/1998	SKEROBLINGARRY		NR271259	140	2 1		4	65	1.6	0.9	0.3 V	N	PH	) surrounding low bank & pebbles
(						7							F	PH	) recumbent Stone 2 metres at 90°
312	22/09/1998	CAMPBELLTOWN		NR724212	45	1		4	100	3.2	1.4	0.4 L	15 N	PH	
313	23/09/1998	HIGH PARK Campbellt'n		NR694257	135	1		2	60	3.1	1.3	0.7 V	N	PH	packing stones; massive Stone
(314	23/09/1998	KILKIVAN FARM		NR653193	110	2 1		3		1.6	1	0.5 V	N	PnK	) packing stones; stands on raised area
(		"				2		3		0.9	0.9	0.9 V	N	PnK	) with cairn 20 metres to East
315	23/09/1998	DUNAVERTY Golf Links		NR698079	20	1		4	0	2.6	2	0.3 V	N	6 PH	many large quartz crystals
355	05/04/1999	INVERARY CASTLE		NN094091	15	1		4	40	2.6	1.4	0.8 L	10 N	PH	
356	06/04/1999	CREGANTERVE N. of Kilmartin		NM857012	40	1		4	40	1.8	1.1	0.4 V	N	PH	1 large uneven furrow
357	06/04/1999	CREAG-an-TAIRBH Beg		NM860016	50	1		4	80	1.8	1.3	0.4 L	10 N	3 PH	packing stones; broke 1879 piece on ground
358	06/04/1999	near FORD village		NM868033	55	1		1		2.8	0.7	0.7 V	D ?	PH	packing stones; stone cairn 20 metres 140o
(359	06/04/1999	on BEALCH MOR		NM840040	220	3 1		1		2.5	0.7	0.6 L	15 N	PH	) also called Salachary; these Stones are
(		" "				2		1		2.5	0.5	0.5 L	55 N	PH	) difficult to find in broken ground
(		" "				7							F	N	PH	) this Stone of 2.5 metres had 30% in ground
360	07/04/1999	CRETSHENGAN		NR707669	20	1		1		1.5	0.5	0.3 L	30 N	3 PH	on rock eminence overlooking sea
361	07/04/1999	ACHADH		NR758601	5	1		4	140	2.1	1.2	0.2 L	20 N	PH	very thin slab
362	07/04/1999	KILMORY CASTLE		NR868865	20	1		4	130	2.3	1	0.2 V	N	PH	very thin with sharp edges
363	09/04/1999	BARBRECK HOUSE		see 182											
364	09/04/1999	STRONTOILER		NM908290	30	1		1		3.8	1.1	1.3 V	N	PH	on mound with small curb cairn at base
(367	09/04/1999	GLENMACHARIE		NM295285	'55	2 1		3		1	0.6	0.6 L	20 N	PnK	) not marked on map; 3 small stones to SW &
(		"				2		3		1.4	0.5	0.5 V	N	PnK	) cairn; all appear to be prehistoric
532	24/04/2000	TORRAN, Ford		NM879059	60	1		1		3.3	1.4	0.6 V	N	PH	large flat stone at base
533	24/04/2000	DUACHY Kilninver south Stone 1		NM205801	55	2 1		1		2.8	0.6	0.6 V	N	2 PH	) square marks on south side of Stone 1
(		" fallen Stone				2		7					F		) 2.5 metres long, fallen between Stones 1 & 2
(		" north Stone 2				1		1		23	0.8	0.7 V	N	2 PH	)
534	24/04/2000	SCALLASTLE Craignure		NM680382	5	1		3		1.3	0.9	0.5 V	N	PH	remains of burial chamber
555	28/04/2000	BRANAULT Ardnamurchan		NM527695	40	1		1		2.1	0.8	0.7 V	N	PH	stands in pool of water
556	29/04/2000	ACHARADUROR		NM986545	5	1		1		3.6	1	0.6 V	N	PH	
(846	06/09/2001	ESCART west stones Tarbert		NR846668	40	5 1		4	40	1	0.8	0.3 V	N	8 PH	) row of 5 Stones in yard
(		"				2		2		2	0.9	0.7 L	15 N	8 PH	) close to farmhouse
(		"				3		1		2.4	0.7	0.4 L	10 N	8 PH	)
(845	06/09/2001	"				4		4	50	3.3	1.3	0.4 V	N	8 PH	)
(		"				5		4	90	2.9	1.1	0.4 V	N	8 PH	)

COWAL peninsula

766	07/09/2001	FEARNOCH Kilfinan		NR926793	10	1		4	150	2.6	1.5	0.3 V	N	PH	
767	08/09/2001	ARDACHERANBERG		NS003861	20	1		4	150	1.6	0.9	0.3 L	20 N	PH	at risk on edge of eroding river bank
768	08/09/2001	AUCHNAGARRON Glenduarel		NS006822	25	1		3		1.2	1.1	0.7 L	10 N	8 PH	packing stones
847	07/09/2001	PORT LEATHEN		NR934678	30	1		4	140	1.8	0.9	0.3 V	N	PH	
(848	07/09/2001	KAMES Post Office		NR972714	40	2 1		1		2.3	0.6	0.6 V	N	8 PH	) both stand on bank 1.5m high, and
(		"				2		4	100	3.5	1.5	0.3 V	N	8 PH	) the heights are that from ground level
(849	07/09/2001	INVERYNE FARM		NR915750	10	3 1		4	55	0.8	0.7	0.3 V	N	8 PH	)
(		" "				2		4	60	0.8	1.1	0.2 V	N	8 PH	)
(		" "				3		3		0.9	0.8	0.4 V	N	8 PH	)
(850	08/09/2001	BALLIEMORE		NS056845	10	2 1		4	20	2.3	1.5	0.2 V	N	8 PH	) packing stones around both
(		"				2		1		1.4	0.6	0.6 V	N	8 PH	)

KILMARTIN area - effectively one large site   in Kilmartin Glen

(179	12/04/1998	BALLYMEANOCH STs		NR834964	25	6 1		1		3.3		L	5 N	PH	) Thom group B
(		& ALINGNMENT				2		4	0	2.8		L	15 N	PH	) " " B
(						3		4	0	4		V	N	PH	) " " A
(		& subsidiary Sts & curb cairn				4		4	0	3.3		V	N	PH	) cup mark " " A
(						5		4	0	2.8		V	N	PH	) " " A
(		Sts numbers by OS notation				6		4	0	2.6		V	N	PH	) " " A
(						7							F	PH	) 2 Stones flat & embedded in the ground
183	14/04/1998	TORBHLAREN		NR864945	15	1		1		2.1	1.3	0.2 V	N	PH	packing stones; 2 cupmarks
181	14/04/1998	STANE ALANE, Achnabreck		NR856899	25	1		4	310	2.3	1.3	0.2 V	N	PH	on small mound
184	15/04/1998	BARSLOISNOCH, Kilmartin		NR821959	25	1		1		2.8	1	0.5 V	N	PH	
187	15/04/1998	LECKUARY		NR876955	30	1		1	340	3.3	0.9	0.4 V	N	PH	packing stones
(189	17/04/1998	MOINE MHOR		NR808941	5	3 1		1		0.7		V	N	PH	) in peat bog; possibly substantial
(		also Crinan Moss				2		1		0.8		V	N	PH	) height under the peat; 4 sts stated
(		" "				3		3		0.5		V	N	PH	) to be here, only 3 found
210	17/04/1998	DUNADD , Kilmartin		NR838936	5	1		1		1.2	0.7	0.3 V	N	3 PH	large prostrate stone 250 metres to south
356	06/04/1999	CREGANTERVE		NM857012	50	1		4	40	1.8	1.1	0.4 V	N	PH	stone cairn 100 metres
(526	22/04/2000	DUNAMUCK FARM SOUTH		NR848925	15	2 1		4		3.7	1.5	0.6 L	8 PH	) packing stones; see 823	
(						2		4		2.7	1.3	2 L	8 PH	) packing stones	
(	23/04/2000	TEMPLE WOOD Setting		NR828976	20	5									) see Templewood outlier at 531
(527		(2 SOUTH STONES						1		2.5	0.8	0.4 L	15 N	PH	) packing stones
(		(					2		1		2.7	0.8	0.5 L	15 N	PH	) packing stones & cupmarks
(528		(CENTRAL STONE					3		4	140	2.8	1.3	0.3 V	N	PH	on mound; packing stones; cup marks
(529		(2 WEST STONES					4		4	160	2.5	1.3	0.4 V	N	PH	) packing stones; through crack; these 2
(		(					5		1		2.8	1	0.6 V	N	PH	) Stones on a low mound
(530	23/04/2000	CARNASSERIE CASTLE		NR835009	110	2 1		4	180	2.6	1.3	0.4 L	20 N	PH	) packing stones; cairn 100 metres southeast
)		" "				2		4	180	2.3	1.6	0.6 V	20 N	PH	)
531	24/04/2000	TEMPLEWOOD outlier		NR828978	20	1		2		1.5	0.6	0.3 L	30 N	8 PH	on small mound

(823	12/08/2001 DUNAMUCK NORTH Stones	NR847929	5	3 1		4 170 2.5 1.4 0.3 L	10 N		PH	) parallel lines on SE corner
(	" "			2		4 170 2.9 1.4 0.4 L	20 N		PH	)
(	" "				7	3.5 0.8 0.4 F			PH	) this large Stone should be re-erected

ARGYLL ISLANDS shown collectively as a separate area;   each Island is however listed separately

ARRAN

831	05/09/2001 MAYISH	Brodick	NS017355	80	1		1	3.2 1.2 0.4 L	10 N	1 PH	large grooves
(832	05/09/2001 HOME FARM East	Stabane	NS006375	5	1		1 200 2.3 0.6 0.4 L	10 N	1 PH	) weathering furrows
(833	05/09/2001 HOME FARM West	Stabane	NS005375							1 PH	) revisited 19-7-02 see 976
(976	19/07/2002 " " "			5	2 1		1	2.5 0.7 0.4 V	N	1 PH	) packing stones & also field stones at base
(	" " "				2		1	3.4 0.7 0.5 V	N	1 PH	) fissures on all 4 sides
835	05/09/2001 STABANE	Brodick	NS010367	5	1		2	2.7 1.6 0.7 V	N	1 PH	weathering furrow
836	05/09/2001 near LOG a BHEITH	Brodick	NS019335	115	1		3	1.3 1.1 0.6 V	N	1 PH	fallen stone & circle nearby
837	05/09/2001 KILBRIDE	Lamlash	SO039330	170	1		4 190 1.5 1.5 0.7 L	10 N	1 PH	packing stones; on small mound
(838	05/09/2001 LARYBEG POINT		NS053234	15	2 1		3	0.9 0.5 0.5 L	10 N	1 PH	) both stand on natural mound
(	" "				2		4 90 1 0.8 0.3 V	N	1 PH	) with severe weathering & furrow
839	05/09/2001 KILDONAN		NS034208	20	1		4 210 1 1.1 0.2 V	N	1 PH	
844	06/09/2001 AUCHENCOR near Machrie		NR890364	15	1		4 135 4.7 1.8 0.3 V	N	2 PH	packing stones & mound; fallen Stone to east
978	19/07/2002 near MACHRIE WATERFOOT		NR894337	5	1		2	1.4 0.8 0.5 V	N	1 PH	deep fissures on north, east & west sides
1053	27-403 MONYQUILL, nr Machrie		NR941353	75	1		4 120 2.5 1.4 0.4 V	N	2 PH	packing stones; chambered cairn nearby

THE STANDING STONES ON MACHRIE MOOR   - a complex area of St Sts & circles

840	06/09/2001 1 - LARGE WEST STONE	NR910325	30	1		4 120 4 1.4 0.5 V	N	1 PH	grooves; cobbled area & circle
(841	06/09/2001 2 - EAST STONES	NR911324	30	3 1		4 120 3.8 1.4 0.3 V	N	1 PH	) form part of ruined circle
(	" "			2		4 220 3.5 1.3 0.6 V	N	1 PH	)
(	" "			3		1 190 4.6 1.3 0.6 V	N	1 PH	) deep grooves on all sides of this Stone
842	06/09/2001 3 - WEST STONE	NR907326	40	1		2	1.4 0.7 0.4 V	N	1 PH	Grooves; strata lie east/west
843	06/09/2001 4 - SOUTH STONE	NR906324	30	1		4 210 1.5 1.1 0.4 V	N	1 PH	grooves; stones at base; cist nearby

BUTE

(851	08/09/2001 LARGIZEAN	NS081554	10	3 1		2	1.4 1 0.8 V	N	8 PH	
(	"			2		2	1.6 1.1 0.8 V	N	8 PH	)
(	"			3		2	1.8 1.7 1 V	N	8 PH	)
(852	08/09/2001 St NINIAN`S POINT	NS046618	0	2 1		4 130 1.1 0.8 0.2 L	20 N	1 PH	) on mound with cobbled area
(	"			2		4 80 0.9 0.5 0.2 L	10 N	1 PH	)
769	08/09/2001 ACHOLTER, Port Bannantyne	NS064669	30	1		2	1.4 0.6 0.3 L	30 N	2 PH	
853	09/09/2001 St COLMAC, Port Bannantyne	NS059671	30	1		4 140 1.4 1.1 0.4 L	10 N	2 PH	
1051	26/04/2003 on hill west of ROTHSAY	NS074636	120	1		4 150 2.4 1.1 0.4 V	N	8 PH	

CANNA

821	11/08/2001 CANNA	NG273044	30	1		1	2 0.3 0.3 V	D	M	damaged Christian cross

COLL

827	14/08/2001 BREACHACHA	Coll	NM151532	10	1		3	1.3 1 0.8 L	20 N	2 PH	a fallen stone lies o.4 metres west
828	14/08/2001 TOTRONALD	Coll	NM160560	30	2 1		4 100 1.4 1.3 0.3 V	N	2 PH	
	"				2		4 100 1.5 1.3 0.4 V	N	2 PH	
829	14/08/2001 COLL WAR MEMORIAL	Coll	NM223581	5	1		1	1.4 0.7 0.4 V	N	2 PH	historic Stone moved for war memorial

COLONSY

(14	25/09/1996 Lower KILLCHATTAN	NR365949	20	2 1		1	3.3 0.6 0.3 L	10 D	2 PH	) tall elegant Sts, with pebble mounds
(	" "			2		1	2.5 0.4 0.4 L	50 D	2 PH	) around the bases
156	17/09/1997 BALNAHARD	NR427995	45	1		2	1.4 0.6 0.4 V	N	2 PH	rough walk

GIGHA   site

209	16/04/1998 OGHAM STONE in south	NR642482	40	1		1	1.6 0.3 0.3 V	D	M	c. 6th. Century; with Ogham script
188	16/04/1998 THE HANGING STONE; north	NR655523	10	1		1	2.3 0.8 0.4 L	20 N	PH	large fissure on West side

ISLAY

5	23/09/1997 FINLAGGAN ST Islay	NR392685	60	1		5	2.2 1.3 1.6 V	D -	8 PH	smooth- like glacial boulder?
(6	23/09/1997 KNOCKLEAROCH Ballygrant	NR399648	115	2 1		6	1.5 0.9 0.5 L	50 N-r	9 PH	) both these Stones show substantial
(	23/09/1997 "			2		3	1.6 1.2 0.7 L	30 N-r	9 PH	) weathering
7	19/09/1997 MULLOCH DUBH Islay	NR403641	150	1		3	1.2 0.9 0.6 L	10 N-r	8 PH	squat square lump on open hill
8	23/09/1997 KNOCKDON Bridgend	NR336643	30	1		2	1.6 0.9 0.6 V	N	PH	
9	23/09/1997 BURCHILL MORE St.	NR311645	30	1		3	1.5 0.6 0.2 V	N	PnK	not marked on OS map
10	)24-09-96 CULTROON Circle	NR187560	80	2 1		2	1.3	V	N	PH	cobble pavement surrounds all stones
11	) " "			2		3	2 1.7 1 V	N	PH	10 other sts never erected
12	24/09/1996 KILCHOMAN CROSS	NR214632	45	1		4	1 0.5 0.2 L	25 D -	8 M	c. 7th. Century Christian Cross; black stone
(13	24/09/1996 BALLINABY Long Stone	NR220672	35	1		4 140 5.4 0.9 0.4 V	D -	8 PH	) another stone 250 metres at 20o; see 153
(&126	15/09/1997 " "			1						) this is the most elegant of all the GB Stones
15	26/09/1996 east of PORT ELLEN	NR372457	30	1		1	4 0.9 0.6 V	D	8 PH	mound or tumulus at base
16	29/09/1996 KILDALTON CROSS	NR458509	20	1			2.3	V	D	13 PH	Christian Cross 7th C; well known
127	15/09/1997 KILBRIDE Farm, Pt Ellen	NR383466	30	1		1	2.9 0.9 0.3 V	D ?	8 PH	
128	17/09/1997 IGEANTSUIDHE Farm	NR294634	10	1		4 135 2.5 1.5 0.6 V	D ?	8 PH	packing stones
153	15/09/1997 BALLINABY Short St	NR221674	40	1		3	1.8 1.1 0.7 V	D	8 PH	veins of quartz; see 13 at 250 metres
154	15/09/1997 TIGH an ARBHAIR	NR383410	45	1		4 135 1.9 1.1 0.4 L	40 N	8 PH	hut circle/ lies 3 meters S
(300	18/09/1998 DRUIM MOR Lagavulin	NR390461	20	2 1		4	2.6 0.8 0.2 L	20 N	PH	) packing stones; with 3 possible fallen Stones
(	" "			2		4	2.4 1.2 0.3 V	N	PH	) packing stones; 0s map shows 3 Stones
301	19/09/1998 GARTAHCARRA	NR282614	70	1		1	2.8 0.8 0.4 V	D ?	PH	similar to Ballinaby - see 13

JURA

(1	22/09/1996 KNOCKROME Jura	NR560718	50	2 1		5	1 1.2 0.6 V	R-s	PH	)
(	"			2		6	1.3 F	R	PnK	) lies flat; excluded
2	22/09/1996 CAMUS-an-STACCA	NR464648	45	1		4 170 3.9 1.4 0.2 V	R-s	PH	stands on cairn
3	22/09/1996 ARDFERNAL Airstrip	NR548715	5	1		4 135 1.3 1 0.3 V	R-s	PH	another small Stone nearby - see 276
(4	22/09/1996)TARBERT Jura	NR609829!	15	1		4 160 2.7 0.7 0.3 V	R-s	8 PH	)packing stones around base
(155	17/09/1997)								) details in book 1 drawing 4
276	20/09/1998 East of JURA AIRSTRIP	NR551715	10	1		4 35 1.4 0.7 0.2 L	10 N	PH	another Stone 300 metres West - see 2

No.	Date	Name	Grid Ref	Alt	a	b	c	deg	L	W	T	O	dist	N/D	Type	Notes
302	02/09/1998	E TARBERT graveyard	NR609829	10	1		1		2	0.4	0.3	V		D	PH ?	`Christianised` early M period; moved? excluded

MULL

No.	Date	Name	Grid Ref	Alt	a	b	c	deg	L	W	T	O	dist	N/D	Type	Notes
534	24/04/2000	SCALLASTLE, Craignure	NM680382	5	1		3		1.3	0.9	0.6	V		N	PH	obvious mound; large flat Stone 5 metres east
535	24/04/2000	above LOCH DON	NM722342	55	1		1		2.3	0.8	0.7	L	5	N	PH	
(536	25/04/2000	LOCH BUIE HOUSE 1	NM618251	5	1		1		3	1	0.4	V		N	PH	) complex site; outlier to circle; see 537 & 390
(537	25/04/2000	LOCH BUIE HOUSE 2	NM617251	5	1		1		2.2	0.8	0.7	V		N	PH	) see 536 & 537 - unknown connection
390	25/04/2000	LOCH BUIE - NORTH St	NM615254	5	1		4	80	1.8	1.7	0.4	L	10	N	PH	see 536 & 537-unknown connection
538	26/04/2000	TIRAGOIL, nr Bunessan	NM353224	30	1		1		2.5	0.8	0.6	L	5	N	2 PH	packing stones; on mound; pink granite
539	25/04/2000	ACHABON Ho Ardinglass	NM313233	30	1		1		2.3	0.8	0.5	V		N	2 PH	in garden; pink granite
340	25/04/2000	POTTIE, nr Fionnaphort	NM325222	45	1		1		2.2	0.8	0.6	V		N	2 PH	packing stones; on mound
541	25/04/2000	AM FAN, UISKEN	NM392196	65	1		4		2.1	1.2	0.3	V		N	3 PH	packing stones; on mound
542	25/04/2000	ARDALANISH, Bunessan	NM378189	10	1		4		1.7	1.2	0.4	L	20	N	PH	stands in water;flat stone 2.5 metres nearby
543	27/04/2000	ROSSAL Fm Pennygael	NM543282	15	1		2		2.1	1	0.6	L		N	PH	
544	27/04/2000	East form PENNYGAEL	NM547300	20	1		2		1.8	1	0.8	L		N	PH	
545	27/04/2000	GRULINE SouthEast ST	NM545396	15	1		1		1.9	0.7	0.5	V		N	2 PH	fell 1999, re-erectd by farmer
546	27/04/2000	GRULINE NorthWest ST	NM543397	10	1		4		2.3	1.1	0.3	V		N	2 PH	lost in rhododenrons
547	27/04/2000	Isle of ULVA	NM426393	80	1		1		2.3	0.8	0.6	V		N	PH	
548	27/04/2000	TOSTARY, Kininian	NM392456	50	1		2		1.6	0.6	0.5	L		N	PH	
549	27/04/2000	CILLCHRIOSA, Calgary	NM378535	35	1		2		2.5	1.2	0.6	V		N	PH	
(550	27/04/2000	ANTIUM Farm, Dervaig	NM439516	90	3	1	2		1.6	0.7	0.5	V		N	PH	) wall now built around this Stone
(		"				2	3		1.3	0.6	0.6	V		N	PH	)
(		"				3	6		0.7	0.8	0.8	V		N	PH	) probably the stump of broken Stone
(		" EXCLUDED from analysis					3		0.9	0.7	0.7	V				possible 4th. Stone in wall nearby
(551	28/04/1999	in DERVAIG forestry	NM439517	130	2	1	1		2.3	1	0.7	V		N	PH	) in forestry glade; with 3 fallen Stones
(		"				2	1		2.3	0.7	0.6	L		N	PH	)
552	28/04/2000	QUINISH HOUSE, Dervaig	NM414552	35	1		1		2.6	0.6	0.5	V		N	PH	packing stones; 2 large flat Stones nearby
(553	28/04/2000	GLENGORM CASTLE	NM434571	40	3	1	4		2.2	0.9	0.3	V		N	PnK	) all have packing stones & have been moved &
(		"				2	2		2.1	0.9	0.4	V		N	PnK	) inside circle (13 by 6 metres) of curb stones?
(		"				3	1		2.3	0.5	0.5	V		N	PnK	) small cairn to northwest
(554	28/04/2000	BALLISCATE, Tobermory	NM500541	90	2	1	2		2.3	11	0.8	V		N	PH	) fallen Stone 2.4 metres lies between
(		"				2	2		1.7	0.7	0.7	V		N	PH	) theses two Stones
1139	03/06/2005	ARDNACROSS, near Salen	NM541491	55	1		2		2.5	1.2	0.7	L	10	N	2 PH	3 fallen Stones?; 2 ruined cairns
(1140	03/06/2005	TENGA, near Salen	NM503462	100	4	1	2		1.6	0.7	0.4	V		N	2 PH	) FOUR POSTER
(		"				2	2		0.8	0.6	0.3	L	10	N	2 PH	)
(		"				3	2		1.8	0.7	0.7	V		N	2 PH	)
(		"				4	3		0.5	0.4	0.4	V		N	2 PH	)

SKYE

No.	Date	Name	Grid Ref	Alt	a	b	c	deg	L	W	T	O	dist	N/D	Type	Notes
(712	05/05/2001	BORVE	NG452480	110	4	1	3		0.9	0.8	0.4	V		N	PH	) these 4 Stones may be part of a
(		"				2	4	90	1.3	1.1	0.3	V		N	PH	) ruined circle
(		"				3	3		0.4	0.4	0.4	V		N	PH	
(		"				4	2		1.6	0.8	0.8	V		N	PH	
901	22/04/2002	CLACH na h-ANNAIT Kilbride	NG589203	40	1		1		2.3	0.5	0.5	V		N	2 PH	on mound with large stones at base
777	23/04/2002	CLACH ARD Pienmore	NG421491	60	1		1		1.3	0.4	0.4	V		N	PnK	carvings on east side
(902	23/04/2002	SORNIACHEAN COIR Eyre	NG414525	10	2	1	2		1.6	0.8	0.6	V		N	PH	)packing stones; on mound; eroded on west
(		" "				2	2		1.6	0.6	0.6	V		N	PH	)packing stones; on mound; eroded on west
903	23/04/2002	CLACH ARD Uig	NG394629	90	1		2		1.4	0.7	0.5	V		N	PH	
904	23/04/2002	OSMIGARRY	NG394718	70	1		2		1.9	1.1	0.8	V		N	PH	large fallen stone nearby, or a gatepost

TIREE

No.	Date	Name	Grid Ref	Alt	a	b	c	deg	L	W	T	O	dist	N/D	Type	Notes
824	13/08/2001	BALLINOE Tiree	NL973526	15	1		4	100	3.6	2.8	1.2	V		N	PH	quartz veins; 2 small stones 7 metres west
825	13/08/2001	BARRAPOL Tiree	NL946430	15	1		5		1.7	1	1	V		N	PH	
826	13/08/2001	CAOLES Tiree	NM074480	25	1		1		2.6	0.9	0.7	L	50	N	PH	leans into pool of water

AYRSHIRE

No.	Date	Name	Grid Ref	Alt	a	b	c	deg	L	W	T	O	dist	N/D	Type	Notes
830	04/09/2001	LYONSTON FARM Maybole	NS310103	40	1		9		1.4	1	0.9	V		N	2 PH	
770	09/09/2001	CRAIGENGOUR Gt Cumbrae	NS176564	55	1		1		1.5	0.4	0.4	V		D	1 M	gatepost? Or used as such?
859	12/09/2001	LIGHTSHAW Murkirk	NS716292	240	1		2		2.1	1.2	1.2	V		N	1 PH	
1052	26/04/2003	CRAIGENGOUR Gt Cumbrae	NS175564	55	1		1		1.9	0.4	0.4	V		N	1 PH	packing stones; grooves; possible cup marks
1062	17/05/2003	FINNARTS HILL Glen App	NX055746	185	1		3		1	0.8	0.7	V		N	PH	small much weathered Stone - glacial boulder?

BORDERS

1.5

No.	Date	Name	Grid Ref	Alt	a	b	c	deg	L	W	T	O	dist	N/D	Type	Notes
730	26/06/2001	WARRIOR`S REST Yarrow	NT354277	200	1		9		1.6	0.6	0.4	V		N	PH	stones around base suggest cobbled area
731	26/06/2001	CARDRONA STONE Peebles	NT300390	160	1		2		1.4	0.8	0.8	L	30	N	PH	on mound
763	08/08/2001	GRISLEFIELD Earlston	NT596398	150	1		3		1.5	1.2	0.7	V		N	1 PH	broken
764	08/08/2001	TOLLISHILL Lauder	NT519580	370	1		2		1.2	0.7	0.4	V		N	8 PH	
862	04/10/2001	HARRIETSFIELD Ancrum	NT634260	150	1		3		1.5	0.8	0.8	V		N	1 PH	surrounded by ridge of field stones
863	04/10/2001	WARRIORS REST 2 Yarrow	NT355278	200	1		1		1.6	0.7	0.4	V		N	PH	
(864	04/10/2001	near LYNE STATION, Peebles	NT201401	200	2	1	3		1.2	1	0.5	V		N	1 PH	) packing stones; probable cobbled area
(		" "				2	5		1.4	1	0.7	L	10	N	1 PH	) packing stones
(909	12/05/2002	BROTHERSTONE HILL WEST	NT619360	250	2	1	2		1.5	0.8	0.6	V		N	PH	) packing stones
(		" "				2	2		2.4	1	0.9	V		N	PH	) packing stones
910	12/05/2002	BROTHERSTONE HILL EAST	NT621362	220	1		3		2.2	1.5	1	V		N	1 PH	packing stones; damaged - by lightning?
1093	04/09/2003	BRUNDEALAWS nr Jedburgh	NT719114	275	1		3		1.4	1.3	0.8	V		N	1 PH	in forestry; second Stone not found
1095	07/09/2003	UPPER CHATTO Hownam	NT759161	305	1		2		1.6	0.7	0.5	V		N	8 PH	packing stones

DUMFRIES

No.	Date	Name	Grid Ref	Alt	a	b	c	deg	L	W	T	O	dist	N/D	Type	Notes
(963	17/07/2002	ERNESPIE Castle Douglas	NX774632	60	2	1	3		1.4	0.8	0.7	V		N	2 PH	) possible cobbled area; stones,
(						2	3		1.3	1	0.7	V		N	2 PH	) probably field stones at base
964	17/07/2002	on LOCH MANNOCH	NX663610	140	1		3		1	1.3	0.7	V		N	2 PH	on mound; glacial boulder with crack
(1072	19/05/2003	by LONGHOUSE Tower Moffat	NT083038	100	3	1	3		0.4	0.8	0.5	V		N	8 PH	) Stone Row on verge of A701
(						2	3		0.8	1	0.5	V		N	8 PH	)
(						3	3		1.3	1	0.7	V		N	8 PH	)
1073	19/05/2003	POLDEAN near Moffat	NT104001	80	1		2		1.5	0.9	0.7	V		N	8 PH	
1074	19/05/2003	LOUPIN STANES Eskdalemuir	NY257966	280	1		10		1	1.8	1	V		N	PH	outlier to circle; 2nd Stone flat nearby

FIFE

	No	Date	Name	Location	Grid Ref	a	n	i	p	q	H	W	D	O	dist	x	c	Type	Notes
(	61	10/07/1997	ORWELL STs	Kinross	NO149044	115	2	1	2		2.3	0.8	0.8	V		N	14	PH	) Stone 1 fell in 1972; both now set in concrete
(	62		" "					2	2		2.8	0.8	0.8	V		N		PH	)
	63	10/06/1997	NEWTON of COLLESIE		NO293133	60	1		1		2.6	0.6	0.7	V		D	2	PH	ring mark on SW side
	64	10/05/1997	EASTER PITORTHIE		NO500040	50	1		4		2.4	1.2	0.4	L	10	N	1	PH	38 cup marks S side; much weathered summit
	65	10/06/1997	BOGLEYS,	Dysart	NO296952	80	1		2		2.3	1	0.5	V		N	1	PH	much weathered summit
(	66	11/06/1997	LUNDIN LINKS		NO405026	65	3	1	1		5.2	1	0.5	L	20	D ?	1	PH	) fourth stone now lost
(			" "					2	4		4.2	1.4	0.8	V		D ?	1	PH	)
(			" "					3	1		5.5	0.5	0.5	L	10	D ?	1	PH	)
	113	26/08/1997	FORDELL		NT159844	35	1		2		2	0.6	1	L	5	N	1	PH	vertical grooves up to 25cm deep
)	115	26/08/1997	LONGLOCH FARM		NT244884	160	2	1	4	320	1.9	1.4	0.4	V		N	4	PH-b	) packing stones; 60o & 5 metres between
)			" "					2	4	340	1.6	1.3	0.7	V		N	1	PH-b	) packing stones; these 2 Stones
(	116	26/08/1997	TULYIES,	nr Newhills	NT028855	35	1		4	20	2.5	1.5	0.5	V		N	1	PH	) deep grooves and probable cup marks
(			(& 3 smaller Sts																) 3 smaller Stones at 170° & 23 metres
	214	20/06/1998	STRATHENRY HOUSE		NO231015	120	1		6		1	1.6	0.8	V		N	1	PH	set in wall on South side of road
	215	21/06/1998	HAWK STONE	Cottown	NO204212	25	1		6		1.3	1.1	1.2	V		N		PH	in cottage garden; may be glacial boulder?
	813	31/07/2001	SALINE GOLF COURSE		NT034919	225	1		3		2.5	1.4	1.3	V		N		PH	
(	980	21/07/2002	BALFARG Henge, Glenrothes		NO282032	100	2	1	3		1.8	1.1	0.9	V		N	2	PH	) stand in impressive henge
	981	21/07/2002	SKIETH St, Easter Anstruther		NO571047	30	1		4	60	0.9	0.9	0.3	V		N	1	PH	cup & grooves; wheel carved on south side
	982	21/07/2002	EAST PICORTHIE Anstruther		NO572071	65	1		4	180	2	1.1	0.4	V		N	1	PH	field stones at base; fissures on N & S ends
	986	02/09/2002	DOGTON STONE Glenrothes		NT236969	100	1		1		1.4	0.5	0.3	V		N	1	M	damaged Cross with weathering furrows/grooves
	987	02/07/2002	EARLSEAT FARM nr Kirkaldy		NT320974	80	1		2		1.3	0.8	0.4	V		N	1	PH	on mound & field stones; cups; crack S to W
	988	02/09/2002	KINGLASSIE	Boarhills	NO552133		1		4	30	2.4	0.7	0.1	L	30	N	1	PH	field stones; flakes of stone falling off
	1133	26/09/2004	ALLOA CROSS	Alloa	NS902927	20	1		4	160	2.8	0.8	0.2	L	10	D	1	M	Lorraine cross on east & west side

GALLOWAY

	No	Date	Name	Location	Grid Ref	a	n	i	p	q	H	W	D	O	dist	x	c	Type	Notes
(	965	17/07/2002	CAIRNHOLY 2 Gatehouse Fleet		NX518450	140	2	1	1		2.6	0.8	0.4	L	15	N	2	PH	) portal Stone of burial chamber
(			"					2	2		1.8	1	0.5	V		N	2	PH	) small portal stone
(	966	17/07/2002	CAIRNHOLY 1 Gatehouse Fleet		NX517538	130	8	1	1		2.4	0.8	0.4	V		N	2	PH	) forecourt stone of burial chamber
(			"					2	4		2	0.7	0.3	V		N	2	PH	) " "
(			"					3	1		1.9	0.4	0.2	V		N	2	PH	) " "
(			"					4	4		2.6	1	0.4	V		N	2	PH	) portal Stone with 6 cup marks
(			"					5	1		2.7	0.7	0.5	V		N	2	PH	) portal stone
(			"					6	1		2.1	0.6	0.4	V		N	2	PH	) forecourt stone
(			"					7	4		1.9	1	0.3	V		N	2	PH	) " "
(			"					8	4		1.9	1	0.3	V		N	2	PH	) " "
	786	17/07/2002	near BAGPIE	Creetown	NX498562	150	1		4	180	1.3	1	0.3	L		N	3	PH	stones at base; quartz veins
	967	18/07/2002	CULGARIE	Wauphill	NX382482	70	1		2		1.4	0.8	0.5	L	10	N	1	PH	weathering (?) grooves on summit
	968	18/07/2002	CUNNIGHAME CROFT Wigton		NX374561	25	1		10		1	1.2	0.8	V		N	2	PnK	rounded glacial boulder
(	969	18/07/2002	TORHOUSE ST STs	Wigton	NX385565	35	3	1	10		0.5	0.5	0.6	V		N	2	PH	) packing stones at base are sandstone
(			" " "					2	10		0.8	1.2	0.4	V		N	1	PH	) not granite
(			" " "					3	10		0.9	1.2	0.6	V		N	2	PH	)
(			" subsidiary Stone																not properly recorded - revisit
	970	18/07/2002	The HOLE STONE	Wigton	NX365557	25	1		3		1.4	1.4	0.7	V		N	2	PH	through hole; glacial boulder
	971	18/07/2002	BARVERNOCHAN	Wauphill	NX390526	40	1		3		1.1	1.5	0.4	V		N	2	PH	glacial boulder
(	972	18/07/2002	DRUMTRODDON Sts Monreith		NX364443	60	2	1	1		3.2	0.9	0.4	V		N	2	PH	) cups & rings; fallen stone
(			"					2	4	220	3.1	1.4	0.5	V		N	2	PH	) marked rocks nearby
(	973	18/07/2002	HIGH GILLESPIE hill Glenluce		NX245527	75	2	1	6		1.4	2	0.8	L	20	N	2	PnK	) unusual Stone on mound; Standing Stones or
(			" "					2	6		1.4	2.5	0.8	V		N	2	PnK	) field stones or glacial boulders
	974	19/07/2002	KNOCK & MAIZE Mull of G`l`wy		NW999579	110	1		3		1.3	0.9	0.6	V		N		PH	on mound with packng and field stones
	975	19/07/2002	TAXING STONE		NX062700	175	1		2		1.6	0.7	0.3	V		N		PnK	graffiti on east side at base
	1057	17/05/2003	STAIRFIELD,Whithorn,Galloway		NX467398	30	1		2		2.2	1.3	0.6	V		N	1	PH	impressive Stone now set in wall
	1058	17/05/2003	BLADNOCH village, Galloway		NX423542	1	1		5		1.5	0.7	0.5	V		N	2	PH	now set in wall beside A746
(	1059	17/05/2003	BORELAND nr Wigt`n Galloway		NX352581	40	2	1	3		1.1	0.9	0.6	V		N	2	PH	) cobbled area around bases
(			"					2	7		1.7	0.9	0.7	F		N	2	PH	) this Stone fell in 1995
	1060	17/05/2003	CARLIN STONE Port William		NX324497	80	1		4	180	1.8	1	0.4	V		N	1	PH	packing stones
	1061	17/05/2003	LONG FORTH,	Glen of Luce	NX230521	25	1		3		2	1.5	1	L	20	N	1	PH	
	1063	17/05/2003	WEST CAIRNGAAN, Drummore		NX133312	50	1		7		1.8	0.5	0.3	F		N	2	PH	fallen recently; small socket
	1064	17/05/2003	HOLLYHOLM,	nr Drummore	NX127380	20	1		2		1.6	0.9	0.7	L	30	N	1	PH	cobbled area
	1065	18/05/2003	TERRALLY,	nr Drummore	NX123414	10	1		4	30	1	1	0.4	V		N	1	PH	
	1066	18/05/2003	on LOGAN Estate nr Sandhead		NX102436	25	1		3		1.4	1.2	0.9	V		N		PH	
	1067	18/05/2003	CAIRNWELL nr Sandhead		NX086486	55	1		2		2.2	1	0.7	V		N	2	PH	parallell lines on south face
	1068	18/05/2003	WHIRLPOOL nr sandhead		NX066489	60	1		7		1.7	0.6	0.3	F		N		PH	no sign of the socket
(	1069	18/05/2003	NEWTON tomb,Gatehouse Fleet		NX551525	25	4	1	1		1.6	0.4	0.3	L	20	N	1	PH	) marked as `burial chamber`
(			"					2	1		1.6	0.5	0.3	V		N	1	PH	) 4 Stones set around others on site
(			"					3	1		1.6	0.5	0.4	L	30	N	1	PH	)
(			"					4	1		2.1	0.4	0.4	L	60	N	1	PH	)
	1070	18/05/2003	BRIGHOUSE, near Kircudbright		NX640455	20	1		3		2	1.4	0.9	V		N	2	PH	packing stones; glacial boulder
(	1071	19/05/2003	PARK of TONGLAND,Kircu`bri`t		NX670561	95	4	1	3		1	0.7	0.4	V		N	2	PH	) a small four-poster?
(			" "					2	3		0.8	0.6	0.6	V		N	2	PH	) packing stones; these Stones lie on a small
(			" "					3	2		1	0.4	0.4	F		N	2	PH	) flattened area.
(			" "					4	7		1					N	2	PH	) this Stone has a very small socket
	1076	16/05/2003	AUCHENLANE Ho, Gat`hs Fleet		NX531524	60	1		4	30	1.5	0.5	0.2	V		D		M ?	Christian cross on prehistoric Stone?
	1077	16/05/2003	ARDWALL Ho, Gatehouse Fleet		NX582547	10	1		4		0.5			V		D		M	moved; small Christian Cross
(	1078	18/05/2003	GLEN TERROW `Four Poster`		NX145626	140	4	1	3		0.6			V		N		PH	) small `four poster` with outlier
(			" "					2	3		0.6			V		N		PH	)
(			" "					3	3		0.6			V		N		PH	)
(			" "					4	3		0.6			V		N		PH	)

GRAMPIAN

	No	Date	Name	Location	Grid Ref	a	n	i	p	q	H	W	D	O	dist	x	c	Type	Notes
	789	26/07/2001	AUCHORACHAN Tomnavoulin		NJ209278	260	1		1		1.8	0.6	0.4	V		N		PH	packing stones; wedged into rock outcrop
	790	26/07/2001	NETHER CLUNY	Dufftown	NJ314381	150	1		3		1.3	0.7	0.6	V		N		PH	packing stones; re-erected in 2000 aafter falling
	791	26/07/2001	near COLEBURN	Elgin	NJ243548	135	1		5		1.3	1.1	0.5	V		N	1	PH	
(	792	26/07/2001	OLD MARNOCH church South		NJ598501	75	2		1		2.4	0.8	0.7	L	10	N		PH	) in churchyard
(	793	26/07/2001	OLD MARNOCH church North		NJ598501	75		2			1.4	0.8	0.8	V		N		PH	)
	794	27/07/2001	NORTH MOMKSHILL	Fyvie	NJ780417	140	1		4	40	2	1.5	0.4	V		N		PH	height etc estimated across crops
	1042	11/04/2003	BATTLE St Kirktown of Mortlach		NJ325393	220	1		4	135	1.4	0.6	0.2	L		N		M	packing stones & Cross; 6th century
(	1043	11/04/2003	BLACKHILLS House, Lhanbride		NJ269584	85	1		1		1.4	0.5	0.5	V		N	2	PH	) packing stones; cup, rings & stipples
(																			) small stone of unknown significance nearby
	1044	12/04/2003	CAMUS`S St near Hopeman		NJ152684	30	1		4	110	2.2	1.5	0.6	V		N	6	PH	8 grooves 5 deep; fallen stones nearby

(1019	04/10/2002	BOGTON,	Lhanbryde Elgin	NJ277607	45	2 1		3	85	1.4	1.5	0.7 V	N	2 PH	) field stones around both, & other
(	"					2		3	30	1.8	1.2	0.6 V	N	6 PH	)
1020	04/01/2002	OGHAM St, Wardend Ho Forres		NJ039554	40	1		4	90	3.4	0.9	0.2 V	D	1 M	ogham marks much weathered
1088	11/04/2003	SUENO`S STONE	Forres	NJ046597	25	1		4		6		V	D	2 M	elaborate carving in glass case; in concrete
(1079	05/06/2003	LOCH CAIREGEAN Aviemore		NH908155	230	2 1		7		2.1	1.2	0.6 F	N	2 PH	) excluded: outlier) 2 fallen outliers to well
(	" "					2		7		2.7	0.8	0.7 F	N	2 PH	) excluded: outlier) preserved ring cairn

HIGHLAND includes Inverness, Ross & Cromarty, Sutherland & Caithness   & some Stones around Loch Llinnhe

556	29/04/2000	ACHARA	Ballahulish	NM986545	5	1		1		3.6	1	0.6 V	N	PH	packing stones; actually in Argyll
820	09/08/2001	CLACH-a-CHARRA	Onich	NN025613	10	1		8	20	2	1.2	0.3 V	N	1 PH	packing stones; 2 holes 8 & 10 cms diameter
765	10/08/2001	LOCHALINE Forest	Morvern	NM659493	330	1		2		1.8	0.7	0.6 V	N	8 PH	difficult to find in forestry
822	12/08/2001	ACHACHRA	Lorne	NM944407	35	1		1		2.3	0.6	0.5 V	N	8 PH	stones at base; diffciult to find
900	22/04/2002	CLACH a BHRANGUI Strontian		NM815613	40	1		2		1.4	0.7	0.4 V	N	PnK	moved; iron ring on south-east side
925	23/06/2002	MONEY`S STONE nr Balnain		NH374300	190	1		4	40	1.4	0.8	0.3 L	10 N	8 PnK	OS bench mark on North side
926	24/06/2002	CLACH an AIRM, Balnafoich		NH682366	200	1		4	30	1.4	1.3	0.4 V	N	1 PH	difficult to find in forestry
927	24/06/2002	MAINS of GASK Balnafouich		NH679359	220	1		4	140	3.1		3	0.2 V	N	1 PH	outlier to ring cairn; splits in stone
953	24/06/2002	DALGAMBICH	near Croy	NH791472	80	1		1		2	1	0.8 V	N	1 PH	packing stones; much weathered
954	24/06/2002	KEBUCK STONE near Nairn		NH825556	10	1		4	190	1.2	1.4	0.4 V	N	1 PH	cups & carvings; grooves developing on top?
955	24/06/2002	BALNAROID	near Cawdor	NH857507	40	1		1		2.1	0.6	0.6 V	N	1 PH	deep straight grooves/furrows; much weathered
(956	24/06/2002	TULLOCHRUM Boat of Garten		NH969201	200	2 1		1		2.3	0.7	0.7 V	N	13 PH	) field stones at base
(	"					2		3		1	1.3	0.4 V	N	2 PH	)
(957	25/06/2002	BALLINTOOMB 1 Dulnain Brg		NJ010246	210	3 1		4	40	2	0.8	0.3 V	N	2 PH	) packing stones; these 3 Stones may be a
(958	25/06/2002	" 2		NJ011245	200	2 1		1		2.2	0.7	0.4 V	N	2 PH	) packing stones; row
(959	25/06/2002	" 3		NJ012247	200	3 1		1		3	0.6	0.6 V	N	PH	) this Stone seen across a deer fence
1021	05/10/2002	PITCHROY, Charlestown of Ab`		NJ178382	160	1		2	80	2.3	1	0.5 V	N	PH	packing stones
(1022	05/10/2002	UPPER PORT, Grant`n on Spey		NJ054302	200	2 1		3		1.5	0.7	0.3 V	N	PH	) on mound; packing & field stones at base
(	"					2		3		1	0.6	0.5 V	N	2 PH	) packing stones
1143	10/06/2001	CLACH CHIARIN Ardnamurchan		NM560619	5	1		4	90	1.8	0.7	0.3 V	D	2 M	Christian cross in ruined churchyard

CAITHNESS

716	31/05/2001	NORTH BILBSTER Watten		ND282538	10	1		3	140	2.7	1.8	1.5 V	N	2 PH	packing stones
717	31/05/2001	GREYSTONES Farm Watten		ND244543	20	1		2	80	1.8	0.8	0.5 L	10 N	1 PH	fallen Stone nearby; significance not known
718	31/05/2001	OLDHALL HOUSE Watten		ND204563	45	1		3	80	1.6	1.2	0.5 V	N	PH	packing stones, some may be field stones
719	31/05/2001	STONE LUD,	- Bowertower	ND221618	70	1		2	150	2.7	1.1	0.6 L	10 N	PH	small depression around base
720	01/06/2001	GANSCLETT SCHOOL		ND338447	75	1		4	0	2.3	1.1	0.2 L	15 N	PnK	S; supported by vertical slabs
721	01/06/2001	ULBSTER SCHOOL		ND324416	90	1		2	120	1.8	0.9	0.5 V	N	PH	S
(722	01/06/2001	LOWER CAMSTER South 1		ND259485	85	2 1		4	110	0.8	1.2	0.3 V	N	PH	) 3 Stones on OS map, one a small boulder
(	" " North 2					2		4	60	0.7	1	0.3 V	N	PH	) stands in peat - may be larger overall
723	01/06/2001	FORSE HOUSE,	Latheron	ND210351	90	1		2		1.3	0.4	0.4 L	20 N	PH	
724	01/06/2001	RANGAG Farm	Dunbeath	ND176448	135	1		1		3	1	0.8 V	N	PH	S; packing stones; 2nd Stone now lost
725	02/06/2001	HOUSTRY School, Dunbeath		NC156343	125	1		1		2.4	0.6	0.3 V	N	PH	S; packing stones
726	02/06/2001	ACHNAGOUL,	Dunbeath	NC161326	110	1		6	10	1.5	1.4	0.6 V	N	PH	S; packing stones; crack
727	02/06/2001	UPPER BORGUE	Borgue	ND126266	130	1		4	30	3.6	1.3	0.5 V	N	1 PH	S; packing stones
728	02/06/2001	CLACH MHIC MHIOS		NC941151	230	1		2	30	3.3	0.8	0.4 V	N	1 PH	S; packing stones; stands in small depression
(729	02/06/2001	CARRDHINAN CLACH Lothbeg		NC937127	130	2 1		2	110	1.3	0.4	0.4 V	N	1 PH	)S; these 2 Stones stand on a prominent
(	" "					2		4	120	1.5	1.1	0.3 V	N	1 PH	)S; spur above 2 rivers
779	26/04/2002	MONAD nan CARN Broubster		ND048584	100	1		3		1.2	1	0.5 V	N	1 PH	packing stones; covered in lichens
780	26/04/2002	LATHERON North-West Stone		ND199338	100	1		3		1.9	1.5	1 V	N	PH	packing stones; covered in lichen; large crack
907	27/04/2002	LATHERON South-East Stone		ND200336	100	1		1		3.5	1	0.8 V	N	PH	packing stones; on mound; coovered in lichen
912	13/05/2002	ACKERGILL MAINS	Wick	ND355542	10	1		4	110	1.8	0.7	0.2 V	N	1 PnK	packing stones; rubbing post?
951	18/05/2002	CREAG BHREAC BHCAG Wick		ND006660	60	1		4	40	2.1	1.3	0.4 V	N	1 PH	packing & field stones; crack & fissures
913	19/05/2002	BEN DORRERY East Stone		ND069550	200	1		4	90	1.4	1.1	0.3 V	N	1 PH	2 splits on east edge
914	19/05/2002	CLACH CLAIS an TUIRC Reay		ND991631	55	1		2		1.8	0.9	0.8 V	N	1 PH	grooves at northeast edge
(922	21/06/2002	BORROWSTON nr Thrumster		ND316431	130	2 1		1		2.3	0.4	0.3 V	N	1 PH	)both on a mound; cairn 25 metres SW and
(						2		1		1.8	0.3	0.3 L	20 N	1 PH	) on hilltop with panoramic wievs
923	22/06/2002	BEN DORRERY West Stone		ND069550	110	1		4	130	1.5	0.8	0.3 L	10 N	1 PH	Stone 319 is intervisible
(962	22/06/2002	ACHNACLY EAST Broubster		ND041048	40	2 1		4		1		V	N	1 PH	) visited in heavy rain - no real records
(	" "					2		4		0.8		V	N	1 PH	)
(1080	06/06/2003	ACEATER 1	near Thurso	ND048601	90	3 1		4	170	1.6	1.1	0.3 V	N	1 PH	) packing stones; furrows or fissures
(1081	06/06/2003	" 2		ND048609	90	2 1		1		2.2	0.8	0.6 V	N	1 PH	) packing stones; 4 Stones for site shown on
(	" 3 small stone					3		3				V	N	1 PH	) OS map - 4th Stone not found

ROSS & CROMARTY   2.2

714	30/05/2001	CLACH a` CHARRA Opisdale		NH716894	35	1		1		3.2	0.6	0.5 L	5 N	2 PH	
908	27/04/2002	EDDERTON	Tain	NH709581	30	1		1		3.3	1	0.9 V	N	1 PH	packing stones; cobbled area; fish symbol
911	13/05/2002	nr BELLE PORT Invergordon		NH681691	10	1		1		1.9	0.6	0.4 V	N	2 PH	symbol markings on SW side
(916	20/06/2002	WINDHILL EAST Muir of Ord		NH533483	25	2 1		1		2.4	0.7	0.4 V	N	1 PH	) packing stones; see 917 200 metres to west
(						2		5		0.6					) subsidiary stone 6 metres at 200o
917	20/06/2002	WINDHILL WEST Muir of Ord		NH531483	25	1		4	200	1.8	0.8	0.3 L	30 N	13 PH	
1136	29/09/2004	OLD EDDERTON church		NH710849	20	1		4	90	2.3	0.7	0.2 V	D	1 M	concreted; horse carvings; excluded
1124	07/06/2004	Badralloch		NH095916											glacial boulder; Other Stones 103
1125	07/06/2004	BADRALLACH Wester Ross		NH080916	65	1		4	20	1.2	1	0.2 L	10 N	PH	
1175	18/10/2006	APPLECROSS monastry		NG713459	10	1		4	315	2.8	1	0.2 L	5 D	M	with Christian Cross on site of monastry

SUTHERLAND

708	31/05/2001	ALT ERIBOLL	Loch Eriboll	NC426559	30	1		3		1	0.8	0.5 V	N	13 PnK	excluded ; small insignificant stone
(715	31/01/1900	CLACH an RIGH StrathNaver		NC680390	65	2 1		4	120	2.5	1	0.2 V	N	2 PH	) 4 flat Stones lie ariound low central
(	" "					2		4		1.8	0.8	0.2 V	N	2 PH	) mound - probably ruined circle?
(915	19/05/2002	MUSEUM graveyard Bettyhill		NC714622	20	2 1		4	90	0.7	0.8	0.2 V	N	2 PnK	) fine Celtic cross at this site - see
(						2		4	160	0.5	0.3	0.1 V	N	2 PnK	) also Other Stones 49
918	21/06/2002	INVERSHIN nr Bonar Bridge		NH587968	5	1		1		1.5	0.8	0.4 V	N	13 PH	packing stones; mound; large fallen Stone south
919	21/06/2002	DALNAMAIN nr Little Torboll		NH728986	75	1		2		1.3	0.4	0.3 L	10 N	13 PH	packing stones; on large mound
(920	21/06/2002	ACHNAGARRON West Rogart		NC732050	160	1		3		1.4	0.8	0.8 V	N	2 PH	) packing stones; see 921 at 32 metres & 70°
(921	21/06/2002	" East "		NC732050	160	1		3		1.4	0.8	0.8 L	20 N	2 PH	) packing stones; on small level platform
(924	23/06/2002	LETTIE`S GRAVE near Rogart		NC692092	130	2 1		4	60	0.8	0.8	0.2 V	N	2 PH	) probably square burial chamber or
(	" "					2		2		1	0.4	0.4 V	N	2 PH	) cairn with surrounding recmbent Stones
1086	10/06/2003	KILDONAN Fm, Strath Kildonan		NC910210	60	1		4	180	1.4	0.8	0.2 V	N	2 M	Christian cross on west side
(1087	10/06/2003	CLEBRIG	Altnahara	NC593340	90	2 1		4	60	1	0.4	0.1 L	20 N	M	) probably early Christian gravestones
(	" "					2		2		1.3	0.3	0.3 V	N	M	)

(	No	Date	Name	Loc	Grid ref	H	n	i	t	az	L	W	Th	o	d	c	m	code	Notes
	1135	29/09/2004	CRIECH CHAPEL	Bonar Bridge	NH637892	40	1		1	130	2.1	0.6	0.3	V		D	2	M	Christian cross on both sides
	1137	29/09/2004	LEARABLE HILL, Helmsdale		NC892236	160	1		4	90	1.6	0.9	0.3	V		N	2	PH	nearby ruined circles & cairns

CANNA

(	No	Date	Name	Loc	Grid ref	H	n	i	t	az	L	W	Th	o	d	c	m	code	Notes
	821	11/08/2001	CANNA		NG273044	30	1		1		2	0.3	0.3	V		D		M	damaged Christian cross

COLL

(	No	Date	Name	Loc	Grid ref	H	n	i	t	az	L	W	Th	o	d	c	m	code	Notes
	827	14/08/2001	BREACHACHA	Coll	NM151532	10	1		3		1.3	1	0.8	L	20	N	2	PH	fallen Stone lies 0.4 metres west
(	828	14/08/2001	TOTRONALD	Coll	NM166560	30	2	1	4	100	1.4	1.3	0.5	V		N	2	PH	) packing stones which form a small mound
(			"					2		100	1.5	1.3	0.3	V		N	2	PH	) packing stones which form a small mound
	829	14/08/2001	COLL WAR MEMORIAL		NM223581	5	1		1		1.4	0.7	0.4	V		N	2	PH	prehistoric Stone now war memorial; moved

SKYE

(	No	Date	Name	Loc	Grid ref	H	n	i	t	az	L	W	Th	o	d	c	m	code	Notes
(	712	05/05/2001	BORVE		NG452480	110	4	1	3		0.9	0.8	0.4	V		N		PH	) these 4 Stones may be part of a ruined
(			"					2	4	90	1.3	1.1	0.3	V		N		PH	) circle
(			"					3	3		0.4	0.4	0.4	V		N		PH	)
(			"					4	2		1.6	0.8	0.6	V		N		PH	)
	901	22/04/2002	CLACH NA h-ANNAIT Kilbride		NG589203	40	1		1		2.3	0.5	0.5	V		N		PH	large stones around base; on mound
	777	23/04/2002	CLACH ARD	Peinmore	NG421491	60	1		1		1.3	0.4	0.4	V		N		PnK	carvings on S-E side
(	902	23/04/2002	SORNIACHEAN COIR	Eyre	NG414525	10	2	1	2		1.6	0.8	0.6	V		N		PH	) packing stones; on mound; eroded on west
(			"					2	2		1.6	0.6	0.6	V		N		PH	) packing stones; on mound; eroded on west
	903	23/04/2002	CLACH ARD	Uig	NG394629	90	1		2		1.4	0.7	0.5	V		N		PH	packing stones; on mound - curb cairn?
	904	23/04/2002	OSMIGARRY		NG394718	70	1		2		1.9	1.1	0.8	V		N		PH	large fallen Standing Stone or gatepost nearby

TIREE

(	No	Date	Name	Loc	Grid ref	H	n	i	t	az	L	W	Th	o	d	c	m	code	Notes
	824	13/08/2001	BALLINOE	Tiree	NL973426	15	1		4	355	3.6	2.8	1.2	V		N	2	PH	2 small stones 7 metres west
	825	13/08/2001	BARRAPOL	Tiree	NL946430	15	1		5		1.7	1	1	V		N	2	PH	
	826	13/08/2001	CAOLES	Tiree	NM074480	25	1		1		2.6	0.9	0.7	L	50	N	2	PH	measured along length; leans into pool

LOTHIANS

(	No	Date	Name	Loc	Grid ref	H	n	i	t	az	L	W	Th	o	d	c	m	code	Notes
	365	10/04/1999	OVERHAILES Farm East Linton		NT581769	65	1		1		2.7	0.7	0.6	V		N	3	PH	PSts
	366	10/04/1999	on CARDINNIS Farm E. Linton		NT578741	100	1		1		2.3	0.6	0.3	V		N	3	PH	moved in 1930s from middle of field to hedgerow
	391	10/04/1999	STANDING ST fm Haddington		NT578737	75	1		2		2.6	0.8	0.8	V		N		PH	
	865	04/10/2001	AUCHENCORTH, Penicuik		NT204576	260	1		1		1.8	0.9	0.7	V		N	1	PH	packing stones; deep grooves on all sides
	1046	13/04/2003	at NEWBRIDGE ROUNDABOUT		NT125725	40	1		1		2.6	0.9	0.5	V		N	2	PH	
	1047	13/04/2003	EASTER NORTON, Newbridge		NT154720	45	1		2		1.1	0.7	0.6	V		N	8	PH	
	1048	13/04/2003	CAMMO, nr Crammond Bridge		NT174746	50	1		5		1.6	11	0.8	V		N	2	PH	
	1055	28/04/2003	REFUGE STONE at Torphichen		NS981731	190	1		3		0.9	0.9	0.5	L	10	N	1	PnK	packing stones; stated to be medieval sanctuary
	1094	05/09/2003	CAT STONE Edinburgh airport		NT149744	30	1		3		1.5	1.2	0.7	V		N	1	PH	
	1107	17/04/2004	WRIGHT`S Houses, Gorebridge		NT364	205	1		3		1.4	0.9	0.9	V		N	1	PH	uninteresting Stone in hedgerow

ORKNEY

(	No	Date	Name	Loc	Grid ref	H	n	i	t	az	L	W	Th	o	d	c	m	code	Notes
	928	14/05/2002	LANGSTONE Croft	Rousay	HX404275	20	1		1		2.2	0.7	0.3	V		N	1	PH	large cracks & splits along strata
	929	14/05/2002	YATNESS St Faraclett	Rousay	HX448328	20	1		4	10	2.5	1.5	0.6	L	10	N	1	PH	packing stones; splits;fallen Stone nearby
	930	14/05/2002	STEWS	South Ronaldsay	ND466890	75	1		4	90	1.9	0.8	0.2	L	15	N	1	PH	packing stones; on mound; cracks appearing
	931	14/05/2002	CLOUDHALL	" "	ND435895	20	1		4	140	2.5	1.2	0.2	L	10	N	1	PH	packing stones; large recumbent stone nearby
	932	14/05/2002	SORQUOY	" "	ND499914	30	1		1		4.4	0.6	0.5	V		N	1	PH	somewhat dumbell shape
	933	15/05/2002	STEMBISTER	Upper Sanday	HY541024	10	1		4	90	1.6	0.8	0.2	V		N	1	PH	packing stones; almost on cliff edge
	934	15/05/2002	STONE of SETTER	Eday	HY564372	35	1		4	100	4.3	1.7	0.3	V		N	1	PH	) packing stones; grooves across strata on S & N, & along strata on narrow E; on cairn?
	935	15/05/2002	SOUTHSIDE	"	HY561292	5	1		1		2	0.6	0.5	V		N	1	PH	
	936	15/05/2002	GALLOW TUAG	South Walls	ND303893	50	1		4	90	0.7	1.4	0.2	V		N	1	PH	on mound with curb cairn
	937	16/05/2002	BARNHOUSE	Mainland	HY312122	10	1		4	100	3.9	1	0.3	V		N	1	PH	cracks filled with cement on E & W
	938	16/05/2002	WATCH STONE	"	HY305126	10	1		4	100	4.8	4.8	1.6	V		N	1	PH	cracks filled with cement N & S edge
(	939	16/05/2002	STONES of ODEN	"	HY306126	10	1		4	150	2.6	0.7	0.4	L	10	N	1	PH	) splits SW end filled cement
(			"					2	1	1	1.6	0.5	0.5	L	10	N	1	PH	)
	940	16/05/2002	COMET STONE	"	HY295133	10		2	4	140	1.8	0.7	0.3	V		N	1	PH	on mound; splits filled with cement
	941	17/05/2002	MOR STEIN	Shapinsay	HY524169	30	1		1		3.2	1	0.5	V		N	1	PH	packing stones; on mound; much weathered
(	942	17/05/2002	STONES of STENNESS M`land		HY308126	5	3	1	4	90	3.2	1	0.5	V		N	1	PH	) another Stone destroyed 1814
(			"	"				2	4	130	5	1.6	0.5	V		N	1	PH	)
(			"	"				3	4	100	5.5	1.3	0.4	V		N	1	PH	)
	943	17/05/2002	STANEY HILL	Mainland	HY320156	50	1		4	60	2.5	1.1	0.3	V		N	1	PH	packing stones
	944	18/05/2002	DEEPDALE	"	HY272118	20	1		4	190	2.3	1.3	0.2	V		N	1	PH	unusual packing stones supporting Stone
	945	18/05/2002	SOUTH BRECKIE	"	HY253263	10	1		4	0	4	1.7	0.5	V		N	1	PH	crack developing on South edge
(	946	18/05/2002	STANERANDY	"	HY268277	70	2	1	4	60	1.8	0.8	0.3	V		N	1	PH	) mound augmented by field stones; Stones
(			"					2	4	40	0.8	0.6	0.2	L		N	1	PH	) partly buried & thus taller than measured:
(	1082	07/06/2003	AUSKERRY 1	Isle of Auskerry	HY671163	10	2	1	4	90	1.3	0.5	0.1	V		N	1	PH	)flat packing stones; fallen Stone at HY 678162
(	1083		" 2		HY673164	10		2	4	80	2.5	1.1	0.1	V		N		PH	) vertical packing stones
	1084	08/06/2003	QUOYBIRSE Isle of Westray		HY442472	45	1		1		3.4	0.5	0.4	V		N	1	PH	field stones; large crack from top to base
	1085	09/06/2003	isle of NORTH RONALDSAY		HY752529	15	1		4	100	3.8	1.3	0.2	V		N	1	PH	vertical packing stones; hole 0.08 metre diameter

OUTER HEBRIDES & OUTER ISLES - see WESTERN ISLES

PERTH includes the 6 Standing Stones on **Druachan Hill** which are shown separately but included in the analysis

(	No	Date	Name	Loc	Grid ref	H	n	i	t	az	L	W	Th	o	d	c	m	code	Notes
(	117	26/08/1997	CROFTHEAD		NN920241	140	2	1	2		2.4	1.8	1.2	V		N -	1	PH	) 10 metres at 90° between Stones; also at 180°
(			"					2	3		1.8	0.8	0.8	L	35	N -	1	PH	) & 150 metres are the 2 larger glacial boulders
(			" & 2 larger sts at		NN920240			2	7							N		PnK	) which are excluded
(	118	27/08/1997	STAREDAM STONES		NO040383	120	2	1	5		1.3	1.3	0.6	V		N	8	PH	) 4.5 metres at 55° between these 2 Stones
(			"					2	3		1.4	1.5	0.5	V		N		PH	)
	119	27/08/1997	CASTLETON, nr Dollar		NN982001	185	1		1		2.4	1	0.9	V		N	8	PH	many cup marks up to 5 cms.; groove on west
(	120	28/08/1997	GELLYBANKS FARM		NO082313	40	2	1	3		1.4	1.2	0.4	V		N	8	PH	
(			"					2	3		1.4	0.9	0.5	V		N	8	PH	packing stones; fissure on summit & west
	121	28/08/1997	BALNAGUARD Farm		NN946521	70	1		4	90	2.2	2.6	0.4	L	10	N	8	PH	2 others thrown down 1910 easily seen
	123	28/08/1997	OVER BENCHILL Farm		NO095322	45	1		2		2.1	1.8	1	V		N	8	PH	quartz strata; sundial on summit
	148	28/08/1997	CRAMFLAT FARM		NO089303	35	1		3		1.8	1.2	0.8	V		N	8	PH	
	149	28/08/1997	PITSUNDRY FARM		NO050344	85	1		2		1.8	0.9	0.7	V		D s	8	PH	one cup mark
	150	28/08/1997	KING`S SEAT Dunkeld		NO014430	60	1		4	60	1.4	1.1	0.5	L	10	N	8	PH	
	217	22/06/1998	KINDALLACHAN		NN993499	70	1		4	175	1.3	1	0.3	V		N		PH	

No	Date	Name	Location	Grid Ref												Notes
218	22/06/1998	E of GRANDDTULLY		NN920532	75	1		5		1.2	0.9	0.5 V	N		8 PH	on small mound; quartz
219	22/06/1998	TOMBUIE,	Aberfeldy	NN872509	120	1		3		0.7	0.6	0.5 V	N		PH	2m fallen; small henge? See 650
220	22/06/1998	BRIDGE of LYON 1		NN731464	115	1		7				F	N		PH	
(232	24/06/1998	LOANHEAD STONES		NO148329	135	2	1	3		1.3	1.3	0.5 V	D ?		PH	)smaller stones nearby; stated to be
(233	"	"					2	3		1.4	1.3	0.7 V	N?		PH	)circle, but no other stones visible
192	21/06/1998	The GREY STONE		NO222213	20	1		5		2.1	1.8	1.4 V	N		1 PH	
197	22/06/1998	MURTHLY CASTLE		NO070396	110	1		5		1.3	1.9	1.3 V			PH	major crack extends around entire St
(198	22/06/1998	EAST CULT FARM		N0072421	205	3	1	2		2.8	1.3	1 L	10 N		PH	
(	"	" "					2	2		2	1.3	0.6 V			PH?	)
(	"	" "					3	7				F			PH?	) broken & lies flat 10m east of St1
(199	22/06/1998	south west of NEWTYLE		NO046415	60	2	1	4	150	1.6	2.5	0.4 V	N		8 PH	
(	"	"					2	4	230	1.9	1.3	0.4 L	30 N		8 PH	
200	23/06/1998	CROFT HOUSE		NO056634	260	2	1	3		1.5	1	0.9 V	N		2 PH	
201	22/06/1998	BALNABROICH Nth St		NO091568	200		2	3		2	1.2	1 V	N		15 PH	) 2 Stones 200 metres to south; see 202
(202	22/06/1998	BALNABROICH Sth St		NO091566	200	1		6		0.6	1.3 na	L	80 N		PH	)
(	"					1		3		1.3	1.2	0.4 L	60 N		PH	
650	27/10/2000	BRIDGE of LYON 2	Fortingall	NN731464	125	1		3		1.5	0.6	0.7 V	N		PH	on mound; packing stones; vertical cracks
(651	28/10/2000	ACHARN	Killin	NN561316	135	2	1	3		1.3	0.8	0.4 V	N		PH	) on mound now cut by road;
(	"						2	3		0.3	0.3	0.2 V	N		PnK	) this subsidiary stone may be modern addition
682	29/10/2000	CLACH an BOILE	Rannoch	NN670580	205	1		3		1.3	1	0.8 V	D		PH	
(683	29/10/2000	CLACH an TOBAIRTE	"	NN617590	210	1		1		1.7	0.3	0.3 L	30 D		PH	) packing stones; on small mound
(684	"	" "	2nd drawing													) or tumulus
706	30/05/2001	CROFT HOUSE,	Enachdhu	NO060630	250	1		3		1.5	1.2	0.8 L	10 D		2 PH	
707	30/05/2001	BLAIR ATHOLL caravan site		NN876653	140	1		2		1	0.6	0.3 V	N		PH	
713	30/05/2001	BRUAR, near Blair Atholl		NN821659	55	1		3		1.4	1.3	0.6 V	N		1 PH	
733	27/06/2001	DUNNING village		NO019147	50	1		2		1.8	1	0.8 L	10 N		2 M	commemorates battle in 965
734	27/06/2001	BELHIE Farm	Aberuthven	NN977165	30	1		4	30	1.6	1.8	0.7 V	N		1 PH	early fissure formation?
(735	27/06/2001	EASTHILL	Auchterauder	NN930124	130	3	1	4	60	1.4	1.2	0.3 V	N		2 PH	) S; stands in hedge
(	"						2	1		1.5	?	? V	N		2 PH	) " " " "
(	"						3	2		1.6	0.9	0.5 L	25 N		13 PH	) on island in road;large horizontal groove
(1002	01/10/2002	BANDIRRAN	nr Balbeggie	NO209310	175	2	1	3		1.6	1.5	0.8 V	N		13 PH	) circle & 4 large &4 small recumbent
(	"						2	3		1.5	1.1	0.8 V	N		PH	) stones may not have been erected
742	28/06/2001	DARGILL FARM	Crieff	NN859201	35	1		9		2.5	1.6	1.2 V	N		6 PH	packing stones; crack
743	28/06/2001	CONCRAIG FARM	Creiff	NN855195	45	1		5		1.9	1	0.8 L	20 N		2 PH	on mound; cup marks
744	28/06/2001	STONEFIELD Dalvreck Creiff		NN852250	230	1		2		2.3	1.7	0.9 V	N		PH	packing & field stones
745	28/06/2001	MONZIE CASTLE	Creiff	NN880243	165	1		3		1.7	1.3	0.8 L	25 N		8 PH	
746	28/06/2001	CLACH an TIOMPAN		NN830329	270	1		3		1.5	1.1	0.6 L	15 N		PH	packing stones & mound
(747	29/06/2001	CREIFF GOLF COURSE		NN873228	135	1	1	3		1.8	1.7	0.8 V	N		PH	) these Stones are the remains of a
(	& 5 other Stones lying flat are excluded						5	7				F			N	) ruined circle
748	29/06/2001	near LOCH MEALLBRODEN		NN924249	245	1		3		1.9	1.7	0.9 V	N		PH	packing stones & mound; outlier - ruined circle
749	29/06/2001	CAR STONE Glen Almond		NN973300	190	1		2		2.8	1.8	1.3 V	N		PH	packing stones
750	29/06/2001	BALNAKEILLY	Pitlochry	NN946595	240	1		1		2.2	0.8	0.6 V	N		8 PH	
751	29/06/2001	COTTERTON	Pitlochry	NO038637	270	1		4		2.3	1.1	0.4 L	15 N		PH	fissures
752	29/06/2001	BORLAND Farm Glen Shee		NO153607	320	1		4	40	0.8	0.7	0.3 V	N		2 PH	packing stones; on mound or cobbled area
(753	30/06/2001	BROUGHDEARG Glen Shee		NO138670	340	2	1	3	30	1.5	1	0.6 V	N		PH	) other stones nearby - revisit
(	"						2	3		1.6	1.3	0.5 V	N		PH	)
754	30/06/2001	BALGARVIE	Scone	NO125263	85	1		3		1.8	0.9	0.8 V	N		8 PH	packing stones; large quartz crystals
755	30/06/2001	MIDDLEBANK,Carse of Gowrie		NO261276	15	1		6		1.8	1.8	1.7 V	N		2 PH	packing stones
759	29/06/2001	by NEW FOWLIS	Creiff	NN926233	100	1		2		1	0.4	0.4 V	N		PH	small Stone on cairn with other small stones
760	29/06/2001	LITTLE FINDOWIE	Pitlochry	NN944387	240	1		3		1.1	0.8	0.7 V	N		PH	on edge of stone cairn/barrow
761	30/06/2001	SPITTAL of GLENSHEE		NN109703	345	1		4		1.7	0.8	0.3 V	N		PH	stands on summit of morraine mound
815	09/08/2001	DALCHIRLA WEST st Muthill		NN822161	115	1		4	20	3	1.1	0.4 V	N		6 PH	pile of field boulders around base
(816	09/08/2001	DALCHIRLA EAST sts Muthill		NN824159	115	3	1	2	50	2.5	1.3	0.6 V	N		1 PH	) packing stones; suggested maybe remains of
(	"	"					2	3		1.5	1.2	0.6 V			6 PH	) ruined circle, but I see no evidence of this
(	"	"					3	7				F				) lies 1 metre long on ground
817	09/08/2001	BISHOPSFAULD	Comrie	NN779190	150	1		3		1.6	1.2	0.7 V	N		1 PH	probable cup marks
818	09/08/2001	AUCHINGARRICH	Comrie	NN788196	135	1		3		2.5	1.2	0.7 V	N		1 PH	packing stones
819	09/08/2001	ROMAN STONE	Comrie	NN774206	65	1		6		2	2.2	1.2 L	30 N		2 PH	cup marks
855	10/09/2001	GLENHEAD SOUTH	Doune	NN754004	120	3	1	2		1.6	0.8	0.5 L	30 N		PH	
	"	" "					2	3	60	1	1.4	0.8 V	N		PH	
	"	" "					3	2		1.9	1	1 L	20 N		PH	
856	10/09/2001	The GREY STONE	Dunning	NO022119	250	1		2		2.2	1.3	0.8 N	N		2 PH	
857	10/09/2001	KING`S STONE	Luncarty	NO097283	5	1		4	90	1.6	1.1	0.4 L	20 N		2 PH	
858	10/09/2001	MOULIN WEST Stone Pitlochry		NN942594	170	1		2		2.2	1.3	1 L	10 N		8 PH	packing stones
(1176	07/03/2007	DRUMLOCHAN Wood, Comrie		NN754225	65	2	1	3		1.4	1.1	0.8 V	N		2 PH	) cup marks on north-west side
(	"						2	3		1.4	1.3	1.2 V	N		2 PH	)
1177	07/03/2007	DALL, Ardeoning, Loch Tay		NN670359	130	1		2		1.5		V	N		LL	erected c. 1995 (info local farmer)
1178	07/03/2007	LURGOMAND Acharn Loch Tay		NN744435	130	1		2		2.3		V	N		LL	erected c. 1995 (info local farmer)

The Six Stones on Dunruchan Hill   including the Craigneich Stone beside the river on north edge of Hill

No	Date	Name		Grid Ref												Notes
736	27/06/2001	CRAIGNEICH	stone F	NN792178	160	1		2		2.2	1.6	1.2 L	20 N		2 PH	packing stones
737	27/06/2001	DUNRUCHAN HILL stone C		NN791171	230	1		4	160	3.6	2	0.8 L	40 N		6 PH	packing stones; complex site
738	27/06/2001	" " " D		NN790168	225	1		2		2.6	1.4	0.8 L	30 N		6 PH	on mound
739	27/06/2001	" " " E		NN789168	225	1		3		1.9	1.2	1.2 V	N		2 PH	packing stones
740	27/06/2001	" " " B		NN792175	200	1		5		1.5	0.8	0.6 L	15 N		6 PH	
741	27/06/2001	" " " A		NN795174	210	1		1		3.5	1.4	0.9 L	10 N		6 PH	packing stones; fissures; 4 Stones intervisible

SHETLAND ISLES

No	Date	Name	Location	Grid Ref												Notes
416	20/05/1999	TROSWICK,	S Mainland	HU408166	10	1		4		2.4	1.2	0.3 V	N		1 PH	packing stones
417	21/05/1999	BRESSAY Island		HU490429	40	1		4		2.8	1.3	0.2 L	20 N		PH	packing stones; large Stone 8 metres south
(418	23/05/1999	GIANT`S STONES		HU243705	30	2	1	2		2.1	1	0.6 V	N		8 PH	packing stones
(	"	"					2	4		1.4	1.4	0.5 V	N		8 PH	)
(419	23/05/1999	GIANT`S GRAVE		HU362855	35	2	1	2		2.3	0.9	0.4 V	N		2 PH	) ruined curb cairn with chamber
(	"	"					2	2		1.5	0.9	0.6 V	N		2 PH	) c. 150 m to North
420	23/05/1999	LUNNING,	Vidlin	HU506666	35	1		4		1.9	1.1	0.4 V	N		2 PH	large quartz crystal inclusions
421	24/05/1999	BUSTA BRAE North Mainl`d		HU349674	30	1		6		3.3	1.3	1.3 V	N		2 PH	packing stones; small stone 8 metres at 100o
422	24/05/1999	SKELLISTER `The Auld Wife`		HU463552	30	1		1		2.8	1	0.7 V	N		PH	large stones at base; quartz veins
(423	24/05/1999	STANEYDALE TEMPLE		HU285502	40	2	1	3		1.1	0.8	0.8 V	N		PH	) smaller stones in uneven row to south
(	"	"					2	3		0.9	1.1	0.6 V	N		PH	) recumbent Stone in pool nearby
424	24/05/1999	GIANT`S St, West Burrafirth		HU251571	10	1		3		1.6	1.6	0.9 V	N		PH	in walled enclosure 7.0 by 3.5
425	25/05/1999	by LOCH BRECK, Walls		HU215489	30	1		1		1.8	0.8	0.6 V	N		PH	irregular unusual shape

No	Date	Name	Location	Grid Ref	Alt	n	i	c	Az	H	W	D	Sh	N	Type	Notes
(426	25/05/1999	YAHAARWELL		HU300433	55	2	1	5		2.3	1.8	0.9	V	N	2 PH	) packing stones; fallen Stone 427 10 metres
(427	"		fallen Stone				2	7					F	N	2 PH	) at 340°, length on ground 2.8 metres
428	25/05/1999	SKAW,	on Whalsay	HU589665	10	1		3		1.4	0.7	0.6	V	N	2 PH	
(429	26/05/1999	MAILLAND,	White Ness	HU378450	45	3	1	2		2.1	1.2	0.7	L	10 N	PH	) 2 recumbent stones to West
(	"						2	7					F	N	PH	) suggest a short row; numerous
(	"						3	7					F	N	PH	) other sts on ground
430	26/05/1999	WORMADALE HILL		HU405465	140	1		2		2.2	0.8	0.5	F	N	2 PH	packing stones & mound 6 m. diameter; quartz
(431	26/05/1999	GREEN MEADOW,	Bixter	HU325558	60	2	1	5		2.1	1.6	0.6	V	N	PH	) packing stones; mound with curb stones &
(	"						2	7					V	N	PH	) 2.1m. Long; ruined circle; cairn nearby
(432	27/05/1999	WALLS village		HU242499	15	2	1	2		1.3	0.6	0.6	F	N	PH	) packing stones; not marked on map; small row
(	" "						2	7					F	N	PH	) stone 5 m. east - significance not clear
(433	01/06/1999	BELMONT South Stone	Unst	HP569009	20	2	1	5		0.9	0.9	0.4	V	N	PH	) not on map; 4 small stones in a row 5 metres
(	"	North Stone	Unst				2	5		1.2	0.9	0.5	V	N	PH	) not on map; to East
434	01/06/1999	CLIVOCAST	Unst	HP606007	40	1		1		2.9	1.1	0.5	V	N	3 PH	small stones 250 metres at 225o - see 435A
435	01/06/1999	CLIVOCAST Small st	Unst	HP604005	30	1		3		0.9	0.6	0.5	L	10 N	PH	pile of field stones at base
435	01/06/1999	BURRAGARTH	Unst	HP575040	70	1		3		0.9	0.7	0.7	V	N	8 PH	now in field bank
(436	01/06/1999	BORDASTUBBLE	Unst	HP579034	30	1		5		4.5	2.7	2	L	15 N	PH	) packing stones; 3 small stones within 0.6 m.
(437	"	"	2nd drawing													) curb stone enclosure 30 metres east
438	02/06/1999	RIPPLE STONE	Fetlar	HU627904	10	1		1		2.2	1	0.5		N	2 PH	
439	03/06/1999	GUTCHER	Yell	HU549986	15	1		3		1.5	1	0.5	V	N	8 PH	
440	03/06/1999	HAMNAVOE	Yell	HU485804	10	5	1	7					V	N	PH?	) packing stones; not on map; on mound
(	"						2	4		0.5	1.1	0.3	F	N	PH?	) made &/or morain? May be ruined
(	"						3	3		0.4	0.6	0.4	V	N	PH?	) circle with central stone; stated to
(	"						4	7					V	N	PH?	) be site of last Shetland leper house
(	"						5	4		0.6	0.8	0.3	F	N	PH?	)
441	06/06/1999	MID FIELD	West Burra	HU370326	30	1		4		1.9	1.3	0.4	V	N	PH	packing stones
442	04/06/1999	ASTA	Golf Course	HU412440	20	1		2		2.2	0.8	0.4	V	N	2 PH	6 cm band of quartz in column
(443	06/06/1999	BRAEMAR Sts,	Skellbury	HU386174	60	2	1	3		1.1	0.7	0.3	V	N	PnK	) see 445 125 m due North; line of small
(	"						2	4		0.9	0.8	0.3	V	N	PnK	) stones 20 metres south
444	06/06/1999	YAA FIELD,	East Burra	HU378382	30	1		4		1.8	1	0.4	V	N	8 PH	may be ruined circle; recumbent stone to NW
445	06/06/1999	MAGGIE FOUR STONES		HU387175	60	1		3		1.3	0.8	0.4	V	N	PkN	many stones - glacial debris? See443

STIRLING

No	Date	Name	Location	Grid Ref	Alt	n	i	c	Az	H	W	D	Sh	N	Type	Notes
854	09/09/2001	GLENHEAD NORTH	Doune	NN755010	90	1		4	70	2.4	2	0.4	V	N	! PH	probable cups - may be weathering
(855	10/09/2001	GLENHEAD SOUTH	Doune	NN754004	120	3	1	2		1.6	0.8	0.5	L	30 N	PH	) Sts stand on elongated mound
(	"	"					2	3		1	1.4	0.8	V	N	PH	) 16 cup marks on this St
(	"	"					3	2		1.9	1	1	L	20 N	PH	) fallen st to North, 2.2 meters long
814	09/08/2001	UPPER WHITSTON	Dunblane	NN806042	150	1		4	10	3	2.1	0.4	L	20 N	PH	packing stones; some may be field stones
960	26/06/2002	DUMGOYACH	nr Strathblane	NS533518	140	1		3		1.3	0.8	0.8	V	N	2 PH	with 5 fallen sts which make a row?
(961	26/06/2002	CRAIG MADIE MUIR1	Mugdock	NS856765	200	3	1	2		1.3	0.5	0.3	V	D?	1 PH	) packing stones; fissures & weathering
(	"	" 2					2	2		1.6	0.5	0.4	V	D?	1 PH	) packing stones, fissures, weathering & cups
(	"	2 " 3					3	2		1.2	0.5	0.3	V	D?	1 PnK	) may be later stone?
979	20/07/2002	KNOCKRAICH	Fintry	NS609878	75	1		3		1.1	0.5	0.4	V	N	2 PH	groove & probable cup marks on west

TAYSIDE

No	Date	Name	Location	Grid Ref	Alt	n	i	c	Az	H	W	D	Sh	N	Type	Notes
772	21/11/2001	FALCON STONE	Longforgan	NO296310	35	1		7		0.8	2	?	F	N	PH	possible cup mark on North face
868	21/11/2001	MacBEATH`S STONE	Meigle	NO434280	55	1		2		3.7	2	1.3	V	N	PH	numerous small cup marks; graffiti
869	21/11/2001	BALBEUCHLEY	Kirkton	NO362381	210	1		2		2.6	1.6	0.7	V	N	PH	large split or crack east to west
(870	21/11/2001	nr HUNTINGFAULDS	Tealing	NO416398	210	2	1	4	100	1.6	2.2	0.8	V	N	PH	)
(	"						2	3		0.9	1.6	0.8	V	N	PH	)
871	21/11/2001	HILL of KIRRIEMUIR		NO546392	170	1		4	110	2.3	2.2	0.7	V	N	6 PH	
872	23/11/2001	DERACHIE	Memus	NO439603	190	1		2	110	2.1	1.4	0.8	V	N	8 PH	Mnd
873	23/11/2001	West from NORMANSIDE		NO463607	150	1		1		1.8	0.8	0.6	V	N	8 PH	Mnd, on summit of natural hillock
874	23/11/2001	PROSENHAUGH	Cortachy	NO388591	160	1		3		2	1.4	0.8	V	N	2 PH	packing stones; quartz veins

WESTERN ISLES   with each Island shown separately but all analysed together

Barra with Vatersay

No	Date	Name	Location	Grid Ref	Alt	n	i	c	Az	H	W	D	Sh	N	Type	Notes
693	27/04/2001	ARDVONRIG	Borve	NF652014	5	1		4	80	1	0.8	0.3	L	35 N	2 PH	small squat st 75m to north
664	27/04/2001	VATERSAY		NL629940	40	1		4		1.6	0.4	0.4	L	5 N	2 PnK	may be boundry mark
665	28/04/2001	DRUIM A`CHARRA	Bervig	NL690990	90	1		1		2.8	0.8	0.6	L	10 N	2 PH	packing stone; fallen & broken stone nearby

Benbecula

No	Date	Name	Location	Grid Ref	Alt	n	i	c	Az	H	W	D	Sh	N	Type	Notes
694	30/04/2001	north GRAMSDALE	North Ford	NF824562	5	1		4	40	1.4	0.8	0.3	V	N	2 PH	packing stones; ruined circle on platform
695	30/04/2001	south GRAMSDALE	South Ford	NF825552	25	1		4	100	1.4	0.8	0.3	L	10 N	2 PH	ruined circle; stones fallen or not erected?
696	30/04/2001	SRIARVAL,	Market Stance	NF812532	35	1		4	140	1.3	1.2	0.3	V	N	2 PH	packing stones; stands in depression

Harris

No	Date	Name	Location	Grid Ref	Alt	n	i	c	Az	H	W	D	Sh	N	Type	Notes
675	02/05/2001	BORVEMORE		NG020939	10	1		4	140	2	1	0.4	V	N	2 PH	packing stones; fallen? Stone 10 metres at 135°
676	02/05/2001	CLACH MHIC CLEOD		NG040972	40	1		4	140	3.3	1.4	0.4	L	10 N	2 PH	packing stones; possible curb ciircle
677	03/05/2001	ENSAY Island		NF980866	20	1		4	60	1.4	0.5	0.2	L	20 N	4 PH	packing stones; on rock eminence

Lewis

No	Date	Name	Location	Grid Ref	Alt	n	i	c	Az	H	W	D	Sh	N	Type	Notes
702	03/05/2001	SUANEBOST		NB507638	20	1		3		0.4	0.3	0.2	L	5 N	2 PH	summit of larger Stone now covered in machair
(703	04/05/2001	CLACH STEI LIN	Siardar	NB398546	50	2	1	2		1.5	0.7	0.3	V	N	PH	)
(	"	"					2	5				0.3		N		) subsidiary stone - significance not clear
704	04/05/2001	BARBHAS Stone		NB369524	60	1		4	30	1	0.7	0.2	V	N	2 PH	no evidence of suggested circle
(705	04/05/2001	CLACH an TRUSEIL, Carloway		NB204430	40	3	1	2	150	2.4	1.1	0.8	V	N	2 PH	) flat area to S - cobbles?
(	"	"					2	7								) west stone fallen & broken
(	"						3	7								) east stone fallen & broken
(710	04/05/2001	GREAT BERNERA BRIDGE		NB164343	15	5	1	2	40	2.1	1.3	0.7	V	N	2 PH	) this area now reorganised
(	"						2	5	120	1	0.5	0.4	V	N	2 PH	) now set in concrete
(	"						3	4	100	1.1	0.4		V	N	2 PH	) now in concrete in original site
(	"						4	1	120	2.8	1.1	0.5	V	N	2 PH	) fell 1910; reset in concrete 1998
(	"						5	4	90	0.6	0.6	0.2	L	30 N	PH	) dangerous; measurements estimated
711	04/05/2001	STONEFIELD , Breasclete		NB215349	10	1		2		1.5	0.5	0.3	V	N	8 PH	now in concrete with pebble plinth
(678	03/05/2001	CLACH STEIN,	Port Nis	NB534641	30	2	1	3	180	0.9	1	0.7	L	15 N	4 PH	) packing stones; small subsidiary stone to NE

(		"	"				2	5		1.4	1	1 V	N	2 PH	)
	679	04/05/2001	CLACH an TRUISEIL	Siadar	NB375537	30	1		1	70	5.7	2	1 L	10 N	2 PH	massive; tallest Stone in Scotland
	906	25/04/2002	CALLANAIS		NB214330	25	1		1	80	3.7	0.8	0.5 V	N	13 PH	the Somerville Stone at north end of avenue
	1123	04/06/2004	SHILTENISH		NB282192	13	1		2		1.6	0.6	0.5 V	N	PnK	5cm through hole
	1190	03/05/2001	GLEN SHADER	Siadar	NB396536	10	1		3		0.8	0.5	V	N	2 PH	glacial boulder listed by County Archaeologist

North Uist

	697	30/04/2001	CRAIG HASTEN, Baile Mor	NF742667	10	1		7		2.4	1	1 F	N	PH	lies flat - measurement on ground; glacial stone?
(698	30/04/2001	CLETRAVAL SOUTH	NF750711	90	1		3		1.5	1	0.8 V	N	2 PH	) is this aa Standing Stone or glacial boulder?
(699	30/04/2001	CLETRAVAL NORTH	NF749713	90	1		6		1.4	1.6	0.8 V	N	2 PnK	) is this a Standing Stone &/or a glacial boulder?
	700	01/05/2001	CROIS MHIC JAMAIN	NF893781	10	1		3		0.3	0.4	0.6 L	20 N	PnK	formerly 2 Stones; burial mounds
	701	01/05/2001	nr BAILE	on Berneray	NF931816	18	1		3		0.5	0.8	0.7 V	N	2 PnK	
	670	30/04/2001	CLACH MHOR A CHE	NF770662	0	1		4	100	2.5	1.2	0.4 V	N	2 PH	packing stones; on drumlin
	671	30/04/2001	BEINN A CHARRA	NF787691	70	1		4	70	3.3	2	0.7 L	30 N	PH	pool water on SE - risk of falling?
(672	30/04/2001	FIR BHREIGE	on Torgas	NF770703	80	2	1	4	30	0.8	1.1	0.4 V	N	2 PH	) in raised ring of peat
(		"	"				2	3		1.1	0.7	0.5 V	N	2 PH	) in raised ring of peat surrounded by water
	673	01/05/2001	CLACH an T-SAGAIRT	NF879760	20	1		6	110	2.6	3.3	1.5 V	N	2 PnK	provenance as Stone not clear - or glacial boulder?
	674	01/05/2001	CLADH MAORLITE Berneray	NF912807	18	1		4	120	2.6	1.1	0.3 L	10 N	2 PH	packing stones & pebbles; enclosure to west
	778	23/04/2002	GREINETOBHT	NF824750	18	1		3		0.9	0.8	0.5 V	N	2 PnK	
(905	24/04/2002	LEACH nan CAILLEACHAN	NF971766	18	2	1	4	0	1.3	1.1	0.3 L	5 N	2 PH	) packing stones; possible cairn to east
(		"	"				2	4	20	1.4	1.2	0.3 L	10 N	2 PH	) packing stones
	1184	01/05/2001	on ferry slip at Berneray	NF914799	5	1	1					V	N	LL	commemorates opening of ferry to Harris 2000

South Uist

	666	29/04/2001	WEST KILBRIDE	NF751148	15	1		2	80	1.4	0.6	0.4 V	N	2 PH	stands on mound with possible curb stones
	667	29/04/2001	POLCHAR INN	NF745145	0	1		1		1.9	0.6	0.5 V	N	2 PH	right on sea shore
	668	29/04/2001	CROIS CHOCA BREACHA	NF734336	10	1		1	50	2	0.4	0.3 L	15 N	2 PH	on substantial mound (of stones?) on machair
	669	29/04/2001	AN CARRA, Lach an Athain	NF770320	60	1		4	60	4.8	1.6	0.5 L	10 N	2 PH	packing stones; stands on levelled platform

APPENDIX 3   The STANDING STONES of WALES from field work betweeen 1997 and 2009

Includes Monmouth and Anglsey as a separate county, with the Valleys, Swansea and the Gower in Glamorgan, and Denbigh and Flint in Conwy.

All measurements are in metres and compass bearings and angles of lean are given to the nearest 5   degrees.

Leaning Stones are measured along the length from ground level to the summit. This thus represents the height had the Stone been vertical

Excluded from the analysis are Stones lying flat, medieval and later Stones, dolmens and circles but outliers and centre Stones are included.

SUMMARY of Welsh sites & Standing Stones

COUNTY	total number of sites	total number of Standing Stones	prehistoric sites & Standing Stones			average height & range of height				number of prehistoric sites with			
			sites	Stones	leaning					1	2	3	>3 Stones
ANGLSEY	31	35	29	33	8	2.5	0.7	to	4	26	2	1	
CARDIGAN	12	19	12	13	3	1.7	0.8	to	4	11	1		
CARMARTHEN	33	44	28	42	11	2	1	to	3.3	22	3	3	
CONWY	10	16	8	11	2	1.7	0.2	to	3.7	7	1		
GLAMORGAN	20	21	17	18	3	2	1	to	3.6	16	1		
GWYNEDD	49	64	40	52	2	1.9	0.8	to	3.3	36	3		1
GWENT	4	4	3	3	1	1.8	1	to	2.3	3			
MONMOUTH	3	5	3	5	3	2.5	1.4	to	3.8	2		1	
PEMBROKE	68	87	58	76	16	2	1.2	to	3.2	46	8	3	1
POWYS	62	80	54	69	12	1.9	0.4	to	4	47	4	1	2
WALES totals	**292**	**375**	**252**	**322**	**61**	**1.9**	**0.4**	**to**	**4**	**216**	**22**	**10**	**4**

prehistoric sites as a percent of all sites — 86%

prehistoric Standing Stones as a percent of all Stones — 86%

percent of prehistoric Standing Stones which are leaning — 20%

percent of prehistoric sites — 85% 9% 4% 2%

designation of columns

A B C   D E F G H I J K L M   O P Q R   S

A — number of drawing & Stone	B — date	C — name of Stone &/or site	D — national grid reference	E — altitude of Stone	F — total Stones on site	G — number of each Stone	H — shape	I — compass orientation	J — height	K — width	L — thickness	M — Vertical Leaning Fallen	O — angle of lean in degrees	P — Natural or Dressed Stone	Q — geology	R — age	S — special features of Stone &/or site

ANGLESY

A	B	C	D	E	F	G	H	I	J	K	L	M	O	P	Q	R	S
231	31/08/1998	SHOP FARM, Boddern	SH318812	15	1		3		1.3	1.2	0.6	V		N	3	PH	
258	30/08/1998	GLAN TREATH	SH268786	25	1		6		1.5	1.3	1.1	V		N		PH	
259	30/08/1998	MEAN HIR TY-MAWR	SH254810	30	1		4		2.3	1	0.4	V		N		PH	
(260	30/08/1998	MEANI HIRION	SH228809	55	2	1	4		2.9	1	O.4	V		N	8	PH	) possibly dressed to obtain
(		PENHROS FEILW				2	4		2.9	0.9	0.2	V		N	8	PH	) the slabs
261	31/08/1998	TREGWEHELYDD	SH341832	20	1		2		2.7	1.1	0.7			D		PH	) in concrete; broken & repaired
262	01/09/1998	BODDEINOL	SH368857	50	1		4		2.5	2	0.7	L	20	?		PH	packing stones
263	01/09/1998	SOAR STONE Llanaethlu	SH319863	60	1		4		2.8	1.8	0.6	V		?		PH	
264	01/09/1998	PENYR ORSEDD 1 South	SH333904	50	1		4		2.8	1.3	0.3	V		?		PH	cup marks; stone 265 at 200 degrees
265	01/09/1998	PENYR ORSEDD 2 North	SH334906	40	1		1		3.6	1.6	0.3	V		?		PH	Stone 264 at 20 degrees & 300m
(266	01/09/1998	LLANFECHELL TRIANGLE	SH364917	40	3	1	4		2.3	1	0.2	L	20	N		PH	) these Stones appear to stand on
(		" "				2	2		2	0.8	0.4	V		N		PH	) small mound
(		" "				3	4		1.5	1.1	0.3	V		N		PH	)
267	01/09/1998	LLANFECHELL Stone by church	SH370916	30	1		4		2.8	2	0.3	L	15	N		PH	packing stones
268	02/09/1998	HIRDRIE-FEIG	SH484746	25	1		2		2.5	1.3	0.6	L	20	N		PH	
269	02/09/1998	BODEWRYD, Rosgash	SH406902	55	1		4		3.8	2.8	0.8	L	10	N	8	PH	packing stones
270	31/08/1998	MEANHIR COTTAGE	SH356746	25	1		2		2	0.9	0.6	V		D		PnK	inscribed
271	02/09/1998	GEARWEN village	SH487714	55	1		3		1.2	0.7	0.4	v		D?		PH	packing stones
272	02/09/1998	N of LLANERCHYMEDD	SH430858	70	1		2		1.8	1	0.8	V		D ?		PH	
273	02/09/1998	CARREG LIEDR Llanerchmyedd	SH446843	75	1		2		1.6	0.5	0.5	V		N	8	PH	unusual hammer shape
274	02/09/1998	BRYNSIENCYN South St	SH476678	15	1		2		1.4	1	0.6	L	15	N		PH	packing stones; Stone 297 300 metres
295	02/09/1998	WERTYR Stone, Almwich	SH414929	55	1		4		3	2	0.8	V		N		PH	packing stones
296	02/09/1998	MEANADDWYN Llannerchymed	SH461833	65	1		2		3	1.3	0.8	V		N		PH	road widening wall built around base
297	03/09/1998	BRYNSIENCYN North St	SH474679	15	1		6		1.5	2.3	0.9	V		N		PH	packing stones; see 274 at 300 mretres
298	03/09/1998	CASTELLIOR	SH554739	50	1		1		2.9	1	0.4	V		N		PH	packing stones
606	04/09/2000	HAFFOTY	SH564781	100	1		6		1	1.5	0.8	V		N		PH	
629	05/09/2000	CREMLYN SOUTH STONE	SH572774	115	1		2		1.9	0.9	0.8	V		N		PH	see Stone 630 at 300 metres south
630	05/09/2000	CREMLYN NORTH STONE	SH571776	120	1		1		3	1	0.8	V		N	3	PH	see Stone 629 at 300 metres north
631	05/09/2000	LLANDDYFNAN Ch Pentreath	SH502786	35	1		1		2.8	0.8	0.8	V		N		PH	
641	05/09/2000	YNYS FAWR Lanerchymedd	SH452831	80	1		2		2.5	1.7	0.9	V		N		PH	
(642	05/09/2000	near CASTEL BRYN-GWYN	SH469669	10	2	1	4		4	3	0.4	L	10	N		PH	) covered in ivy
(		" " "				2	6		3.1	1.8	1.3	V		N		PH	) massive Stone
1160	01/09/2006	BRYN CELLI DDU, Llanddaniel	SH508702	35	1		1	90	2.8	0.7	0.3	V		N		PH	surrounded by field stones
1161	01/09/2006	LLEDWIGAN, near Llangefni	SH457740	25	1		4	240	2.1	0.8	0.2	L	45	N		PH	packing stones
1162	01/09/2006	TREFDREATH, Maltreath	SH409693	10	1		2		3.3			V		N		PH	seen from 125 metres (wire fence!)

CARDIGAN

A	B	C	D	E	F	G	H	I	J	K	L	M	O	P	Q	R	S
252	19/08/1998	NANTYMEAN	SN762583	395	1		3		3	1.3	1	L	45	N		PH	packing stones; cups?; 4 quartz veins
253	19/08/1998	LECH GRON, Cross Inn	SN543648	200	1		4		3	3	1.3	L	20	N	6	PH	
254	19/08/1998	HIRFEAN, of Lampeter	SN624465	340	1		1		4	1	0.4	V		D		PH	stands on field bank
(561	04/06/2000	YSYBTY CYNFYN church	SN752791	240	1		1		2.4	1.3	0.6	V		N		PH	) all one site with Stones 562
(562	"	" " "	SN752791	240	2	1	4		1.6	0.8	0.3	V		N		PnK	) 2 Stones which form gateposts into
(						2	4		1.3	0.8	0.2	V		N		PnK	) churchyard

No	Date	Name	Grid Ref	Alt	Grp	St	N	Brg	L	W	H	O	Ln	C	n	Per	Notes
(563	04/06/2000	COW & CALF Ponterwydd	SN722833	320	2	1	11		1.75	1.2	1.2	V		N		PH	) glacial boulder
(						2	3		0.9	0.8	0.8	V		N		PH	)
586	04/06/2000	CWHSYMLOG	SN685837	240	1		3		0.8	0.75	0.4	V		N		LL	drill hole on NW side
564	05/06/2000	PLAS GOGERDDAN East stone	SN626835	30	1		11		1.4	1.4	0.8	V		N		PH	see Stone 538 east at 300 metres
565	05/06/2000	PEN MEAN GWYN	SN752650	230	1		6		1.3	1.3	0.6	V		N	4	PH	on mound;large lump of quartz
583	07/07/2000	PLAS GOGGERDAN West st	SN624835	30	1		3		1.4	0.9	0.9	V		N		PH	see Stone 538 east at 300 metres
896	07/04/2002	The PILLAR STONE, Aberporth	SN289513	140	1		2		1.6	0.7	0.7	V		D	3	M?	mound; fell & re-erected; inscription
1148	06/08/2006	CAREG LWYD, nr Morfa Farm	SN309530	140	1		2		1	0.6	0.5	L	45	N	1	PH	now beside field bank
1149	06/08/2006	CARREG FAWR south Morfa Fm	SN308530	180	1		2		1.5	1	0.7	V		N		PH	field stones? Around base
1150	05/08/2006	CARREG FAWR north Morfa Fm	SN308532	180	1		5		1.2	1.1	1.3	V		N		PH	developing crack on east face
1151	05/08/2006	nr NANTLLO club Brynhaffant	SN341522	140	1		4	140	1.2	0.7	0.2	V		N	3	PnK	may be small rubbing post
(1152	05/08/2006	PARC PWDWR or RHYDLEWIS	SN345476	110	1	1	2		1.1	0.6	0.4	V		N	4	PH	) will be made a scheduled monument
(		" "				2	?		1.4	0.4	0.3	V		N	4		) in hedge nearby

CARMARTHEN

10

No	Date	Name	Grid Ref	Alt	Grp	St	N	Brg	L	W	H	O	Ln	C	n	Per	Notes
76	05/08/1997	STYTHFEAN LLWYN DU,	SN675244	125	1		2		2.8	0.9	0.4	L		N	2	PH	on Llwyndu Faarm, Bethlehem
97	05/08/1997	PENTREFYNYS, Peniel	SN429248	80	1		3		1.6	0.9	0.6	V		N	1	PH	
100	12/08/1997	MEAN ELWYD Lwr Crt F	SN308149	5	1		6		2.3	1.8	1.5	L	45	N		PH	almost fallen
(101	12/08/1997	MEAN I ELMYDION 2	SN314140	15)	2	1	5		1.7	1.2	1	V		N		PH	) Stones 1 & 2 are 40 metres apart at 50o
(102	12/08/1997	" 1	SN314140	15)		2	7					F		N		PH	) see Stone 103 west at 300 metres
103	12/08/1997	MEAN LLYWD	SN312140	5	1		6		1.3	1.3	1.1	V		N		PH	see Stones 100, 101, & 102
230	19/08/1998	PENDRAINLLYN	SN783410	205	1		2		1.9	0.4	0.4	V	10	D ?		PkN	square; looks to be prehistoric
396	18/06/1999	BRYMEAN, Llannon	SN554068	140	1		4		3.3	1.2	0.4	L		N	1	PH	packing stones
397	19/06/1999	LLANCWM, Pontyates	SN445111	130	1		3		1.8	1.1	0.8	V		N	1	PH	grooves 0.25m.wide) these two Stones
398	19/06/1999	nr HALF-WAY HOUSE INN	SN452121	120	1		2		2.8	1.4	1	V		N	1	PH	packing stones) are similar
(399	19/06/1999	LLECHDWNN, Stone 3	SN432101	110		3	3		1.1	1.1	1.1	V		N		PH	)
(400	19/06/1999	" Stone 1	SN432101	110	4	1	5		1.7	1.3	0.5	V		N		PH	)
(		" Stone 2				2	2		2.4	1.2	1	V		N		PH	)
(401	19/06/1999	" Stone 4	SN432101	110	4		5		1.3	1.3	1.3	V		N		PH	)
402	19/06/1999	PENLAN UCHAF, Kidwelly	SN412083	110	1		3		1.8	1.4	1	V	20	N	4	PH	packing stones; opaque crystaline rock
403	19/06/1999	MEAN ELWYD	SN381112	75	1		2		1.9	0.9	0.8	L		N	8	PH	packing stones; furrow around Stone
404																	ERROR - no drawing or Stone
405	20/06/1999	MYNYDD LANGYNDEYRN	SN483132	250	1		2		2.6	1.3	0.6	L		N	7	PH	packing stones; on mound
(406	20/06/1999	nr PLASBACK FARM	SN455151	135	2	1	3		1.8	0.8	0.5	V		N	1	PH	) dumbell shape
(		" "				2	3		1.6	1.2	0.8	V		N	1	PH	) grooves on S & W; moved now in hedge
407	20/06/1999	GLANRHYDW, Pontantwn	SN439139	110	1		1		3.3	1.4	1.3	V	10	N	1	PH	packing stones
408	20/06/1999	near PENIEL village	SN429241	70	1		4		1.9	1.3	0.4	L	30	N	7	PH	
(409	20/06/1999	LECH CISTE, Horeb	SN515281	230	3	1	2		2.2	0.8	0.8	L		N	4	PH	) two other recumbent Stones, one
(		" "				2	7					F		N	4	PH	) each side to east & west
(		" "				3	7					F		N	4	PH	) quartz stones
(466	02/09/1999	CROSS HANDS, Llanboidy	SN186229	195	3	1	5		1	0.8	0.8	V		N	2	PH	) in garden & overgrown, with
(		" "				2	4		1.5	1.2	0.3	V		N	2	PH	) two tumuli nearby
(		" "				3	7					F	10	N	2	PH	)
467	02/09/1999	MEANHIR Fm SOUTH St	SN154254	200	1		3		1.6	1.5	0.8	L	10	N	2	PH	
468	02/09/1999	MEANHIR Fm, NORTH St	SN154259	190	1		4		1.6	0.8	0.2	L		N	2	PnK	packing stones ; medieval or later marks
521	09/04/2000	ST PAUL's MARBLE nr Cylgwyn	SN747301	160	1		3		2.1	1.4	0.9	V		D	8	PH	modern inscription
388	09/04/2000	nr BETHLEHEM	SN695260	80	1		2		2	0.8	0.4	V		D	8	LL	c1900
522	09/04/2000	ABERMARLAIS PARK	SN695293	30	1		3		2.6	2.5	1.7	V		N	1	PH b	mound
523	09/04/2000	LLANDEILO BRIDGE	SN627217	30	1		3		1.4	1	0.7	V		N	1	PH	second Stone no longer extant
524	09/04/2000	BRYN-Y-RHYD Llanedi	SN589084	90	1		4		2.5	2	0.4	V		N	1	PH	packing stones
587	27/06/2000	LLANDDOWROR village	SN256149	20	1		4		1.3	0.5	0.2	V		N	1	PH	packing stones
573	29/06/2000	MEAN ELWYD Llanibi	SN360135	105	1		3		2.2	2	1	V	10	N	11	PH	packing stones
574	29/06/2000	GILFACH Llangain	SN386145	50	1		3		2	1.2	0.6	L	10	N		PH	
575	29/06/2000	MEAN ELWYD nr Ferryside	SN381112	35	1		2		2.3	1.1	1.1	L	3	N		PH	packing stones; medieval or later marks
692	21/02/2001	BRYNGWYN Stone, Llandielo	SN670224	220	1		2		1.6	0.65	0.45	V	20	D	1	LL	marker post? C18 or C19?
(661	21/02/2001	NANTGAREDIG village	SN494211	30	3	1	2		1.75	1.2	0.7	L	20	N	1	PH	) irregular rough Stones with
(		"				2	2		1.6	1	0.6	L		N	1	PH	) intricate quartz veins.
(		"				3	7					F		N		PH	) stands 1.5 NE from Stone 2
(662	21/02/2001	BRYNCER-MEINI GWYN Peniel	SN459261	255	1	1	6		2.1	1.75	1.75	V		N	4	PH	) stands in depression
(						2	7					F		N	6	PH	) small quartz second Stone nearby
663	21/02/2001	FOSSY MEAN nr Llanpumsaint	SN414283	150	1		1		2.6	1.1	1	V		N	6	PH	moved; now loose in socket
883	04/04/2002	CARREG FYRDDINT,Tyllwd farm	SN459211	10	1		4	90	1.6	1.2	0.4	V		N	7	PH	crack at west end

CONWY with DENBIGH & FLINT

No	Date	Name	Grid Ref	Alt	Grp	St	N	Brg	L	W	H	O	Ln	C	n	Per	Notes
(624	04/09/2000	BWLCH DDEUFEAN WEST st	SH714717	420	4	1	2		1.8	1.3	0.6	V		N		PH	) packing stones
(		" " "				2	3		0.8	0.9	0.4	V		N		PH	) these three small stones are
(		" " "				3	3		0.3	0.3	0.2	V		N		PH	) almost in line
(		" " 2				4	3		0.2	0.2	0.2	V		N		PH	)
625	04/09/2000	BWLCH Y DDEUFEAN EAST st	SH715717	410	1		5		2.8	1.4	1.3	V		N	3	PH	packing stones
626	04/09/2000	CAE COSH 1 , above Roewan	SH735717	380	1		4	80	2.3	2	0.6	V		N	3	PH	
627	04/09/2000	MEAN CAMPIAU near Hafodty	SH748749	375	1		2		2.3	0.8	0.7	V		N		PH	
628	04/09/2000	MEAN PENDDU above Henryd	SH739736	435	1		3		1.8	1.3	0.5	V	15	N		PH	
1131	30/07/2004	ARTHUR'S SPEAR, Roewan	SH740717	360	1		1		2.3	0.3	0.3	L		N		PH	
1132	30/07/2004	CAE COSH 2, above Roewan	SH734716	380	1		2		1.5	0.3	0.3	V		N		PH	now gatepost in stone wall
1027	30/03/2003	CARREG-y-BIG, near Poulfadog	SJ224397	365	1		1		2.6	0.4	0.2	L	20	N		PH	) inscription on east side
1129	30/07/2004	MEAN ACHWYFEAN, Whitford	SJ129788	150	1		1		3.7					D		M	carved;Christianised Standing Stone?
(1130	30/07/2004	in GWYTHERIN churchyard	SH877615	220	4	1	2		1.1	0.3	0.3	V		N		M	) possible runes
(		"				2	2		1	0.4	0.2	V		N		M	)
(		"				3	4	180	1	0.6	0.2	V		N		M	)
(		"				4	2		0.8	0.4	0.3	V		N		M	)

GLAMORGAN — includes the GOWER (9 Sts), the VALLEYS & SWANSEA

No	Date	Name	Grid	Alt													Notes
168	30/01/1999	EGLWYS NUNYDD	SS803845	35	1		3		1.1	0.6	0.4	V		D	8	PnK	dressed with square edge
331	31/01/1999	KENFIG HOUSE Fm, Pyle	SS802838	25	1		2		2.5	1.8	0.8	V	20	N	8	PH	packing stones; on mound
332	31/01/1999	MOUNT PLEASANT	SS873826	120	1		5		1.8	1.2	1.2	L		N	1	PH	a second stone not found
(333	31/01/1999	TINKINSWOOD Burial site	ST092732	80	2	1	4		1	1.3	0.5	V		N	9	PH	) beside Tinkinswood burial chamber
(						2	4		1.1	1	0.3	V		N	9	PH	) packing stones
334	31/01/1999	DRUIDSTONE HOUSE	ST242834	65	1		5		2.5	2.3	0.9	V		N	1	PH	moved
567	27/06/2000	CWRT SART School, nr. Neath	SN744953	20	1		1		2.8	1.8	0.8	V		n	1	PH	moved; in concrete in school yard
525	09/04/2000	BON-Y-MEAN Inn Swansea	SS678953	80	1		3		1.3	1	0.5	V		N	1	PH	scheduled monument in housing estate
166	30/01/1999	STOUT HALL 1 Knelston Gower	SS475985	50	1		6		1.3	1	0.8	V		N	7	PnK	contains quuartz pebbles
167	30/01/1999	BURRY Fm 2, Bury Green Gower	SS461901	55	1		2		1.5	0.7	0.6	V		N	7	PH	packing stones; grooves; scheduled
325	29/01/1999	OLD WALLS Gower	SS484920	70	1		4		2.5	2	0.6	V		N	7	PH	packing stones; quartz crystals; scheduled
326	29/01/1999	SAMSON JACK Old Walls Gower	SS477922	56	1		2		3	1	1	V		N	7	PH	quartz crystals; scheduled
327	29/01/1999	BURRY Fm 1 Burry Green Gower	SS462901	55	1		7					F		N	7	PH	scheduled; fell in 1947; 2.8 metres long
328	30/01/1999	STOUT HALL 2 Knelston Gower	SS476891	50	1		2		2.7	0.7	0.8	V		N	7	PH	grooves; quartz crystals
329	30/01/1999	KNELSTON Gower	SS469892	50	1		4		2.3	2.5	0.8	V		N	7	PH	packing stones; quartz crystals
330	30/01/1999	TRYCOED Fm Old Walls Gower	SS475917	60	1		2		2.6	1	0.6	V	10	N	7	PH	in new earth bank; scheduled
880	03/04/2002	LLANFIHANGEL ROGIET	ST444878	10	1		4	60	2.2	1.8	0.7	L		N	1	PH	weathered fissures on SW & NE
881	04/04/2002	CARREG BICA Birchgrove Neath	SN724994	255	1		4	120	3.6	1.3	0.5	V	40	N	1	PH	many graffiti
1098	16/09/2003	CEFN GELLIGAER nr Rhymney	SO104034	440	1		1		2.4	0.5	0.4	I		N?	2	PNK	cup marks (?)
1099	16/09/2003	TAIRGWAITH	SN707124	180	1		7		2.8	1.8	1	F		N	6	PH	no drawing or photo
1145	05/08/2006	BRIDGEND in front of Bowls club	SS902795	30	1		2		1.3	0.6	0.4	V		N	1	PH	moved; in concrete; 5 straight grooves on N

GWYNEDD — includes LLEYN PENINSULA (21 sites) and HARLECH ALINGMENT (7 Sts)

20

No	Date	Name	Grid	Alt													Notes
576	06/07/2000	LECH IDRISS, near Bonaber	SH731311	260	1		4	160	3.3	2.5	0.3	L		N	8	PH	packing stones
577	06/07/2000	PLANWYDD HELYG, nr Athog	SH651132	250	1		1		1.8	0.6	0.6	V		N		PH	stands on small knoll
(578	06/07/2000	BRYN SEWARD 1, Bwlchgyn	SH627117	220	2	1	1		2.2	0.9	0.6	V		N		PH	) stand in wall of glacial
(579	"	" 2	"			2	2		1.4	0.8	0.5	V		N		PH	) boulders
(580	07/07/2000	WAUN OER Llwyngwril	SH618113	220	4	1	6		1.4	1	1	V		N		PH	) packing stones; 4 Stones from a row,
(	"	"	"			2	7					F		N		PH	) with 5th Sstone not found
(	"	"	"			3	1		1.6	0.8	0.6	V		N		PH	) on mound, stones at base
(	"	"	"			4	3		0.8	0.6	0.3	V		N		PH	) stones around base
581	07/07/2000	WEANFACH, Llanegrynn	SH594048	35	1		2		1.5	1	0.8	V		N		PH	packing stones
582	07/07/2000	PONT Y STUMANNER, Dyffryn	SH661080	10	1		2		2.1	1.1	0.8	V	35	N		PH	surrounded by hedge
(589	06/07/2000	MEAN ELWYDD, Bronaber	SH706330	215	2	1	2		1.3	0.6	0.6	L		N		PH	) Stone 2 is an organised small
(	"	"	"			2	3		0.4			V		N		Pkn	) outlier
590	06/07/2000	HAFFOTY FACH, near Arthog	SH664137	240	1		3		0.9	1	0.5	V		N		PH	has 2 quartz outliers
591	07/07/2000	LLYNAU Lake, above Arthog	SH659145	240	1		1		1	1	0.7	V		N		PH	
592		no drawing or stone for this number															
593	07/07/2000	on CEFN COCH Ceminais Rd	SH835032	220	1		6		1	1	0.5	V		N		PH	
594	17/07/2000	St. JOHN`S Church Meantwrog	SH664406	15	1		2		1.2	0.7	0.4	V		N		Pkn	beside church
601	20/07/2000	GARTH FARM Tremadog	SH553422	220	1		2		2.6	1	0.7	V		N		LL	erected 1999 as a "joke"
603	21/07/2000	Stone 1 on HARLECH HILL	SH598309	245	1		2		1.8	0.6	0.3	V		N		PH	one of 6 Stones forming an alingment
604	21/07/2000	Stone 6 0n HARLECH HILL	SH608322	290	1		3		1.2	0.8		V		N		PH	part of alingment
605	21/07/2000	TYNEWYDD, Dyffryn	SH625236	350	1		5		0.8	0.9	0.5	L	10	N		PH	packing stones; may be circle or cube cairn
607	05/09/2000	near GARTH, Port Dinorwic	SH542683	65	1		2		1.2	0.7	0.7	V		N	3	PH	field stones at base
621	20/07/2000	FACH GOCH, Tremadog	SH568411	180	1		2		2.2	0.6	0.4	V		N		PH	packing stones
(647	06/09/2000	PARTH-Y-GWYDDWCH South	SH603104	220	2	1	2		1.7	1.5	0.7	V		N		PH	) stones around base
(	"	" North	"			2	3		0.9	0.8	0.5	V		N		PH	) " " "
680	07/09/2000	TTYN-Y-DOL, Llanegryn	SH671091	25	1		3		1.1	0.9	0.4	V		N		PH	packing stones; flat stone; ruined cairn
1103	17/09/2003	St. CADFAN`S Church Tywyn	SH588010	5	1		1		1.7	0.3	0.2	V		D		M	
1101	17/09/2003	in PENRHYNCOCH Aberystwyth	SN661856	45	1		3		1.4	1.2	0.8	V	10	N		PH	moved; quartz; now war memorial
1102	17/09/2003	CROES FAEN Tywyn	SH597015	10	1		1		2.2	0.4	0.4	L		D	8	PnK	7 sides
1104	17/09/2003	TALYWERN nr Machynlleth	SH827005	200	1		3		2.3	1.2	1.2	V		N	8	PH	large stone
(1100	17/09/2003	St PADARN`s church Llanbadarn	SN598810	30	2	1	1		2.6	0.3	0.3	V		D	2	M	) both moved into church in 1916;
(	"	"				2	2		1.5	0.7	0.5	V		D		M	) Christianised PH stones?
1163	02/09/2006	MUR-MOCH near Llanrug	SH551620	280	1		2		1.5	0.7	0.4	V		N		PnK	prehistoric Stone &/or gatepost?
1166	04/09/2006	CERRIG Y CLEDD, nr Barmouth	SH643197	255	1		2		1.4	0.5	0.5	V		N		PH	

Lleyn Peninsula — 23 sites; 21 prehistoric Stones; 1 later stone & 2 provenance not known

No	Date	Name	Grid	Alt													Notes
595	19/07/2000	GLASFRYN, nr Y For, Lleyn	SH403425	140	1		2		1.8	0.6	0.4	F		N		PH	fell 2000; to be re-erected
596	19/07/2000	FRON OCHAU, Y For, Lleyn	SH418425	140	1		6		1.2	0.8	0.8	V		N		PH	seen across growing crops
597	20/07/2000	MEAN ELWYD Penygroes Lleyn	SH445542	10	1		2		2.5	1.5	0.8	V		N		PH	
598	20/07/2000	PEN-Y-BYTHOD, Lleyn	SH442553	5	1		2		1.5	0.8	0.7	V		N	3	PH	packing stones
599	20/07/2000	PLAS DU Farm, Llangybi Lleyn	SH412403	80	1		7		3.2	1	1	F		N		PH	lies flat in farmyard
600	20/07/2000	N of LLANYSTUMDWY, Lleyn	SH465406	75	1		1		2.8	1	1	V		N		PH	seen across growing crops
602	20/07/2000	TRYFFLYS, Penrtefelin Lleyn	SH526397	20	1		1		3	0.35	0.35	V		D		LL	tall square pillar, erected 1712
609	18/07/2000	PANDY, nr Botwnnog, Lleyn	SH288322	90	1		1		2.1	0.4	0.3	V		N		PH	2 flat stones at base
610	18/07/2000	St PETER`S CHURCH, Lleyn	SH238329	60	1		1		2.8	0.5	0.4	V		D		PH	in churchyard
611	18/07/2000	TRWYN MEAN MELVYN Lleyn	SH138252	50	1		6		1.5	1.4	1	V		N		PH	stands on edge of sea cliff
612	18/07/2000	PENY-BONT MEAN HIR Lleyn	SH325325	80	1		1		3	0.6	0.5	V		D		PH	packing stones
613	18/07/2000	ERFAIL-GALEDRYDD Lleyn	SH293365	65	1		1		2.3	0.8	0.7	V		N		PH	field stones at base
614	18/07/2000	on MOEL GWYNUS Lleyn	SH346420	170	1		2		1.8	0.9	0.7	V		N		PH	field stones at base
615	19/07/2000	HENDRE PENPRYS S st Lleyn	SH390344	95	1		2		3	1.2	0.9	V		N		PH	packing stones
616	19/07/2000	HENDRE PENPRYS N st Lleyn	SH392344	95	1		2		2.3	0.8	0.8	V		N		PH	packing stones; small Stone nearby
617	19/07/2000	PENFRAS OCHAF Lleyn	SH379417	120	1		5		1.9	0.8	0.5	V		N		PH	
618	19/04/2000	TIR BACH nr Y For, Lleyn	SH401401	55	1		5		1.8	0.8	0.7	V		N		PH	four small Stones forming a row
619	20/07/2000	MEAN DYLAN Llanllifni, Lleyn	SH455492	135	1		1		3	0.8	0.6	V		N		PH	ruined curb cairn 10 metres to NW
620	20/07/2000	below TYDDYN-MAWR Lleyn	SH431444	180	1		2		1.8	0.8	0.8	V		N		PH	packing stones; other Stones in bank
643	06/09/2000	MEAN LLWYD Lleyn	SH447542	15	1		2		2.8	1.1	1	V		N		PH	see 597
644	06/09/2000	near BETWS FAWR Lleyn	SH465406	65	1		1		2.7	1.2	0.8	V		N	2	PH	packing stones; see Stone 600
(1164	02/09/2006	LLANAEHAEREN church Lleyn	SH295289	140	1		4	0	1.2	0.3	0.1	V		N	2	PnK	) in churchyard, with another
(1165	02/09/2006	" " Lleyn	SH295289	140	1		2		0.8	0.4	0.3	V		D	2	PnK	) small st nearby

The Harlech Alingment — 9 sites with 10 stones over 6.5 kilometres at 35°

ID	Date	Name		Grid Ref											Notes
(603	21/07/2000	HARLECH ALINGMEBT	Stone 1	SH599309	245		1	2	1.8	0.6	0.3 V	N		PH	) stones at base
(622	21/07/2000	"	" 2	SH601313	275		2	2	2.2	1	0.5 V	N		PH	) stones at base; largest Harlech Stone
(	06/09/2000	"	" 3	SH604317	240		3	3	0.6			N		PH	) no drawing
(646A	06/09/2000	"	" 4	SH606320	280		4	2	1	0.5	0.3 V	N		PH	) stones around base
(645B	06/09/2000	"	" 5	SH607321	280		5	3	0.8	0.9	0.6 v	N		PH	)
(604	21/07/2000	"	" 6	SH608322	290		6	3	1.2	0.8	0.8 V	N		PH	) stones at base & stone caim
(645A	06/09/2000	"	" 7	SH609325	295		7	3	1	0.6	0.6 V	N		PH	) packing stones; cairn & circle to west
681	19/10/2000	LLANFAIR FARM	" 8	SH584290	120	1		1	2.75	0.6	0.6 V	N		PH	part of Harlech alingment?
(623	21/07/2000	LLANBEDR VILLAGE	" 9	SH583279	5	2	1	4 180	1.8	0.6	0.2 V	N	3	PH	)north side covered in white lichen; this
(		" "					2	1	3.1	0.8	0.6 V	N	4	PH	**site in direct line with the other Stones**

GWENT

ID	Date	Name	Grid Ref										Notes
108	12/08/1997	LLANGIBI ST ST	SO381965	15	1	4	1.8	1.6	0.6 V	N	8	PH	small mound of stones at base
517	07/04/2000	LLANGENY Lane Crickhowel	SO223184	150	1	4	2.2	1.8	0.5 V	N	1	PH	
686	19/02/2001	CARREG MEAN TARO	SO238113	430	1	2	1	0.7	0.5 V	15 N	1	LL	probably marker Stone C19
658	19/02/2001	CARREG WAUN LECH	SO164173	395	1	4	2.3	1.1	0.4 L	N	9	PH	fissures on south & north ends

MONMOUTH

ID	Date	Name	Grid Ref											Notes
(392	27/04/1999	HAROLD STONES Trellick	SO499051	210	3	1	1	3.8	1.5	0.8 L	30 N	7	PH	) all three have quartz crystals
(		"	"			2	1	3	0.8	0.8 L	10 N	7	PH	)
(		"	"			3	4	2.8	1.3	0.4 L	5 N	7	PH	)
(394	28/04/1999	GRAY HILL Stone 1	ST439936	250	1	2	1.4	1	0.5 V	N	7	PH	) possible grooves; part of ruined circle
(395	28/04/1999	GRAY HILL Stone 2 outlier	ST438937	250	1	2	1.6	1	0.5 V	N	7	PH	) Stone 394 60 metres at 130°

PEMBROKE   includes SKOMER ISLAND

ID	Date	Name	Grid Ref										Notes
77	11/08/1997	HAROLD STONE Stackpole Fm	SR968958	40	1	4	2.2	1.4	0.4 V	10 N		PH	packing stones and on mound
78	11/08/1997	LONG ST Liddeston	SM892072	65	1	4	2.2	1.4	0.2 L	10 N	8	PH	packing stones and on mound
79	11/08/1997	LONG ST Mabesgate	SM828076	50	1	4	3.1	2	0.3 L	D?	8	PH	
98	11/08/1997	NEW HOUSE Farm	SN152115	175	1	5	1.6	1.6	0.6 V	N		PH	
99	11/08/1997	AMROTH Longstone	SN146069	120	1	4	1.3	1.3	0.4 V	N	4	PH	
105	11/08/1997	STACKPOLE WARREN	SR981950	35	1	4	2	1.5	0.3 V	20 N	4	PH	moved; also called DEVIL'S QUOIT
106	11/08/1997	HAROLD STONE Broad Haven	SM862148	60	1	2	1.6	1	0.7 L	N?		PH ?	grooves; moved
107	11/08/1997	DRUIDSTON Broad Haven	SM864168	60	1	6	2.5	1.8	1.1 V	N	2	PH?	not marked on map; not a glacial erratic
369	03/09/1999	TREMEAN HIR; WEST ST	SM825262	80	1	6	1.3	1	0.8 V	N	2	PH	packing stones; see 370 c. 300 metres E
370	03/09/1999	TREMEAN HIR; EAST ST	SM828262	80	1	5	1.9	0.8	0.8 V	N	1	PH	now in bank; taller than as measured
371	03/09/1999	TREHALE HOUSE, Mathry	SM885299	120	1	3	0.9	0.9	0.9 V	N	8	LL	drill hole in stone
372	03/09/1999	CLYN FFWRN, Mathry	SM898289	145	1	5	1.4	1	0.5 V	N	2	PH	stones at base appear collected off field
(373	05/09/1999	EFAILWEN WEST ST	SN131253	205	1	2	1.6	0.8	0.5 V	N	2	PH	three other modern Stones to west
(374	05/09/1999	EFAILWEN EAST ST	SN139254	210	1	2	1.7	0.7	0.5 V	N		PH	
375	17/10/1999	BRITHDILL MAWR	SN072374	110	1	6	0.9	1.3	0.6 V	N		PkN	five other sessile Stones in same field
376	18/10/1999	PUNCHESTON Common	SN010303	180	1	3	2.4	1.1	0.8 V	N		PH	in field bank projecting above 1.8 metres
377	18/10/1999	CIL-MOOR, WEST STONE	SN080269	195	1	5	1.4	1	0.5 V	45 N	12	PH?	Prescelli bluestone ?
378	18/10/1999	on BED MORRIS hill	SN038364	295	1	6			L	N		PnK	not measured; see Other Stones 130
469	03/09/1999	RHYNDASTON-FAWR	SM896243	110	1	6	2.2	1.5	1.2 V	N	2	PH	
470	03/09/1999	east from ST. DAVID'S	SM766257	65	1	2	2.1	1.4	0.6 V	N	2	PH	packing stones; in concrete
471	02/09/1999	MEAN DEWI, Dowroy C`mn	SM775275	55	1	5	2.8	1.5	1 V	10 N	2	PH	in garden
472	04/09/1999	TYNEWYDD-GRUGG	SM924287	75	1	1	2.4	1	0.6 L	N	5	PH	
473	04/09/1999	Dolmen	SM848335	40	transferred to Other Stones 131							5	PH	CARREG SAMPSON spectacular dolmen
474	04/09/1999	RHOS Y CLEGYRN	SM913354	125	1	2	2.8	0.8	0.5 V	N	2	PH	packing stones; tumulus 50 metres west
(475	04/09/1999	FYNNON DRUIDON	SM921364	105	1	2	2.1	1	0.8 V	N		PH	) other Stones nearbt - ruined circle?
(		" at Fynnon Druidon farmhouse	SM919369			5	2		V	20 N		LL	) erected by Owen James 1998; excluded
476	04/09/1999	GARNWNDA, nr Goodwick	SM933390	145	1	6	2.1	1	1 L	N		PH	fallen? Stone 5 m. to SE & other stones
(477	04/09/1999	PARC y MERW row, Llanllawer	SM999359	190	4	1	2	2.3	1	0.7 V	N		PH	) row of 4 sts now in field bank;
(		"				2	4	2.5	1.3	0.4 V	N		PH	) measurments from bottom of bank
(		"				3	2	2.1	0.5	0.5 V	N		PH	)
(		"				4	2	2	0.6	0.6 V	N		PkN	) this used as gatepost; medieval or later?
478	04/09/1999	nr TREDAFFYD, Pontfean	SN029354	230	1	1	2.6	0.8	0.6 V	D?	2	PkN	now gatepost but prehistoric? See 485
479	05/09/1999	PRISK Fm, Meanclochog	SN097271	330	1	3	1.9	0.9	0.6 V	N		PN	
480	16/10/1999	RHYDYGSTH, Llanfirnach	SN211311	175	1	2	2	1	0.5 V	N	8	PH	
481	16/10/1999	BRYNHEINI SOUTH Stone	SN207314	205	1	2	2.4	1.8	0.8 V	N		PH	packing stones
482	16/10/1999	BRYNHEINI NORTH Stone	SN207314	205	1	1	3.2	0.8	0.7 V	N		PH	in field bank projecting above 1.8 metres
(483	16/10/1999	DOLAUMEAN, Crynych	SN158312	220	2	1	2	2	0.8	0.8 V	N		PH	)
(		"				2	4	2.3	1.2	0.4 V	N		PH	)
(484	16/10/1999	RHOS FACH, Mynachlog	SN135305	215	2	1	2	1.8	0.8	0.7 V	N		PH	) many stones here; small circle at 160o
(		" "				2	2	1.4	0.5	0.5 V	N		PH	)
485	17/10/1999	nr TREDAFFYD, Pontfean	SN024351	210	1	1	2.5	0.8	0.6 V	N		PkN	now gatepost but prehistoric? See 478
486	17/10/1999	on MYNYDD CARNINGLI	SN061379	190	1	4	1.3	1.2	0.4 V	N		PH	surrounding cobble stone pavement
487	17/10/1999	TREFACH, Cilgwyn	SN063351	230	1	1	2.3	0.9	0.7 V	N	8	PH	packing stones
(488	17/10/1999	TREBWICH, Cilgwyn	SN091358	230	2	1	2	1.4	0.6	V	N		PH	) deep groove or fissure
(		"				2	4	1.2	0.9	V	10 N		PH	)
489	17/10/1999	DINAS CROSS	SN088388	35	1	4	2.1	1.4	0.4 L	20 N		PH	looks like a slab split/prised off rock face
490	17/10/1999	west of BWLCH-MAWR	SM995376	75	1	2	2.4	1.2	0.8 L	20 N		PH	
491	18/10/1999	FAGWYR-FRAN	SN004315	210	1	1	2.2	0.6	0.8 L	20 N		PH	
492	18/10/1999	BUDLOY, Meanchlochog	SN065285	195	1	1	2.5	0.7	0.4 L	N	12	PH	deep groove? Weathered? On south
(493A	18/10/1999	MEANCLOCHOG Stone 2	SN081280	220	1	5	1.6		1.1 V	N	12	PH	) large stones around base; both Stones
(493B		" North A			1	5	1.8	1.4	1 V	10 N	12	PH	) are Prescelli bluestone
494	18/10/1999	MEANCLOCHOG STONE 1	SN088278	210	1	1	2.1	0.6	0.6 V	10 N	12	PH	on mound; flagstone at base; bluestone
495	18/10/1999	CIL-MOR EAST Stone	SN085270	185	1	1	2.1	0.8	0.6 L	N		PH	packing stones
568	27/06/2000	DEVIL'S QUOIT ST Petrose	SR962964	40	1	3	1.8	1.6	0.7 V	N		PH	deep crack on S-W border
569	27/06/2000	HAROLD STONE Skomer	SM732096	55	1	2	1.4	0.8	0.5 V	N	12	PH	

No	Date	Name	Grid Ref	Elev					H	W	T	Lean	Code	Notes
(570	27/06/2000	NORTH BROADMOOR Fm	SM952276	90	1		2		2.8	1.4	0.8 V	N	PH	) packing stones; massive
(	" "											N	PnK	) 5 cuboidal stones 50 metrse to west
(571	27/06/2000	CWM-GARW Mynachlog Ddu	SN119310	230	3	1	1		2.2	0.8	0.4 V	N	12 PH	) packing stones round both; fallen stone?
(	" "					2	2		2.6	1.1	0.8 V	N	12 PH	) lies 2 metres at 160o from stone 2
(	" "					3	2		2.6	1.1	0.8 V	N	12 PH	) fallen Stone at base
(572	27/06/2000	GORS FAWR Efailwen	SN135295	195	2	1	2		1.4	0.6	0.5 V	N	12 PH	) stated to line up to midsummer sunrise
(	" "					2	2		1.5	0.7	0.5 V	N	12 PH	)
884	05/04/2002	MANORWEN FARM, Fishguard	SM933360	80	1		1		1.4	0.6	0.25 V	N	12 PnK	square; rubbing post?; not prehistoric
885	05/04/2002	PUNCHESTON council house	SN006298	160	1		2		2.3	1.3	0.6 V	20 N	12 PH	in garden of council house (no. 6?)
(886	05/04/2002	south sts TAFARN-y-BWLCHst1	SN081337	310	2	1	3		1.2	0.75	0.6 L	20 N	2 PH	)
(886	05/04/2002	south sts TAFARN-y-BWLCHst1	SN081337	290	2	1	3		1.2	0.8	0.6 L	20 N	12 PH	) could be glacial boulders
(	" " st2					2	4	60	1.3	0.9	0.3 L	N	2 PH	) see 887 300 metres N & 890 400 m NE
887	05/04/2002	north st at TAFARN-y-BWLCH	SN080339	300	1		2	145	2.1	1.3	0.6 V	N	12 PH	stands in pool of water
888	06/04/2002	PANTYGARN Farm Eglwyswrw	SN136379	120	1		3		1.2	1	1 V	N	12 PH	broken by explosive c. 1900
889	06/04/2002	near BRYNBERIAN	SN091355	230	1		5		1.8	1.3	0.5 V	N	12 PH	
(890	06/04/2002	WAUN MAWN, Tafarb-y-Bwlch	SN083340	310	3	1	2		1.6	0.9	0.7 V	N	PH	) this appears to have been a row of
(						3	7		3		F	N	PH	
776	06/04/2002	nr TAFARN-y-BWLCH on B4329	SN081332	310	1		5		1.6	1.3	0.6 V	N	12 PH	on roadside; taller than measured
891	06/04/2002	GLYNSAITHMEAN on Preseli	SN112311	255	1		2		2.3	1	0.7 V	10 N	PH	two other stones nearby not found
(892	06/04/2002	MEINI GWYN, Glandy Cross	SN140266	200	2	1	2		1.6	0.7	0.5 L	N	PH	) remains of circle of 17 stones
(						2	3		1.1	0.7	0.7 L	N	PH	)
(893	06/04/2002	west of GLANDY CROSS Preseli	SN139267	200	2	1	2		1.6	1.2	0.8 V	20 N	PH	)
(	" " "					2	4	10	1.7	1.1	0.3 L	N	PH	)
(894	06/04/2002	PANTYRODYN, near Efailwen	SN150255	200	2	1	3		1.4	0.75	0.75 V	N	PH	)
(						2	7		2.5	0.8	0.8 F	N	PH	)
895	06/04/2002	in BRIDEL churchyard	SN177421	50	1		1		2.1	0.8	0.2 L	D?	M	Christian cross, ogam & cup marks
1153	06/08/2006	NEVERN CHURCH	SN083400	50	1		1		1.8	0.6	0.5 V	N	11 M	ogam Stone
1154	06/08/2006	near TRELLYFFANT	SN082423	130	1		5		1.3	11	0.6 V	N	11 PH	cromlech at 250 metres & 240°
(1155	06/08/2006	PENTRE IFAN dolmen Newport	SN100370	150	5	1	4	155	2.5	1.1	0.3 V	N	12 PH	) spectacular Stones of burial chamber
(	" "					2	4	90	2.4	1	0.3 V	N	12 PH	) large capstone; see outlier1156 at 250
(	" "					3	4	170	2.5	1	0.4 V	N	12 PH	) metres south
(	" "					4	4	110	2	1.5	0.3 V	N	12 PH	
(	" "					5	5		1.7	1	0.4 V	N	12 PH	
1156	06/08/2006	PEN FEIDR COEDAN Newport	SN099369	150	1		4	145	2.2	2.5	0.5 V	N	PH	packing stones; outlier to 1155
1157	06/08/2006	NEVERN church Christian cross	SN083400	50	1		1		3.9	0.7	0.7 V	D?	11 M	extensive Saxon carving on all sides
1158	09/08/2006	DYFFRYN-MEIGAN nr Boncath	SN180381	180	1		3		1.2	1.1	1 V	N	4 PH	quartz boulder

POWIS

No	Date	Name	Grid Ref	Elev					H	W	T	Lean	Code	Notes
												5		
(69	11/07/1997	QYRT-Y-COLLEN	SO233168	65	1		1		4	1.3	0.6 L	N	1 PH	) cup marks
(74	04/08/1997	" "												)
(92		" "												)
70	12/07/1997	TRETOWER	SO181219	95	1		2		2.5	1.1	0.8 V	N	1 PH	fissures
71	12/07/1997	The FISH STONE	SO183198	90	1		1		4.5	0.8	0.5 V	N	1 PH	
72	12/07/1997	LLANGYNIDR BRIDGE	SO156203	110	1		2		4.2	1.4	1 V	N	PH	square stone
73	12/07/1997	GILESTONE FARM	SO116235	115	1		6		3	2.3	2.3 V	N	7 PH	
75	04/08/1997	NOYADD FARM	SO127412	155	1		2		2.5	1.4	0.8 V	N	1 PH	
89	03/07/1997	DRUIDS ALTAR	SO240178	100	1		2		1.3	0.7	0.4 V	10 D	1 ?	cup marks; packing stones
90	10/07/1997	on HAY BLUFF	SO239373	460	1		4		1.2	1.3	0.2 L	N	1 PH	cup marks; ruined circle?
91	10/07/1997	BLEAN-BWCH	SO236328	450	1		4		1.8	1.2	0.2 V	N	3 PH	
93	12/07/1997	PEN MYARTH	SO188199	80	1		3		1.4	0.7	0.5 V	D	1 LL	placed in 1995
94	12/07/1997	BWLCH	SO150219	195	1		2		1.8	0.5	0.5 V	30 D	1 M?	circular depressions S face
95	04/08/1997	LLANGOED, Llyswen	SO124396	95	1		2		2.2	0.8	0.7 L	N?	1 PH	square, "cut off"top
96	04/08/1997	by PETERSTONE Court	SO089268	130	1		2		1.3	0.4	0.4 V	N?	?	square, "cut off"top
(222	04/07/1998	KINNERTON SW Stone	SO246628	120	2	1	5		1	0.8	0.8 V	N	2 PH	) another uninteresting Stone c. 250 m.
(	" NW "		SO245629			2	7				F			) to North lies flat beside road
223	15/08/1998	The CWM near Radnor	SO101563	310	1		6		0.8	1.6	1.3 F	N	PH	on mound; part of larger site with cairns
227	17/08/1998	near FOUR STS Walton	SO248610	200	1		6		0.9	1.6	1.3 V	N	PH	no name; see Four Stones 239
228	18/08/1998	GWERNCYNYDD	SO020651	235	1		5		1.4	1.3	0.6 V	N	PH	sheet of quartz down one face
(229	18/08/1998	CWMIRFON	SN859499	245	2	1	3		1.8	1	0.6 V	N	3 PH	) stand on low bank in undergrowth; if
(	" "					2	3		0.8	0.7	0.7 V	N	3 PH	) Stone is prehistoric so is the bank
(237	04/07/1998	CARREGY-Y-GWYNT	SN951769	310	2	1	4		1.9	2.3	0.5 V	N	3 PH	) Stone 2 lies 2.0 metres from NW end
(	" "					2	7				F	N	3	) 2.2 by 0.8 metres on ground
(238	04/07/1998	ALTWYD STONE	SN964776	300	1		2		2.2	1.4	0.6 V	N	3 PH	) S; tumulus to south
(	" 2										F			) other recumbent Stones nearby to north
(239	04/07/1998	The FOUR STONES			4	1	5		1.8	1.5	1.3 V	N	11 M	) smooth spherical glacial boulders;
(	" "					2	5		1	1.3	1.3 F	N	11 M	) see 227 nearby
(	" "					3	7		1.7	1.3	1.3 V	N	11 M	
(	" "					4	5		1.7	1.3	0.8 V	N	11 M	)
(245	17/08/1996	UPPER WOODMASTON	SO263613	185	1		5		1.3	1.3	1.3 V	10 N	2 PH	
246	17/08/1998	BLEAN EDW	S0142588	280	1		5		1.5	1	0.8 L	30 N	2 PH	
247	18/08/1998	NEWBRIDGE-on-WYE	SO014580	155	1		3		1.8	1.2	0.8 L	20 N	PH	packing stones; angle of lean increased
248	18/08/1998	TY MAWR,	SN990570	190	1		5		1.9	1.3	0.9 V	15 N	6 PH	packing stones; on mound
249	18/08/1998	DOLYFELIN	SN977550	185	1		2		2.8	1.8	1.3 L	N	PH	packing stones
250	18/08/1998	BWLCHCILAU	SN948558	290	1		3		1.9	1.4	0.7 V	15 N	PH	large packing stone; 2 fallen stones 310o
251	18/08/1998	LLANWRTYDD WELLS	SN885474	220	1		2		2.5	1.3	0.8 L	D	PH	packing stones
255	20/08/1998	USK RESEVOIR	SN833284	325	1		5		2.3	2.3	1.2 V	N	6 PH	packing stones
(256	20/08/1998	MEAN MAWR, also listed as	SN852207	390	1		3		2	1.4	0.8 V	N	PH	) 2 small stones to west & Cerrig Duon
(	" CERRIG DUON													) ciircle to east; all on platform
257	20/08/1998	PONT-ar-YSCIR on battle mound	SO006306	175	1		1		3.7	1.1	1.1 V	N	PH	packing stones; on mound10 by 6 metres
386	08/04/2000	near PENTRE Farm nr Bwlch	SO144235	200	1		2		0.9	0.7	0.4 V	N	PnK	milestone? - but looks like Bronze Age
387	08/04/2000	LLANFILHANGEL CHURCH	SO343290	185	1		1		1.5	0.4	0.4 V	D	PH	moved inside church porch; see 59
497	19/10/1999	MEAN LLENAI	SN855215	500	1		4		1.9	1.3	0.2 V	N	PH	
498	19/10/1999	MEAN ELIA, on Bryn Melyn	SN924192	440	1		4		3.5	2.5	0.6 V	N	8 PH	packing stones
517	07/04/2000	LLANGENNY Lane St Crickhowel	SO223184	150	1		4	100	2.2	1.8	0.5 V	N	1 PH	
518	08/04/2000	nr CRADDOCK nr Brecon	SO018306	180	1		4		2	0.9	0.6 V	N	1 PH	

No	Date	Name	Grid	Alt	Stones	#	a	deg	H	W	T	Or	Lean	N	b	Type	Notes
519	08/04/2000	MEAN RICHARD nr Brecon	SN967347	415	1		3		1.5	0.8	0.5	V		N	7	PH	packing stones
520	08/04/2000	CILYCWM north of Llandovery	SN755473	390	1		4		1.8	1.2	0.2	V	10	N	3	PH	2 holes on N_W side
584	03/06/2000	CROSS FOOT Farm, Clyro	SO219458	235	1		3		1.3	0.9	0.7	L	10	N	1	PH	stones around base may be field stones
585	03/06/2000	St MICHAEL`S CHURCH	SO187496	360	1		1		2			V		D	1	Pkn	Christianised; damaged; inside church
(557	03/06/2000	REHWAY nr New Radnor	SO157569	410	4	1	6		0.7	1.7	0.6	V		N	11	PH	) 4 glacial boulders; large cairn 55 metres
(		"				2	6		0.7	1	0.6	V		N	11	PH	) at 50o
(		"				3	5		0.4	0.6	0.6	V		N	11	PH	)
(		"				4	5		0.3	0.5	0.3	V		N	11	PH	)
558	04/06/2000	St GWRTHWL`S Church	SN975637	180	1		3		1.5	1.6	0.8	V		N	11	PH	glacial bouder in church yard
559	04/06/2000	RHIWNANT Elan Valley	SN882613	450	1		5		1.6	1.3	0.8	V		N	8	PH	packing stones; quartz veins & crystals
(560	04/06/2000	above ELAN VALLEY	SN905631	405	5	1	3		0.5	0.4	0.3	V		N		PH	) row of 5 stones, 2 now fallen
(		"				2	3		0.6	0.8	0.3	V		N		PH	)
(		"				4	2		1.6	0.8	0.4	V	15	N		PH	)
588	06/07/2000	MEAN BUENO, Dyffry	SJ204013	80	1		5		1.3	0.9	0.6	L		N		PH	large crack filled with cement
608	17/07/2000	MAES MONCHNANT	SJ136247	120	1		1		3.5	1	0.5	V		N		PH	
687	19/02/2001	No Name - above Sennybridge	SN939260	315	1		4	0	1.4	0.8	0.25	V		N	1	PH	small Stone hidden in belting
688		there is no drawing number 688 due to a numbering error by me															
689	20/02/2001	TY-LOSIN west st Usk resevoir	SN833293	310	1		6		0.9	1.3	0.65	V		N	8	PH	see 690, 200 m. at 300 degrees
690	20/01/2001	TY-LOSIN east st Usk resevoir	SN830293	320	1		4	90	0.7	1.25	0.4	V	35	N	8	PH	see 689, 2000 m. at 180 degrees
659	20/02/2001	above USK RESEVOIR East St	SN805285	365	1		4	70	1.3	1.5	0.5	L		N	1	PH	see 660, 150m. at 110degrees
(660	20/02/2001	above USK RESEVOIR West st	SN807284	365	2	1	2	60	2.2	1.4	1	V		N	1	PH	)see 659, 150m. At 290 degrees
(		"				2											small satellite St 3m. NE
691	20/02/2001	east of TY-BRYCH, Llanandog	SN765226	310	1		7		1.25	0.8	0.6	F	45	N	9	PH	uncertain Stone, on small ruined cairn
(882	04/04/2002	SAITH MEAN st row Craig-y-Nos	SN835145	370	7	1	3		0.75	0.75	0.3	L	45	N	4	PH	) stone row
(		"				2	4	40	0.8	0.8	0.25	L	45	N	4		
(		"				3	3	40	0.8	0.8	0.3	L		N	4		
(		"				4	7		2.8	1.1	0.3	F		N	4		
(		"				5	3	40	1.1	0.9	0.4	V		N	1		
(		"				6	7		2.2	0.7	0.25	F		N	4		
(		"				7	4	40	1.6	0.9	0.3	V		N	4		
897	07/04/2002	MEANGWYNGWEDDWRhayder	SN925925	480	1		6		0.8	0.8	0.8	V		N	4	PH	
898	07/04/2002	MEAN-SERTH Rhayder	SN943699	460	1		1		1.9	0.6	0.3	V		N	3	M	in concrete
899	08/04/2002	on PEN MEAN WERN Rhayder	SN863620	545	1		3		1.6	1.7	0.8	V		N	4	PII	stone 559 is intervisible
1105	18/09/2003	PANTYCARGLE Beguildy	SO200791	250	1		7		1.8	1.4	0.9	F		N	6	PH	may never have stood?
1128	29/07/2004	St GARMON Church	SJ158328	220	1		4	200	0.4	0.6	0.2	V		N		M	5th/6th century? On preaching mound
1146	05/08/2006	TAFARN-y-GARREG Glyntawe	SN849168	210	1		4	160	1	0.4	0.2	V		N	1	PnK	behind chapel
1147	05/08/2006	BLAENAU UCHAF, Usk resevoir	SN835256	360	1		3		1.5	0.6	0.5	V		N	1	PH	
1127	04/04/2002	LLANRHEADR-yn-MOCHANT	SJ125260	200	1		1		2.6	0.6	0.3	V		N	8	PH	in concrete; small pits; phallic?

WALES SUMMARY sites 277.......... Stones 348 number leaning 60 17.3%

APPENDIX 4   **35 STONES STILL EXTANT & seen from a distance or other reliable information**
               130 STONES LOST or DESTROYED
               75 STONES of STATUS not KNOWN - no reliable information

abreviations -

M - MARKED on ordnance survey map	EX extant
NM - NOT MARKED on ordnance survey map	SD seen from distance
CArch - COUNTY ARCHAEOLOGIST	L lost or destroyed
	NF not found
some Stones are not prehistoric and the list cannot be comprehensive	NV not visited
	P photo

no. of STONE	date	STONE /SITE name etc	COUNTY	Grid Ref on OS map	OS map no.	sources of info	STATUS today	

36 STONES EXTANT

no. of STONE	date	STONE /SITE name etc	COUNTY	Grid Ref	OS map no.	sources	STATUS today	
7	21/7/98	in GLEANN DROIGHEACH	ISLAY	NR211594	60 M	OS map	EX	SD inacessible; seen over peat bog
8	20/9/98	south from STRONE CROFT	JURA	NR508638	61 M	OS map	EX	SD seen from Strone; difficult access
9	20/9/98	near SANNAIG old croft	JURA	NR518649	61 M	OS map	EX	SD seen across impassable forestry
11	23/9/98	GLEN MUCKLACH,	ARGYLL	NR703124	68 M	OS map	EX	SD inaccessible across impenetrable gorse
27	8/4/00	nr DOLFALLT Fm Randirmwyn	CARMARTHEN	SN794431	147 M	OS map	EX	NV small 0.75m. Stone - farmer information
69	1/3/99	above NANTY-MOCH RESEVOIR	DYFED	SN783895	135 M	OS map	EX	SD 2 Stones difficult access; another nearby marked on OS map not seen
97	2/6/01	EAST CLYTH Caithness	HIGHLAND	ND295396	11 NM	CArch	EX	SD 2 small stones seen across heather
101	6/9/01	THE DOON FORT Isle of Arran	ARGYLL	NR886292	66 M	OS map	EX	SD P; seen from distance; rough walk
103	8/9/01	south from PORTAVADIE Cowal	ARGYLL	NR931684	62 M	OS map	EX	SD 2 Stones marked; difficult rough walk
104	3/10/01	DOD`S COURSE St Ledgerwood	BORDERS	NT582464	74/73 M	OS map	EX	NF not found in forestry
105	May `01	CLACH an TEAMPAIL, Taransay	WEST. ISLES	NB013008	18 M	OS map	EX	NV farmer information; difficult island access
114	9/9/01	THE CAMP STONE Callender	PERTH	NN700061	57 M	OS map	EX	NF farmer information; not found in forestry
123	13/10/02	BEARDOWN MAN	DARTMOOR	SX598796	191 M	OS map	EX	NV information estate office; dangerous walk
124	19/5/02	BEN DORRERY	CAITHNESS	ND060550	11 M	OS map	EX	SD steep stiff climb
125	19/5/02	ACHNACLY Broubster village	CAITHNESS	ND044599	11 M	OS map	EX	SD seen across swamp; small stone
(126	17/5/02	Isle of SWITHA in Scapa Flow	ORKNEY	ND362907	7 M	OSmap	EX	NV) easily seen from passing boat - info from
(		" " "	"	ND365910	M		EX	NV) local boatman
136	22/6/02	ACHNACLY WEST st, Broubster	CAITHNESS	ND045599	11 M	OS map	EX	SD smaller st in rough area
138	26/6/02	KNOCKRAICH Fintry	STIRLINGshire	NS609878	64 M	OS map	EX	SD revist
145	3/9/02	DRUMFOURS, Muir of Fowlis	ABERDEENshr	NJ561110	37 M		EX	P; lies uprooted beside silage pit; PNK
(147	2/9/02	NEWTON of AUCHINCLECH	ABERDEENshr	NJ828088	38 NM		EX	SD) P; PNK - rubbing post? small conical
(		nr Kirton of Skene						) stone; seen driving past
152	5/9/02	DRUM STONE nr Kirton of Skene	ABERDEENshr	NJ811100	38 M	OS map	EX	SD small tower not a Stone (as marked!)
153	29/10/01	BRAENEIL nr Kemnay	ABERDEENshr	NJ721123	38 M		EX	SD small uninteresting stone
154	11/3/03	EAST CLYTH nr Bruan	CAITHNESS	ND295396	12 NM		EX	SD two small uninteresting Stones
166	12/4/03	MEADOWFIELD, nr Auldearn	MORAY	NH931549	27 M	OS map	EX	P row of 4 small stones; PNK uninteresting
171	10/6/03	HELLIAR HOLM isle of Shapinsay	ORKNEY	ND484153	6 M	OS map	EX	SD large prominent stone cairn;
186	19/4/04	CAIRNTRADLIN 2 nr Blackburn	ABERDEENshr	NJ816137	38 M	OS map	EX	SD small columnar stone - rubbing post?
190	1/7/00	DOLFALLT farm Rhandirmcwyn	DYFED	SN974431	147 M	OS map	EX	NV info from farmer; small stone
191	30/8/03	MYNYDD MALLAEN Llandovery	DYFED	SN734447	147 M	OS map	EX	SD quartz stone; long rough walk
174	10/6/03	GRUMMORE nr Altnahara	SUTHERLAND	NC603366	16 M	OS map	EX	SD small Stone on hillside; not visited
210		CARFUNG MENHIR Tredinnick	CORNWALL	SW440340	203 NM		EX	SD 3.0m. Pillar inaccessible in undergrowth
211		near NANT-y-MOCH resevoir	GWYNNED	SH784896	135 M	OS map	EX	SD isolated, difficult acess
(192	29/4/04	LEYLODGE 1 near Kintore	ABERDEENshr	NJ613129	38 M	OS map	EX	SD) two small uninteresting stones
(193	20/4/04	LEYLODGE 2 near Kintore	ABERDEENshr	NJ763133	38 M	OS map	EX	SD) two small uninteresting stones
205	21/7/98	on CARN MOR Islay	ARGYLL	NR224606	60 M	OS map	EX	SD too far to see any detail

130 STONES LOST or DESTROYED

no. of STONE	date	STONE /SITE name etc	COUNTY	Grid Ref	OS map no.	sources	STATUS today	
1	1/7/97	GIANT`S STONE, Bisley	GLOS	SO918062	163 M	OS map	L	removed by farmer c. 1990
2	1/7/98	ODO & DODO Nottingham hill fort	GLOS	S0981289	163 NM	CArch	L	NF 2 Stones recorded but not found
3	1/7/98	nr WINDRUSH in valley bottom	GLOS	SP191138	163 NM	CArch	L	NF
4	19/9/98	BAILLE THARBHACH	ISLAY	NR363677	60 M	OS map	L	NF P; site visited, no Stones, complex site
12	12/8/97	LONG STONE, Sandy Haven	PEMBROKE	SM848084	157 M	OS map	L	NF 3 searches - now lost
(14	30/3/97	WESTERN COMMON 2 stones	EXMOOR	SS7267371	180 M	CArch	L	NF) lost - searched for 3 times
(		Near Simmonsbath		SS729368	M	CArch	L	NF) without success - both lost
17	30/1/99	LONGSTONE FIELD west end of	GOWER	SS421924	159 M	CArch	L	Famer says not there
18	30/1/97	COETY GREEN west end of	GOWER	SS426910	159 NM	CArch	L	NF
19	30/1/99	west of HENLYS	GOWER	SS443843	159 NM	CArch	L	lost - info from farmer
32	1/6/99	BURN of FORSCPAPIL Yell	SHETLAND	HP537042	1 NM	CArch	L	NF cannot find it - now removed?
34	2/6/99	nr cairns on STACKABERG Fetlar	SHETLAND	HU616928	1 NM	CArch	L	NF cannot find them
37	2/6/99	GALLOW HILL Mainland	SHETLAND	HU392141	4 NM	CArch	L	NF may be 3 stones here
41		SAITH MEAN above Llanwithwl	POWYS	SN949603	147 M		L	NF not seen/found - 3 searches
42		ST nr Saith Mean Llanwithwl	POWYS	SN954606	147 M		L	NF not seen/found - 3 searches
49	1/6/00	LITTLE HILL nr Llandrindod Wells	POWYS	SO071594	147 M		L	NF area searched

50	1/6/00	CARREGWIBER Llan`dod Wells	POWYS	SO084598	147 M			L		destroyed by farmer c. 1987
53	1/6/00	LLANYBYTHER on Banc Melyn	DYFED	SN543396	146 NM			L	NF	should be beside cross-roads
56	4/2/97	nr DORSTONE beside B4348	HEREFORD	SO305422	161 NM	CArch		L	NF	searched for 3 times
58	21/6/05	GLYNSAITHMEAN - WEST ST	PEMBROKE	SN112303	145 M			L	NF	searched for 3 times
59	21/6/05	GLYNSAITHMEAN - EAST ST	PEMBROKE	SN115305	145 M			L	NF	searched for 3 times
60	21/6/05	nr YSTRAD AERON	DYFED	SN518562	146 NM			L		
61	7/7/00	BRYN Y MEAN nr Tregaron	DYFED	SN635572	146 NM			L	NF	difficult search area
62	20/6/05	BICTON nr St Ishmeals	PEMBROKE	SM848084	157 M			L	NF	searched for 3 times - lost?
63	20/6/05	SANDY HAVEN	PEMBROKE	SN736447	157 NM	CArch		L	NF	searched for - lost?
64	1/6/00	MEAN DEWI Puncheston	PEMBROKE	SN006294	157 NM	CArch		L	NF	searched for - lost? In garden?
68	1/3/00	beside LLYN NNANNTYCAGL	DYFED	SN729908	135 NM	CArch		L	NF	site seen from road - no stone
78	1/6/00	MEANGWYN HIR Nr Llanfrynach	DYFED	SN238302	145 NM	AStW		L	NF	
79	1/6/00	LLANFIHANGEL church nr Rogiet	MONMOUTH	ST448876	171 NM	AStW		L	NF	AStW no167; area searched
80	1/6/00	FOUR CROSSES, nr Aerbech	GWENT	SH400389	123 M	AStW		L	NF	searched area; AStW no172
82	1/6/00	DOL GARREG Llangadfan	CLYWD	SH974119	125 NM	AStW		L	NF	not found in open fields
84	16/5/01	Isle of VATERSAY Barra	WEST. ISLES	NL640940	31 NM	CArch		L		lost - info from Farmer
94	18/5/01	ACHMORE Lewis	WEST. ISLES	NB308299	13 NM	CArch		L	NF	not seen on rough hillside
96	16/5/01	HEISHIVAL on Vatersay, Barra	WEST. ISLES	NL643958	31 NM	CArch		L	NF	
109	26/7/01	LEY FARM Fordyce	GRAMPIAN	NJ536639	29 M			L	NF	info from farmer`s son
120	19/5/01	CLACH STEIN Eye, Lewis	WEST. ISLES	NB516311£	8 M	OS map	L		NF	not found after 2 searches
132	18/5/01	RANGAG (off east sidE OF A9	CAITHNESS	ND184452	12 M			L		farmer says now lost
140	19/7/02	near TERALLY, Drumore, Mull of	GALLOWAY	NX123414	82 M			L	NF	not found at site
143	19/7/02	KNOCKINAAM lodge Port Patrick	GALLOWAY	NX028524	82 M			L	NF	apparently lost; site now a silage pit
148	2/9/02	AUCHINCLECH, Kirton of Skene	ABERDEENshr	NJ828092 *	M	OS map	L		NF	* map 38
151	5/9/02	MUIR of KINELLAR nr Blackburn	ABERDEENshr	NJ817139	38 M	OS map	L		NF	
162	9/4/03	GREENHILLS Coldwells	ABERDEENshr	NK097401	30 M	OS map	L			destroyed? Stump still in ground
164	9/4/03	HOWE nr Stuartfield	ABERDEENshr	NJ984416	30 M	OS map	L			farmer says disappeared recently
163	9/4/03	STONE CROSS at TARFSIDE	ANGUS	NO484799	44 M	OS map	L		NF	NF on open hillside - not there
24	7/4/99	SENNYBRIDGE RANGES south	POWIS	SN921366	160 NM	CArch		L	NF	searched open moorland not there
28	8-88-99	FORTINGALL near Aberfeldy	PERTHSHIRE	NN732463	52 M	OS map	L		NF	stated tumulus & small flat stone
166	25/4/03	MONREITH HOUSE Monreith	GALLOWAY	NX335642£	83 M	OS map	L		NF	2 sculptured sts marked - not found
71	1/3/99	disused mine near Devil`s Bridge	DYFED	SN722746	135 NM	CArch		L	NF	cannot be seen; circle large sts
71	1/3/99	LLETHR near Ysbyty Ystwyth	DYFED	SN742702	135 NM	CArch		L	NF	
72	1/3/99	BRON CARADOG, Tynygrad	DYFED	SN694702	135 NM	CArch		L		info from farmer
74	19/2/01	BEDD GWYL ALTYD nr Brecon	POWYS	SN978267	160 NM	AStW		L	NF	open hill - not there
75	19/2/01	on TREATH MAWR nr Brecon	POWYS	SN903256	160 NM	CArch		L	NF	error in grid ref; 2 small stones PnK
168	8/5/03	WHITTONDEAN, Rothbury	NORTHUMB'LD	NU062003	81 M	OS map	L		NF	
169	3/7/03	BAMPTON COMMON Haweswatr	CUMBRIA	NY490162	90 M	OS map	L		NF	not found on open hillside
183	1/6/00	CARREGWIBER,LlandrindodWells	POWYS	SO094599	147 M	OS map	L			destroyed b farmer c. 1985; 2 stones
184	18/4/04	LONGREENS FARM nr Dyce	ABERDEENshr	NJ917147	38 M	OS map	L		NF	
185	18/4/04	CAIRNTRADLIN 1 nr Blackburn	ABERDEENshr	NJ824137	38 M	OS map	L			stated by farmer lost over 20 years ago
187	19/4/04	EAST BALHALGARDY nr Inverurie	ABERDEENshr	NJ760243	38 M	OS map	L		NF	farmer says fell down in 3 pieces 1999
188	19/4/04	CAMIES STONE nr Kintore	ABERDEENshr	NJ769179	38 M	OS map	L		NF	
189	20/4/04	above FOOT o` HILL nr Blackburn	ABERDEENshr	NJ838131	38 M	OS map	SD			glacial boulder
190	20/4/04	CLINTERTY HOME fm Blackburn	ABERDEENshr	NJ845150	38 M	OS map	L		NF	
191	20/4/04	SOUTH RUCHINLECH nr Westhill	ABERDEENshr	NJ828092	38 M	OS map	L		NF	
196	21/4/05	on SADDLEWORTH MOOR	DERBYSHIRE	SE037055	110 M	OS map	L		NF	searched for, not found
199		near Llandegley	POWYS	SO142612	148 M	OS map	L		NF	three searches
200		MEAN MELYN Llantbri	CARMARTHEN	SN347129	139 M	OS map	L?		NF	stated 2 m. high - not there
201		HENDY farm Llangain	CARMARTHEN	SN384149	139 M	OS map	L?		NF	should be in hedgerow

75 STONES of STATUS UNKNOWN

Stones in forestry & undergrowth are usually not found

reasons not known -   **NOT VISITED** (NV)   possibly because the site was **INACCESIBLE** (IN)

or   **the STONE was not FOUND**

	5	19/9/98	BIENN CHAM hill	ISLAY	NR349679	60 M	OS map	NK	IN	inaccessible - rough walk
	6	21/9/98	east of KILCHRIAN HOUSE	ISLAY	NR213605	60 M	OS map	NK	SD	inacessible across rough hill walk
	10	20/9/98	CURRAGH a` BHLINNE	JURA	NR511665	61 M	OS map	NK	IN	inacessible in forestry
#	16	30/1/99	in OLD WALLS village Gower	GOWER	SS486920	159 M	OS map	NK	NF	must be re-checked
#	23	7/4/99	north of LLANGENNY	POWYS	SO234188	161 M		NK	NF	in deep undergrowth, several searches
	30	21/7/98	CLACH an TIOMPAIN	ISLAY	NR338698	60 M	OS map	NK	IN	very long rough walk
#	31	1/6/99	SNARRA VOE Unst	SHETLAND	HP575021	1 NM	CArch	NK	IN	walk not attempted
#	33	1/6/99	in YELL NATURE RESERVE Yell	SHETLAND	HU487964	1 NM	CArch	NK	IN	alingment?; long rough walk
#	35	2/6/99	SOTERSTA Mainland	SHETLAND	HU261446	4 NM	CArch	NK	NV	
#	36	28/5/99	WHITE ST of TOUFIELD Mainland	SHETLAND	HU418373	4 M	OS map	NK	NV	long hill walk
#	39	20/6/99	HENDY near N	CARMARTHEN	SN384145	159 M	OS map	NK	NF	looked for it 3 times
#	43		MEAN-SERTH above Rhayder	POWYS	SN943699	147 M	OS map	NK	NF	I have searched 3 times for this
#	44		MEANGWYNGWEDDW Rhayder	POWYS	SN926706	147 M	OS map	NK	NF	I have searched 3 times for this
	45		DARREN Standing St	POWYS	SN911567	147 M	OS map	NK	NV	long hill walk; not visited
	46		MEAN CAM on Faned hill	POWYS	SN917558	147 M	OS map	NK	NV	long hill walk; not visited
	47		MEAN BACH on Mynydd Mallen	DYFED	SN731451	147 M	OS map	NK	NV	long hill walk; not visited
	48		MYNYDD MALLEN Standing St	DYFED	SN735447	147 M	OS map	NK	NV	long hill walk; not visited

#	51		above ABOECWMHIR	POWYS	SO048696	147 M	OS map	NK	NF	not found in forestry
	54	1/6/00	FFYNON IAGO nr Llanybyther	DYFED	SN548426	146 NM	CArch	NK	NF	may be difficult to find in houses
#	55	21/6/05	beside B4310	DYFED	SN513261	146 NM	CArch	NK	NF	supposed remains of 4 stone row
#	57		MEAN ELWYD on Twun Du	POWYS	SO228272	161 M	OS map	NK	NV	not visited; long hill walk
	77	19/2/01	nr FELINCAMLAIS, Mynnyd Illtud	POWYS	S0963254	160 NM	AStW			P; 2 small stones found of unknown status
(	83	16/5/01	Isle of SANDRAY Barra	WEST. ISLES	NF632920	31 NM	CArch	NK	NV	) did not visit this island
(			"		NF640904	NM	CArch	NK	NV	)
(			"		NF655910	NM	CArch	NK	NV	)
	85	16/5/01	isle of MINGUALAY Barra	WEST. ISLES	NL568835	31 NM	CArch	NK	NV	did not visit island
	86	16/5/01	GOIRTEN Barra	WEST. ISLES	NL633983	31 NM	CArch	NK	NV	not seen on open hill
#	87	16/5/01	SKALLARY above Bervaig, Barra	WEST. ISLES	NL688984	31 NM	CArch	NK	NF	re-check
	88	17/5/01	SLIGEANACH KILDONAN S Uist	WEST. ISLES	NF727286	22 M	OS map	NK	NF	not found in machair
	89	17/5/01	POLLACHAR, Adivachar S Uist	WEST. ISLES	NF745448	22 NM	CArch	NK	NF	not found in machair; grid error?
	90	18/5/01	ISLE of VALLEY North Uist	WEST. ISLES	NF770760	18 NM	CArch	NK	NV	
#	91	16/5/01	NA FIR BHEIGE North Uist	WEST. ISLES	NF887717	18 M	OS map	NK	NV	long rough walk
#	92	16/5/01	on MAARI North Uist	WEST. ISLES	NF864729	18 M	OS map	NK	NV	long rough walk
	95	16/5/01	CUL a` CHLEIT, Garynahine Lewis	WEST. iSLES	NB246303	13 M		NK	IN	across peat bog
	98	AUG /O1	GLEN AIRGH near Lochgilphead	ARGYLL	NR931981	55 M	OS map	NK	NV	difficult acess in forestry
	100	4/9/01	WALLACE`S STONE Ayr	AYRSHIRE	NS332166	72 M	OS map	NF		site searched
	106	6/9/01	CAOLAS Isle of Coll	HIGHLAND	NM122532	46 M	CArch	NK	NV	not looked for in machair - long walk
	107	27/4/00	CRAIGAIG, Isle of Ulva Mull	ARGYLL	NM402390	47 M	Rcahms	NK	NV	long walk
	108	28/4/00	MAOL MOR Dervaig Mull	ARGYLL	NM435530	47 M	RcahmS	NK	NV	in forestry; difficult to find
	110	30/7/01	CONEYHATCH on Kempstone hill	ABERDEEN	NO877895	45 M	OS map	NK	IN	2 sts marked; now in thick gorse
#	115	1/4/00	GLEN GORM FOREST Mull	ARGYLL	NM436531	47 M		NK	IN	in forestry - not searched for
	118	1/7/01	LAMINGTON nr Oyne	ABERDEEN	NJ661267	38 M		NK	IN	not found in thick gorse
	119	16/5/01	RUEVAL Benbecula	WEST. ISLES	NF826531	22 M		NK	NF	not seen on open hillside
#	121	19/5/01	CLACH MHUIRE Barhabas Lewis	WEST. ISLES	NB355518	8 M	OS map	NK	NF	in machair
	139	20/7/02	BLAIRBUIE, Montrieth	GALLOWAY	NX362415	83 M	OS map	NK	NV	in standing crop; revisit
(	131	18/5/01	nr HALSARY east of A9	CAITHNESS	ND177492	12 M		NK	NF	) in dense forest area - not looked for
(					ND177498	M		NK	NF	)
	133	17/5/02	BURNS of MUSETTER, Eday	ORKNEY	HY556329	5 M		NK	IN	not seen - acess across thick heather
	141	19/7/02	LONG TOM near Cairnryan	GALLOWAY	NX081719	76 M		NK	NV	in forestry - not searched for
	144	24/6/05	near CRAGAIG, Isle of Ulva	Isle of MULL	NM402390	48 M	OSmap	NK	NV	2 stones marked on OS map
	155	11/3/03	near HALSARY south of Mybster	CAITHNESS	ND178492	12 M	OS map	NK	NV	2 sts marked on map in thick forest
	166		on SHIEL HILL Glenquicken Moor	GALLOWAY	NX515586	83 M	OS map	NK		in forestry - not looked for
	170	16/5/03	SHIEL HILL near Creetown	GALLOWAY	NX515585	83 M	OS map	NK	IN	difficult acess & in forestry
	172	9Jun `03	near STRATHY - CROSS SLAB	SUTHERLAND	NC831650	10 M	OS map	NK		not looked for across peat cuttings
	173	10/6/03	on LEARABLE HILL Kildonan	SUTHERLAND	NC892234	17 M	OS map	NK	NV	complex site not visited
	176	16/8/03	WHITE MOSS above Eskdale	CUMBRIA	NY172024	89/90 NM	A Burl	NK	NV	very rough walk
	177	29/8/03	PACKET STONE, on Long Mynd	SHROPSHIRE	SO422913	137 M	OS map	NK	NV	
	178	29/8/03	CANTLIN STONE, in Clun Forest	SHROPSHIRE	SO202870	137 M	OS map	NK	NV	
	179	29/8/03	CWM-BEDW, above Abbycwmhir	POWIS	SO049696	136 M	OS map	NK	NV	
	180	29/8/03	CARREG WEN in Hafren Forest	DYFED	SN830885	136 M	OS map	NK	NV	
	181	29/8/03	TALYWERN, nr Machynelleth	POWIS	SH827005	136 M	OS map	NK	NV	needs re-check
	182	29/8/03	in valley of AFON MYDDGEN	GWYNEDD	SN874895	135 M	OS map	NK	NV	re-visit
	184	5/9/03	STANDARD ST, on Culross Moor	FIFE	NS954872	70 M	OS map	NF	NF	not found in forestry
	185	10/9/03	THREE KINGS in Redesdale	NORTH`b`LAND	NT774009	80 M	Burl/OS	NK	NV	not looked for in forestry
	186	11/9/03	MAEN ELWYD near Crickhowell	POWYS	SO227272	161 M	OS map	NK	NV	long rough walk
	187	13/9/03	on DARREN HILL north of Beulah	POWYS	SN911567	147 M	OS map	NK	NV	inaccessible; 2 sts marked
	188	13/9/03	MEAN CAM on Fanfed hill Beulah	POWYS	SN917558	147 M	OS map	NK	NV	long rough walk
	189	30/8/03	CEFN CNWCHIETHINOG	DYFED	SN757497	147 M	OS map	NK	NV	long rough walk
	192	30/8/03	MAEN BACH on Mynydd Mallaen	DYFED	SN734451	147 M	OS map	NK	NV	long rough walk
	193	18/4/04	LOCH GREENS Farm nr Dyce	ABERDEENshr	NJ971147	38 M	OS map	L	NF	searched for
	194	21/4/05	PANCAKE Stone, Ilkley Moor	W YORKshire	SE134463	104 M	OS map	NK	NV	
	195	21/4/05	DABGER Stone, Ilkley Moor	W YORKshire	SE114461	104 M	OSmap	NK	NV	
	196	21/4/05	on SADDLEWORTH Moor	DERBYSHIRE	SE037055	110 M	OSmap	NF	NV	rough walk; not seen
	198		near Llangenny	POWYS	SO236188	161 M	OSmap	NK	NF	not found in dense undergrowth
	220		near Llanwthwl	POWYS	SN955606	147 M	OS map	NK	NV	
	221		in forestry near Abbeycwmhir	POWYS	SO048696	147 M	OS map	NK	NV	

APPENDIX 5   OTHER STONES not included as 'standing stones'

many of these Stones & other monuments are of uncertain provenance & age
some circles & dolmens are included

stone no.	date	SITE & COUNTY	OS map no.	grid ref	altitude	total Sts at site	St no.	height	photo #	Age etc. Not Dressed or Dressed	COMMENT etc.
		ENGLISH STONES									
(1	31/3/98	on HOWL MOOR N. Yorks	94	SE818984	205	2	1	1	#	N PnK	) 2 small Stones in stonefield
(							2	1		N PnK	) which are clearly different
(2	1/4/98	JENNIE BRADLEY N. Yorks	94	NZ612022	425	2	1		#	D M	) dated 1838
(							2	1		D	) small St at base
3	2/4/98	BLAKEY RIDGE N. Yorks	94	SE695935	325	1		1.5	#	PnK	cobbled surround suggest antiquity
	20/5/97	transferred to Standing Stones 1189									
5	23/5/97	DODDINGTON MOOR Northub'land	75	NT984367	100				#	PH	spectacular Cup & Ring Marks
6	10/7/97	ARTHUR'S STONES Hereford	161	SO319431	280				#	PH	burial chamber c. 3000-2000BC?
7	10/7/97	WILLMARSH Stones Hereford	161	SO342402	150	6		1.5	#	N PnK	6 large cuboidal stones; clearly moved
8		error	161	SN670224				actual stone is nearby			
10	7/5/98	EDGERLY Stone Exmoor	180	SS720408	410	1		1.8	#	D M	County & parish boundry markc. 1675
15	21/2/99	GLEN MINE Cornwall	203	SW502371	200	1		1.5	#	N PnK	listed by CountyArcheaologist - boulder?
16	14/11/99	on CROUSE COMMON Cornwall	204	SW775201	105	1		1.8	#	N PnK	probably 'rubbing posts'
17	15/11/99	Cornish granite gatepost	201	SX232689	200	1		1.5	#	D LL	now free standing gatepost
18	15/11/99	KING DONIERT's Stone Cornwall	201	SX237689			transferred to Standing stones 510					Cornwall England
19		deleted - just a boulder									
20	1/4/00	WEST MIDDLETON Fm Exmoor	180	SS649458	240 c. 30				#	N PH	complex setting ofc. 40 small stones up to o.8m.
		no 23									
39	13/10/01	BLACKATON Cross Dartmoor	20	SX571631	270	1		1.7	#	D M	medieval Cross somewhat damaged
43	16/3/02	WRITTEN ST Longridge Lancs	102	SD625379	130	1			#	D LL	lies flat 2.8 metres; inscribed
55	29/5/02	ELSDON GREEN Northumberland	80	NY936933	165	1		NA	#	M	bear-baiting stone on village green
56	29/5/02	PERCY'S LEAP Northumberland	81	NU050199	90	2			#	N PnK	site of battle
64	21/7/02	CALNE Millenium St Wilts	173	SU007700	115	1		1	#	N Mod	erected 2000
65	21/7/02	GREY WETHERS off A4 Wilts	173	SU700034	115	++			#		part of large sarsen stonefield
67	22/9/02	BELSTONE jubilee stone Dartmoor	191	SX620936	300	1		2.1	#	D Mod	jubilee 1977 & millenium 2000
69	22/6/05	BISLEY Cross Gloucestershire	163	SO982066	255	1		1.5	#	N M	Saxon Cross, damaged; not my photos
70	19/3/03	on DOUGLAS RIDGE N York Moor	100	SE502952	265	1		1.5	#	D LL	fallen; gate post or boundary mark
(71	19/3/03	BILSDALE east moor N York Moor	100	SE611953	335	5	1	0.7	#	D LL	) 5 boundary marks 17th or 18th centuary ?
(		"		SE611956	345		2	1	#	D LL	) set in almost straight line at c. 350 degrees
(		"		SE608959	340		3	1.25	#	D LL	) for 2km across the moor
(		"		SE608961	350		4	1.4	#	D LL	) considerable weathered erosion of summit
(		"		SE606973	400		5	1.25	#	D LL	)
71A	20/3/03	STUMP CROSS Todd Intake NYM	94	SE606982	410	1		0.7	#	D LL	) broken column set into stone plinth
72	31/3/03	KIT BROW, Galgate Lancashire	102	SD491565	30	1		1.6	#	D LL	stone gatepost left in middle of field
76	23/4/03	SEDBERGH millenium st Cumbria	98	SD003919	110	1		2.4	#	D Mod	erected 2000; sculptures S & W sides
79	18/5/03	INGLE Stone Campbeltown Argyll	83	NX660533	80	1					large erratic glacial boulder
84	15/8/03	KEMP HOWE, Shap, CUMBRIA	90	NY567132	270	6		max1.1	#	N PH	ruined circle of glacial boulders
86	15/8/03	THREE SHIRES St CUMBRIA	90	NY276028	393	1		1.5	#	D LL	inscribed, dated 1816
87	5/9/03	Roman milestone, Northumberland	80	NY911815	300	1		1.9	#	D	TRANSFERRED to Standing Stones ; fallen
89	17/8/03	GREAT URSWICK Cumbria	96	SD262745	50				#	N PH	burial chamber
90	15/8/03	MOOR DIVOCK,Askham Cumbria	90	NY499220	235	9		max0.7	#	N PH	9 squat stones of ruinous Cairn Circle
93	30/9/03	COMPTON BEACHAMP OXON	174	SU282868	140	1		2.3	#	D	1950 war memorial
94	13/4/04	HANGMAN'S st Lambourn BERKS	174	SU320812	185	1		1	#	N PNK	small uninteresting Stone
95	17/4/04	BOLAM CROSS Co DURHAM	93	NZ207225	190	1		2.8	#	D M	weathered & damaged
104	7/7/04	CANTLIN Stone, west SHROPshire	137	NS203870	485	1			#	D M	concrete modern monumental pillar
105	26/7/04	HANGMAN'S st Boxford, BERKS	174	SU431784	120	1		0.7	#	N PnK	small uninteresting St
108		no stone for this number									
109	28/9/04	CULNAKIRK Drumnadrochit Invern's	26	NH499311	200	1		fallen	#	PH	cup marks; fallen Standing Stone?
111	21/4/05	SWASTIKA St Ilkley Moor W York	104	SE096470	330	1		NA	#	NA PH	carved into natural outcrop
112	22/4/05	ARBOR LOW henge Derbyshire	119	SK160636	370	50		NA	#	N PH	impressive henge & prostrate circle
113	21/4/05	NINE STANDARDS Cumbria	91	NY825066	600	9		?	PC		dry st columns on summit; not visited
114	21/4/05	CURSING STONE museum Carlisle	85	NY397562	30	1		1.8	PC	D 2000	polished granite boulder with curse
117	24/8/05	CASTLERIGG circle, CUMBRIA	90	NY291237	215				#	N	stone CIRCLE
118	13/4/06	BRATTON CAMP, Bratton WILTS	184	ST901517	210	1			#	N 2000	commemorates Ethandune 878
119	14/4/06	nr MARK CAUSEWAY, Somerset	182	ST360481	5	1		1.5	#	D M	isolated gatepost in field
120		no enrty for this number									
121	16/8/97	GREAT ST, High Bentham, Lancs.	98	SD671663	280	1		5	#	N	large glacial boulder
122	16/3/97	NINE STONES circle, Dorset	194	SY610904	110	9		2.1	#	N PH	magnificent Stone circle
123	23/2/97	HEATHER BRAE West Cornwall	203	SW451362	190	1		2	#	N LL	modern stone; looks like PH stone
124	22/10/96	STANTON DREW circle Somerset	172	ST601633	40			2.4	#	N PH	see Cove Sts drawing 19
125	21/2/97	CORK STONE Derbyshire	119	SK245626	310	1		6		N	windworn natural feature
126	5/3/97	FERNWORTHY Dartmoor Devon	191	SX265082	380	1			#	N PH	circle of small stones
127	25/8/97	CORBY CRAGS Northumberland		TRANSFERRED to Standing Stones England, Northumberland 145								
128	30/9/03	AVEBURY West Kennet Avenue	173	SU109603	190	1		2.6	#	N PH	outlier in the Avenue
132	9/5/98	BRAMDEAN memorial sts Hants.	185	SU630271	90				#	N LL	circle of sarsen trilithons, late 19th. Century
133	19/6/06	MEMORIAL St, Anstey Common	181	SS840297	355	1		2.2	#	N Md	inscribed; erected 1937
134	1/7/06	SARSENS in garden nr Arundel Sx	197	SU943068	15	6			#	N LL	erected 2000 by O. Swarbrick
138	11/9/06	HIGHER TOWN St.Martin, Scilly	203	SV933154	10 NA				#		LL	horticultural settings
139	12/9/06	MEMORIAL St, Hayle Cornwall	203	SW559373	5	1		1.6	#	D Md	commemorates New York death in2001
140	12/9/06	KING ARTHUR'S Stone Cornwall	200	SX110857	210	1		3	#	D M	fallen by river;c. AD 540; Ogham marks

No	Date	Name	Map	Grid	Alt	Count		Ht	#	D/N	Type	Comment
141	12/9/06	medieval CIDER PRESS Cornwall	200	SX110857	210	1			#	D	M	
142	15/9/06	HAYTOR TRAMWAY Dartmoor	191	SX769776	350	1		1.7	#	D	LL	Granite tramway built 1820 & Standing Stone
148	20/4/07	Nine Stones Close Derbyshire	119	SK227627	270	4		2	#	N	PH	ruined circle

SCOTLAND

No	Date	Name	Map	Grid	Alt	Count		Ht	#	D/N	Type	Comment
13	24/6/98	KIRKTON of KINOLDRUM Angus	53	NO317541	240	1		1.3	#	N	PH	TRANSFERRED to Standir]
19	28/5/99	FOULA Shetland	4	HT071389	10	1		0.6	#	N	PnK	originally 2 sts; one moved & lost in burn
22	29/4/01	stone fence posts on South Uist	31	NF765141	5	3			#	D	LL	look like Standing Stones;erected c. 1900
23	1/5/01	BERNERAY slipway North Uist	18	NF914799	5	1			#	D	Mod	modern (c 2000?) to comemorate new ferry
24	3/5/01	GLEN SHADER, Sirdar, Lewis	24	NB396536	10	1			#	N	PnK	glacial boulder, but standing up
25	31/5/01	REAY village Caithness	11	NC959645	25	1			#	N	M	damaged market cross; moved from Old Reay
26	31/5/01	ACHVARSADAL H`se Caithness	11	NC983647		1			#	N	PH	fallen, 3.6 meters on ground
27	1/6/01	HILL o` MANY STANES Caith`ss	11	ND394383	100	c200			#	N	PH	complex setting of c. 200 small Stones
28	1/6/01	GREY CAIRNS,Camster,Caith`ss	11	ND260455	110				#		PH	2 large chambered rock cairns, restored
29	28/6/01	CLACH OSSIAN Sma`glen Perth	52	NN895306	210	1		2.1	#	N		large cuboidal glacial bouldere
30	25/6/01	GIBBET Stone Aboyne Grampian	44	NO569999	160	1		1	#	D	M	now cemented into garden wall
31	26/7/01	SHEEP PARK Aberdeen	29	NJ604504	90	3			#	N	PH	probably ruined recumbent circle
32	29/7/01	KIRKTON of BOURTIE Aberdeen	38	NJ800241	155				#	N	PH	ruined recumbent circle
33	28/7/01	CARLIN STONE Turriff, Grampian	29	NJ674466	140	1						large boulder, not St St
34	29/7/01	PEATHILL Inverurie Aberdeen	38	NJ821191	90	1			#	N	LL	erected 2000; dug up in garden;scratch marks
35	29/7/01	EASTER AQUHORTHIES Aberdeen	38	NJ732209	170				#	N	PH	recumbent stone circle, all complete
36	10/8/01	CLACH CHIARIN Ardnamurchan	47	NM560619	5	1		1.8	#	D	PH	Christianised PH StSt & chambered toomb
37	9/9/01	SAMSON`S STONE Perth	57	NN604078	150	1			#	N		seen from distance; probably glacial boulder
38	4/10/01	LADY LILLIARD`S St Borders	74	NT619275	170				#		LL	19C memorial to Battle of Ancrum Moor 1545
40	24/11/01	near MOSSTOWER Borders	74	NT722268	100				#		LL	memorial slab dated 1645 & 1860
41	23/11/01	GIRDLESTANE Tayside	54	NO528498	115	1			#	D	PH	cup & ring marks; used as boundary stone?
42	21/11/00	MARTIN`S STONE Tayside	54	NO385375	150	1		0.7		D	LL	uninteresting
47	22/4/02	INVER MEADALE Skye Highland	32	NG388352	120	1		2	#	N	M	probably erected when road widened
48	25/4/02	BARVAS CEMETARY Lewis	8	NB353517	30	c200	NA		#	N	PH	many small headstones - typical of area
49	26/5/02	BETTYHILL churchy`d Sutherland	10	NC715622	30	1+3		1.6	#	D	M	Celtic Cross & 3 small headstones?
(50	16/5/02	SNELSETTER Hoy Orkney	7	ND325887	20	3		1.4	#	N	PnK	) 3 sts on cliff edge listed as possible arch-
(	"							1.9	#	N	PnK	) ealogical sts, but are probably fencing posts
(	"							1.5	#	N	PnK	) of local stone
51	18/5/02	DEEPDALE, Mainland Orkney	6	ND271116	40	1		1.2	#	N	PnK	probably fencing post
52	27/4/02	CARN nam FIANN Ross/Cromarty	21	NH631742	220	C			#	N	PH	possible remains of ring cairn
53	18/5/02	nr STROMENESS Orkney	6	HY265151	10	1		1.6	#	N	PnK	gatepost; shows it similar to smaller St Sts
54	18/5/02	LUNGA FIONA Stromness Orkney	6	HY254155	60	6		1.5	#	N	PnK	fencing posts?
(57	22/6/02	FIELD BOUNDARIES Caithness	12	ND218648	12	3	1		#	N	LL	) typical traditional Caithness field
(	" "			ND102664			2		#	N	LL	) boundaries
(	" "			ND061638			3		#	N	LL	)
58	22/6/02	KYLE of TONGUE Sutherland	10	NC556591	10	1		2.7	#	N	PH	probable St St - see drawing
59	24/6/02	PRICESS St Glenferness Invern`s	27	NH937427	180	1		1.3	#	D	M	sculptured stone, much weathered
60	24/6/02	RODNEY`S St Brodie Cst Forres	27	NH984577	20	1		1.5	#	D	M	moved; Celtic cross & sculpture
61	26/6/02	AVIEMORE Grampian	36	NH897135	220	circle		1.5	#	N	PH	C - ring cairn, double circle; many sts lost
62	22/7/02	St MARGARET`S St Dumfermline	65	NT109850		1			#	N	PH	cupmarks; moved; glacial boulder
63	17/7/02	Wren`s Egg & circle Galloway	83	NX361420	30				#	N	PH	ruined circle
66	2/9/02	Corsedardan Hill, Aboyne Aberdeen	37	NO597940	37	1		2.2	#	N	LL	millenium Stone
68	20/10/02	Park House, Peterculter Aberdeen	38	NO780977	40	1			#	N	M	Pictish symbols, much weathered & new stone
73	11/4/03	HUNTLY Square Grampian	29	NJ529400	120	2			#	N	M	2 small symbol sts, no symbols visible
74	12/4/03	UPPER MANBEEN, Elgin, Moray	28	NJ188577	65	1		0.9	#	N	M	symbols not easily recognised as Pictish
75	12/4/03	MEADOWFIELD Auldearn Moray	27	NH931459	30	4			#	N	PnK	row of 4 smaller sts & nearby cairn
79	18/5/03	Ingle Stone, Twynholm Galloway	83	NX660533	60	1						large glacial boulder; seen from distance
80	28/4/03	KNOCK nr Torphicen Lothians	65	NS991713	280	1		1.3	#	N	Mod	on spoil heap; modern circle 50m. South
81	7/6/03	isle of AUSKERY ORKNEY	5	HY672164	10	1		2.2	#	N	LL	quarried & set up c. 1980 by island owner
(82	9/6/03	NORTH RONALLDSAY ORKNEY	5	HY750530	5	2	1		#		LL	) square cairn; both built of flat sandstone
(							2		#		LL	) conical cairn; slabs; significance not clear
85	16/5/03	NEWTON burial chamberGalloway	83	NX550525	25	4						
88	5/9/03	REFUGE St Torphichen Lothian	65	NT991728	290	1		0.7	#	D	M	with Lorraine cross; now set in wall
97	18/4/04	TEMPLE STONES Aberdeen	38	NJ953164	75		NA			N	?	marked; large group of boulders
98	18/4/04	in DYCE CHURCH Aberdeen	38	NJ876154	60	3			#	D	M	magnificent Pictish Stones inside ruined church
99	21/6/04	Druidsfield, Montgarrie, Aberdeen	37	NJ589178	140	2			#	N	PH	marked as "remains of circle"
100	3/6/04	by SCALPAY BRIDGE West` Isles	14			1		1.6	#	N	M	by new road & bridge
101	7/6/04	Knockan visitor centre Wester Ross	15	NC189091	230	1		2.1	#	N	M	erected 2001; prehistoric Stones were `found`
102	8/6/04	CUAIG nr Applecross Wester Ross	24	NG702571	50	1			#	N		could be erected to make a St St
103	7/6/04	nr BADRALLACH Wester Ross	19	NH075916	55	1		1.1	#	N		glacial boulder? Which looks like a St St
109	28/9/04	CULNAKIRK INVERNESSshire	26	NH499311	200	1		NA	#	N		cup marks on flat stone
110	1/10/04	HELIARHOLM ORKNEY	6	HY483153	25	1			#		M	dry stone pillar on ruined cairn
115	3/6/05	nr ARMOLICH, Moidart, HIGHLAND	40	NM721712	60	2	1 ?		#	N	PnK	2 small sts
129	22/6/98	Courthill Stones Rattray Angus	53	NO184481	190	4			#	N	PH	4 large recumbent Stones, one broken
143	16/10/06	DWARFIE STONE Hoy, ORKNEY	7	HY243005	120	1			#	N	PH	large glacial boulder; internal chamber
144	19/10/06	DUN TELVE BROCH, Glenelg	33	NH834173	15				#		M	one of best examples of broch
145	7/3/07	FAIRY STONE, St. Fillians PERTH	51	NN698242	100	1		1.6	#	N		glacial boulder with 'fairy' legdens
25	31/5/01	REAY Cross, Caithness Highland	11	NC959645	25	1		1.25	#	D	M	medieval Cross provenance not known
27	1/6/01	HILL o` MANY STANES Caithness	11	ND394383	100	many			#	N	PH	Bronze Age chambered cairn covered in stone
28	11/6/01	Grey Cairns of Camster Caithness	11	ND260455	110				#		PH	chambered cairns; Neolithic
29	28/6/01	CLACH OSSIAN Sma` Glen Perth	52	NN895306	210	1		2.1	#	N		glacial boulder
30	25/6/01	GIBBET STONE Aboyne Aberdeen	37	NO566999	160	1			#			circular stone set into garden wall
31	26/7/01	Sheep Park, Aberchirder, Aberdeen	29	NJ604504	90	3			#	N	PH	ruined recumbent circle
32	29/7/01	Kirkton of Bourtie Aberdeen	38	NJ800241	155							
34	29/7/01	Peathill Farm, Inverurie Aberdeen	38	NJ821191	90	1		2.1	#	N	?	dug up in garden - a thrown down Stone?

No	Date	Name	Map	Grid				#	D/N	Type	Notes
22	29/4/01	fencing posts? S Uist West. Isles	31	NF765141	5	3				LL?	stone fencing post c. 1900
40	24/11/01	nr MOSSTOWER Eckford Borders	74	NT722268	100			#	D	LL	memorial stones dated 1645 & 1860
47	22/4/02	Invermeadale, Skye, Highland	32	NG388352	120	1	2	#	N	LL	commemorates road widening
48	25/4/02	Barbhas Uarach cemetary Lewis	8	NB353517	30			#		LL	Scottish gravestones 18 & 19 centuries
49	26/4/02	Celtic grave Bettyhill Sutherland	10	NC715622	10	1	1.6	#	D	M	fine carved Celtic gravestone & later ones
50	16/5/02	Snelsetter Hoy Orkney	7	ND325887	20	3	1.4-1.9	#	N	?	Standing Stones? Farmer says fence posts
51	18/5/02	Deepdale Stromness Orkney	6	ND271116	40	1	1.2	#	N	PnK	small stone - probably fence post
52	27/4/02	near Alness Ross & Cromarty	21	NH631742	220			#	N	PH	possiible ruined curb caim or burial chamber
53	18/5/02	Voy near Stromness Orkney	6	HY265151	10	1	1.6	#	N	?	gatepost or Standing Stones - they look alike
54	18/5/02	Lunga Fiona Hill, Stromness Orkney	6	HY254155	60	4	1.5	#	N	?	probably fencing posts
57	22/6/02	Wester Olrig, Castletown Caithness	12	ND218648	40	3		#	N	LL	traditional Orkney field boundary stones

WALES

No	Date	Name	Map	Grid				#	D/N	Type	Notes
146	21/4/07	OGMORE stepping stones GLAM.	170	SS882770	0			#	D	M?	40 cuboidal stepping stones; tidal area
147	21/4/07	St Brides stepping stones GLAM	170	SS882770	10			#	D	M?	17 stepping stones
14	29/1/99	KING ARTHURs STONE Gower	59	SS491906	150			#	N	PH	dolmen with huge capstone
9	5/8/97	near DEFYNNOG village Powys	161	SN939260	305	1					small uninteresting Stone in field bank
21	19/10/99	wall at GILLYDAN Gwynedd	124	SH693392	190			#		PNk	unusual wall structure - see attached letter
44	4/4/02	PANTYGLIEN nr Carmarthen	159	SN459218	70	1		#	N	PnK	moved c. 1990; listed by county Archaeologist
45	5/4/02	Hangstone Davey Haverfordwest	158	SM895147	90	1	0.8	#	N	PnK	moved; uninteresting
46	5/4/02	on Bed Morris Pembroke	145	SN038365	295	1	2.1	#	N	PnK	boundary inscription, graffiti & bench mark
91	16/9/03	WHILGARN Talgarreg DYFED	146	SN448851E	310			#	N	PH	circle of uncertain origin
92	18/9/03	BRYN-Y-MAEN,New Radnor Powis	148	SO167573	490	1		#	N		glacial boulder marked as Standing Stone
106	30/7/04	PILLAR of ELISEG LlangollenClywd	117	SJ203445	120	1	1.8	#	D	M	broken Cross, moved
107	30/7/04	nr LLANFERRES Bridge CLYWD	116	SJ202262	200	1	NA	#	N	LL	boundary stone from 1793
108	30/7/04	nr CAE COCH, Roewan, GWYEDD	115	SH734716	320	1	1.5	#	N	PnK	gatepost in wall;looks like a Standing Stone
130	18/9/99	on BEDD MORRIS Pembroke	145	SN038364	295	1		#	N	PnK	may have been raised by humans?
131	4/9/99	Carreg Sampson, Pembroke	157	SM848335	40		3	#	N	PH	dolmen with 6 understones & large capstone
135	5/7/06	in field Rhos Ymryson Powis	146	SN467505	280	1	0.7	#			small quartz boulder
137	2/9/06	STEPPING STONES on Anglesey	114	SH441648	0	28		#	N	M	28 cuboidal stones across tidal Afon Briant
146	21/4/07	Ogmore stepping stones Glamorgan	170	SS882770	30	40		#	N	?	40 cuboidal stepping stones scross tidal area
147	21/4/07	St Bride Major stepping stones Glm.	170	SS909758	20	20		#	N	?	25 stones

OTHER STONES etc.

No	Date	Name						#			Notes
83	3/8/03	INUKSUIT replica Winnipeg						#			replica in Winnipeg museum

ILLUSTRATIONS

The STONE of SETTER, EDAY, ORKNEY
15 May 2007 from South
4.3 metres   HY564372

Sketch 1, Stone of Setter, 4.3 metres, with large cracks
(934 Orkney HY564372)

CORRACHREE, Tarland near Aboyne ABERDEENSHIRE
3° Sept 2002 from South East. Has been broken, possibly by lightning strike
1.4 metres   NJ461047

Sketch 2, Corrachree, now 1.4 metres, broken probably by lightning strike
(992 Aberdeen NJ461047)

Sketch 3, Upper Fernoch Stone 2, 3.3 metres,
tall slim Stone with square cross-section
(185 Argyll NR729864)

Sketch 4 Midmar Kirk, 2.7 metres, leaning
pillar of red granite *(804 Aberdeen NJ699066)*

Sketch 5, Beckhampton Stones, sarsens both Stones 3.5 metres, at end of West Avebury
avenue *(111 Wiltshire SU088963)*

Sketch 6 Tulyes, 2.5 metres, with unfinished (?) holes on east & west sides *(116 Fife NT028855)*

Sketch 7   Easter Pitorthie Farm, 2.35 metres, with 33 cup marks on southside *(64 Fife NO500040)*

Sketch 8, The Hole Stone, 1.4 metres, penetrating hole 22cms diameter narrowing to 10 cms. in granite *(970 Galloway NX365557)*

LANGSTANE CROFT, Frotoft, Rousay ORKNEY 928
14° May 2002 from East
2.2 metres HX 404275

1.0 metre

GANSCLET SCHOOL, Thrumster, CAITHNESS:
1st June 2001 from North East
2.25 metres ND 338 447

Sketch 9, Langstone Croft, 2.2 metres, between public road and croft house *(928 Orkney HX404275)*

Sketch 10, Gansclett School, 2.3 metres, showing packing stones around a Slab *(720 Caithness ND338447)*

photo. 1 Wimblestone , 1.7 metres, triangular *(24 Somerset ST434585)*

photo. 2 near Woolacombe, 2.0 metres, unrecorded quartz Stone
stump *(1183 Exmoor SS465443)*

photo. 3 Park Neuk, four poster' *(204 Angus NO196515)*

photo. 4 Long Meg, 3.7 metres, pillar outlier to Stone circle
(132 Cumbria NY507372)

photo. 5 Boscowen Un, 2.7 metres, leaning quartz pillar at the centre of a stone circle
(1173 Cornwall SW412273)

photo. 6   Stontoiler, 3.8 metres, column beside ring cairn *(364 Argyll NM908290)*

photo 7 Cairnholy, up to 2.7 metres, tall forecourt Stones of burial chamber *(966 Galloway NX517538)*

photo 8. Maiden Stone, 3.3 metres, carved Pictish & Christian
Stone 8th. or 9th. century *(1036 Aberdeen NJ703248)*

photo 9. Tristan Stone, 2.5 metres, 6th. century mediaeval monument *(503 Cornwall SX112252)*

photo 10 Tryfflys Cross, 3.0 metre, carved tall column with Cross, dated 1712 *(602 Lleyn Peninsula Gwynedd SH526379)*

photo 11. Garth Farm, Stone 2.6 metre, erected 1999 as a 'joke' *(601 Gwynnedd (SH553422)*

photo 12 Ballymeanoch, up to 3.3 metres, complex Stone setting *(179 Kilmartin, Argyll NR834964)*

photo. 13 An Carra, 4.8 metres dominates the surrounding landscape *(669 South Uist, Western Isles NF770320)*

photo 14 Mean-Searth, Powys *(898, Powys SN943699)*

photo 16 Pen Mean Wern, Powys *(899 Powys SN863620)*

photo 15 Suainebost, 0.4 metre, small insignificant Stone 0.4 metre *(702 Lewis, Western Isles NB507638)*

photo 17 Stanton Drew cove Stones, 5, 3 & 1.6 metres *(19 Avon ST601631)*

photo 18   Pen Mean Wern , 1.6 metres, a quartz stump,   1.6 metres at 545 metres *(899 Powis SN863620)*

photo 19 The   Stones of Stenness, up to 5.5 metres, slabs *(942 Orkney HY306126)*

photo 20 Maeni Hirion Penhros Feilw, 2.8 &
2.8 metres, slabs *(260 Anglsey SH228809)*

photo 21 Llangoed, 2.0 metres long, large heavy Stone
leaning at 30° *(95 Powis SO124396)*

photo 22 Mottistone Long Stone, 3.8 metres with fallen stone at
base *(60 Isle of Wight SZ407842)*

photo 23 Lundin Links, 4.2, 5.2 & 5.5 metres, three unusual Stones *(66 Fife NO405026)*

photo 24 Merrivale Stone Row, 1.4 metres, blocking Stone *(653 & 654 Dartmoor, Devon SX655784)*

photo 25 Cat Stone, 1.5 metres high, cuboidal
(1094 Lothians NT149744)

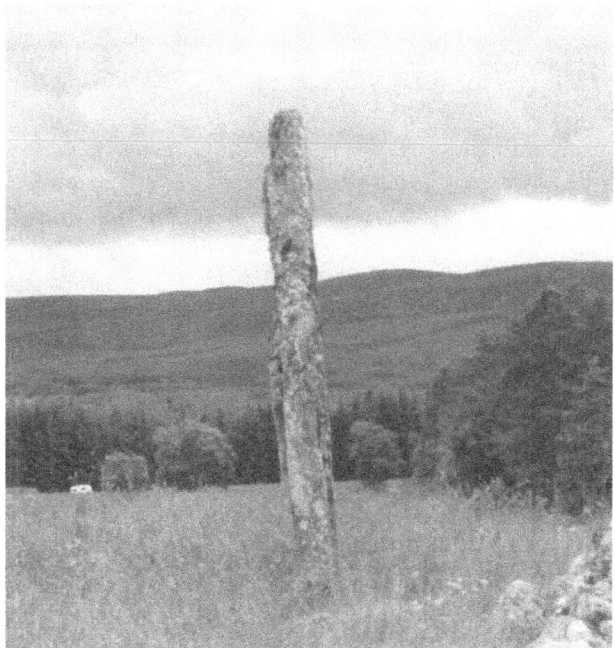

photo 26 a & b Mains of Gask , 3.1 metres, large slab   *(927 Highland NH679359)*

photo 27 Barnhouse, 3.5 metres & 0.3 metre thick *(937 Orkney HY312122)*

photo 28 Latheron, 1.9 metres with large split *(780 Caithness, Highland ND199338)*

photo 29 Creag-an-Tairbh Beg, now 1.75 metres, top of Stone 'blown down' in1879 leaving stump
(357 Argyll NM860016)

photo 30 Pipers granite west Stone, 4.0 metres with large splits *(319 Cornwall SW435247)*

photo 31 Tregwehelydd Mean Hir, 2.7 metres held together with bronze bands *(261 Anglsey SH341832)*

photo 32 a & b   Balinaby Stone, 5.4 metres, an elegant tall smooth dressed slab
(13 Islay, Argyll NR220672)

photo 33 Watlington Park, medieval (?) stone with hand cut grooves
(82 Northumberland NZ034842)

photo 34 Multiple grooves on the Queen's Stone
(415 Hereford SO561181)

photo 35 Machrie Moor, slab 4.0 metres high with grooves 3 metres above ground level *(840 Arran Argyll NR910325)*

photo 36 Fordell Stone, 2.0 metres with multiple deep weathered grooves , 2.0 metres *(113 Fife NT156844)*

photo 37 Castallack east Stone, 1.5 metres, a granite stump 1.5 metres with weathered summit *(284 Cornwall SW453254)*

photo 38 Sythfean Llwyndu, 2.75 metres, granite column with weathered furrow
(76 Carmarthen SN675244)

photo 39 Tresvennack Pillar, 3.7 metres, pillar with an east to west crack which needs conservation *(339 Cornwall SW442289)*

photo 40 Bogleys, sandstone 2.3 metres, short
grooves with square ends
(65 Fife NO296952)

photo 42 Yarberry Farm, 2.2 metres, weathered
limestone *(25 Somerset ST390578)*

photo 41 Largybeg Point, 0.9 & 1.0 metres, rough surface and deep uneven
furrow in sandstone *(838 Arran, Argyll NS053243)*

photo 43 Corby`s Crag boulder with one straight man-made groove *(145 Northumberland NU3011054)*

photo 44 Auchencorth Farm 1.8 metres, with no erosion on the S-W side *(865 Lothians Nt204567)*

photo 45 Easthill, 1.6 metres, with originally (?) horizontal groove *(735 Perth NN930124)*

photo 46 Fyfield Down, recumbent 'polishing stone' with five grooves
and axe (?) polishing area *(1187 Wiltshire SU128715)*

photo 47 Machrie Moor, recumbent 'polishing stone' with five grooves and axe (?) polishing area
(840 Arran, Argyll NR910325)

photo 48   Long Stone , 2.4 metres, oolitic Stone with two holes and much weathering *(136 Gloucester ST884999)*

photo 49   The Edderton Stone with Pictish carvings (including a salmon not shown) *(908 Ross & Cromarty NH709851)*

photo 50   Mean Addwynn, 3.0 metres, now built into a roadside wall by official vandalism *(296 Anglsey SH461833)*

photo 51   Medieval Stepping Stones over small tidal estuary *(Other Stones 137 Anglsey SH441648)*

photo 52   Tolvan Cross Stone , 1.6 metres, with hole 0.25 metre diameter through 0.3 metre of granite *(501 Cornwall SW706277)*

photo 53   The Picardy Stone , 2.0 metres, with Pictish carvings
(1013 Aberdeen NJ610303)

photo 54   Skeith Stone , 0.9 metre high, with wheel (?) carving *981 Fife NO571047)*

photo 55 Unexplained and undated setting of 40 stones up to 0.8 metre high *(Other Stones 20 Exmoor SS649458)*

photo 56 Old Man of Gugh, 2.4 metres, granite pillar
with three straight grooves
(1168 Isles of Scilly, Cornwall SV891084)

photo 57 near Merry Maidens, 1.7 metres, granite
with clean cut perforating hole
(1172 Cornwall SW432246)

Printed in January 2023
by Rotomail Italia S.p.A., Vignate (MI) - Italy